WITHDRAWN BY THE
UNIVERSITY OF MICHIGAN

Expressive Politics

Expressive Politics: Issue Strategies of Congressional Challengers

ROBERT G. BOATRIGHT

The Ohio State University Press

Columbus

Copyright © 2004 by the Ohio State University Press

Library of Congress Cataloging-in-Publication Data

Boatright, Robert G.
  Expressive politics : issue strategies of congressional challengers / Robert G. Boatright.— 1st ed.
    p. cm.
  Includes bibliographical references and index.
  ISBN 0-8142-0943-2 (cloth : alk. paper) — ISBN 0-8142-9050-7 (cd-rom)
  1. Political campaigns—United States. 2. United States. Congress—Elections. I. Title.
  JK1976.B57 2004
  324.7'0973—dc22
                                            2004003369

Cover design by Dan O'Dair
Type set in Sabon
Printed by Thomson-Shore, Inc.

The paper used in this publication meets the minimum requirements of the American National Standard for Information Sciences—Permanence of Paper for Printed Library Materials. ANSI Z39.48–1992.

9 8 7 6 5 4 3 2 1

Contents

List of Tables and Figures	vii
Acknowledgments	ix
Introduction	xi
Chapter 1: Parallel Histories: The Incumbency Advantage and Electoral Competition	1
Chapter 2: The Rational Candidate and the Hopeless Cause	17
Chapter 3: Incumbents and Challengers Compared	48
Chapter 4: "It's Not Like Rocket Science": How Candidates Understand Public Opinion	74
Chapter 5: "Like Throwing Golf Balls against the Wall": The Candidates Talk About Issues and Ideology	102
Chapter 6: "You Don't Know Me, But Here I Am": Candidate Perceptions of Party Strength	142
Chapter 7: Expressive Campaigning in 2000 and Beyond	183
Chapter 8: Conclusions: Expressive Politics and Invisible Politics	211
Notes	227
Interviews	231
Works Cited	235
Index	245

List of Tables and Figures

Figure 1.1:	Incumbents' Rate of Reelection and Rate of Comfortable Reelection, 1956–2000	3
Figure 1.2:	Percent of Uncontested Seats by Year, 1956–2000	5
Table 2.1:	Candidate Competition Theories Compared	29
Figure 2.1:	Candidate Positions for Multiple Races, Median Voter Model	31
Figure 2.2:	Candidate Distance in Median Voter Model	32
Figure 2.3:	Candidate Positions for Multiple Races, Expressive Campaigning Alternative	38
Figure 2.4:	Candidate Positions for Multiple Races, Party-Based Campaigning Alternative	41
Figure 2.5:	Candidate Positions for Multiple Races, Null Hypothesis	44
Table 3.1:	Candidate Issue Positions in the 1996 House Elections	53
Figure 3.1a:	Candidate Ideology by 1988 Party Presidential Vote	55
Figure 3.1b:	Candidate Ideology by 1992 Party Presidential Vote	56
Table 3.2:	Tobit Estimates of LQ Scores by 1988 and 1992 District Presidential Vote	57
Figure 3.2:	Candidate Ideology and Ideology Differentials for First-Term and More Senior Republicans	59
Table 3.3:	Comparison of Candidates Interviewed with All Nonincumbent 1996 Candidates	65
Table 4.1:	Candidate Polling by Competitiveness	90
Table 4.2:	Candidate Information Sources by Competitiveness	93
Table 4.3:	Candidate Attitudes toward Opinion Polling	95
Table 5.1:	Candidate Evaluations of Their Opponents	110
Table 5.2:	Candidate Issue Focus by Competitiveness	116
Table 5.3:	Candidate Issue Strategies	118
Figure 5.1:	Candidate Motivations for Running	124
Table 6.1:	Candidate Ideology and Polarization by Party Organization and Party Culture	148
Table 6.2:	Summary Statistics on Party Assistance	152
Table 7.1:	1996 and 2000 Candidates Compared	192

Acknowledgments

This book began as a term paper in Jim Fearon's "Topic in Game Theory" course in the spring of 1995. From that term paper, I embarked upon the research that became this book because of my interest in developing a research trajectory that went beyond the library, the classroom, and the computer lab. Apart from my academic interest in the subject of congressional campaigns, I undertook this project out of a desire to travel and to see political campaigns "on the ground." This desire led me to put over 13,000 miles on an already aging graduate student car, to become stuck in a blizzard in southern Minnesota, to endure a flood in southern Ohio, and to log many a midnight drive from remote parts of the Midwest back to my home in Chicago. And, in the course of what many of my friends considered a crazy project, I incurred many, many debts.

The most important debt is to the candidates discussed in the following pages. I cannot thank them enough for their willingness to open up their homes to me and to speak at length about their campaigns. In particular, I am greatly indebted to the ten candidates who comprise the case studies here. I also wish to thank Susan Hynes and Lydia Spottswood for coming to Chicago to speak with my students and colleagues about their campaigns; to Tom Coyne and Ian Maitland, who used their own campaign experience to help me develop my interview questions; and to Tom Chandler and Gary Revier for helping me to get my car through the aforementioned flood and blizzard. I also thank Julie Dwyer of the Democratic Congressional Campaign Committee and Terry Nelson of the National Republican Congressional Committee for their assistance in contacting candidates and in understanding the workings of their respective party committees.

Back in Chicago, Mark Hansen served as a model dissertation chair and adviser. He was instrumental in helping me with the dissertation from start to finish, and his guidance in developing the dissertation into a book was also invaluable. Lynn Sanders provided much-needed advice on interviewing techniques, moral support, and, when I needed it most, employment while I was conducting my dissertation research. And Susan Stokes was also a vital part of my research, helping me to place my findings within a theoretical and comparative context. Others at the University of Chicago who helped me to develop the ideas here include John Baughman, Rob Eisinger, Kevin Esterling, Jim Fearon, Jonathan Katz, Roger LaRocca, Steve Laymon, Norman Nie, Brian Portnoy, Emily Vogt, and the participants in the university's American Politics Workshop.

Beyond the dissertation, I benefited from conversations during my APSA Congressional Fellowship with Andy Taylor and the staff of Rep. David Price's office. The Political Science Department at Swarthmore College also provided a congenial place from which to conduct the second round of candidate interviews discussed here. In particular, I wish to thank Rick Valelly and Carol Nackenoff for their comments, and to thank the college for providing research grants that helped to fund the transformation of this project into a book. And in my current position at the Campaign Finance Institute, Michael Malbin, Marlinda Menashe, and Steve Gunderson have also provided valuable comments and advice.

This project was also much improved by the thoughtful comments of Kathy Barber, John Green, Susan Herbst, Paul Herrnson, and Robin Kolodny. I also appreciated the help of my former undergraduate professors at Carleton College, Steven Schier and Catherine and Michael Zuckert. Another member of the Carleton faculty who provided a unique form of assistance to this project was the late Paul Wellstone; the long-shot, expressive campaign Paul waged while I was at Carleton must certainly have influenced my fascination with congressional challengers (and made me less cynical about their lot, as well). The interviews could also not have been conducted without the generous hospitality of numerous college and graduate-school friends. And, certainly not least, my parents, John and Claudia Boatright, helped me out in many a jam during my travels.

An earlier version of chapter 6 appeared as a chapter in *The State of the Parties,* Third Edition. I thank Rowman and Littlefield for allowing me to include that material in this book. The survey questionnaire in chapter 3 appears courtesy of *Time* magazine.

Finally, I greatly appreciate the patience and assistance of my editors at The Ohio State University Press, Malcolm Litchfield and Eugene O'Connor. Both Malcolm and Eugene ably guided me through the publishing process, helped to sharpen my writing, and deftly accommodated many last-minute questions.

In 1995, when I began this project, my two greatest sources of support for this project were my dog, Omar, and my car. At the time I could not have guessed that my greatest support as I was finishing this journey would come from two people whom I had not even met when the project began. My wife, Audrey, has provided much-needed support and encouragement throughout the latter stages of this project. And our son, Jacob, has taught me that having a dada who can write a book is wonderful, but having a dada who can read a good bedtime story is often more wonderful. This book is dedicated to Audrey and Jacob.

Introduction

When Americans awoke on the morning following Election Day 2000, the outcome of the previous day's presidential contest had not yet been decided. When residents of New Jersey's Twelfth Congressional District awoke that morning, they also did not know who their congressman would be. In this race, incumbent Democrat Rush Holt had faced a stiff challenge from the district's former representative, Republican Dick Zimmer. It would not be until November 29 that Zimmer finally conceded that Holt had won the race, after a recount showed Holt with a scant 746-vote edge out of almost 300,000 votes cast (Siegel 2000).

Zimmer, who had given up the seat in 1996 to run for the Senate, attracted the attention of the national news media in his campaign because of his own formidable stature and because the Republican primary to take on Holt had featured a high-stakes battle as well, pitting Zimmer against yet another former representative from the district, Mike Pappas. Pappas had succeeded Zimmer in 1996 only to be defeated by Holt in 1998. As a member of the House from 1990 to 1996, Zimmer had established a moderate profile as a fiscal conservative who fought the Clinton administration on healthcare issues but had sided with chamber Democrats on environmental issues and had sought to establish a cautiously pro-choice stance. Among the achievements he was most proud of was his work on "Megan's Law," a provision of the 1994 crime bill requiring that communities be notified when a paroled sex offender moves into the area.

Holt had sought to establish a record not dramatically different from Zimmer's; in order to court the district's affluent, well-educated voters, Holt had gained a seat on the House Budget Committee and had sought to position himself, as well, as a fiscal conservative and as a defender of scientific and medical research funds. The two candidates argued vigorously over federal budget priorities and over their competence at understanding fiscal issues, but there were few great ideological differences in the positions they took. Most of the conflict between the candidates revolved around each other's campaign tactics. Many local newspaper endorsements took a stance similar to that of the *Hunterdon Review* (2000), which concluded its endorsement of Zimmer by saying, "The Twelfth District would be very well-served by either candidate."

The Holt-Zimmer race was watched by political analysts and congressional experts around the country; it was seen by many as a "must win" for both parties in their quest to come out of the election with majority status in the House. Both candidates received generous support from their parties and from donors around the country; each candidate spent just under two million dollars in hard money, with soft money expenditures in excess of that amount (see Berinsky and Lederman 2003). Zimmer surely had a fair shot at explaining his views to voters and at drawing contrasts between himself and Holt.

Other New Jersey candidates, however, were not so fortunate. Among the neighboring races were a contest in the Cape May area of the state which pitted Democrat Edward Janosik, an eighty-two-year-old former political science professor, against third-term Republican incumbent Frank LoBiondo; a race in the overwhelmingly Democratic district around Camden featuring Republican challenger Charlene Cathcart, a young attorney, running against fifth-term Democratic incumbent Rob Andrews; and a contest in the Trenton area between Democratic state legislator Reed Gusciora and Republican incumbent Chris Smith. Spending by the challengers in these three races combined was under $120,000, and the combined vote total for these three challengers was less than Zimmer received.

What happened in these races? Did these candidates commit any gross strategic errors? It seems unlikely that even had they done so these errors would have been noticed, because the budgets of these candidates seem insufficient to gain media attention. The local media paid scant attention to the three candidates. Janosik received some coverage merely because of his age; he was quoted in one newspaper article acknowledging, "I'm running because I always wanted to, and to give Frank LoBiondo some competition. No one should have a free ride into Congress" (Curran 2000). Gusciora received coverage in the Trenton newspapers, but even despite the dramatic contrasts he drew between himself and Smith, he was unable to force Smith to debate or to acknowledge him. In each of these races, the competing issue platforms were far more diverse than in the Holt-Zimmer race: Gusciora savaged Smith for his views on healthcare, civil rights, and abortion; Cathcart took issue with Andrews' opposition to the George W. Bush's tax plan; and Janosik criticized LoBiondo's views on healthcare and gun control. To judge merely by the degree of difference between the candidates, these races ought to have been livelier than the race between Holt and Zimmer, for these races represented what voters often claim to want from elections—issue-based competition and real choices. However, these races were neither close nor particularly prominent on the radar screen of New Jersey voters.

Despite the drama behind their campaigns, this is not a book about the Dick Zimmers and Rush Holts of the world. Their race was atypical. This book is about the way the majority of contests for Congress take place. For every congressional campaign like the Holt-Zimmer race there are more than a half dozen like the challenges to Rob Andrews, Chris Smith, and Frank LoBiondo. And the ratio of uncompetitive races to competitive races has been growing more lopsided over the past decade. Holt was one of only thirty-nine incumbents who garnered less than 55 percent of the vote in 2000; had he lost, he would have joined a group of only six incumbents who were defeated in the general election. Political scientists have the tools to document these rising inequalities, and they have the tools to explain why this trend is occurring. This trend, however, has begun to make political scientists' understanding of campaign dynamics less and less applicable to congressional races. We may know why more and more congressional races are as unbalanced as the challenges to Andrews, Smith, or LoBiondo were, but we do not know why someone in the position of Cathcart, Gusciora, or Janosik would run, how he or she would choose to campaign, or why the existence of candidates such as these makes any difference. This book is about such challengers. It is about how people run for election to "the people's house" in the races where most people are not paying attention.

The Challenger's Dilemma

For the past four decades, the study of campaigns and electoral competition has been dominated by a view of elections as pitched battles between two relatively evenly matched adversaries. Empirical studies have focused upon the winners of these battles. They have told us much about how the holders of political office got there, what characteristics they share, and how they maintain their grip on their offices. Meanwhile, theoretical studies have told us much about "rational" campaigning, about what ideological or policy stances candidates will take if they are aware of what opinions the voters hold.

Over these same four decades, however, the degree, or the frequency, of electoral competition in American politics has been declining at the national level. Since 1948, the average vote share of House of Representatives incumbents who even face major party competition has never dipped below 60 percent (Jacobson 1997a, 23). In this same period, over 80 percent of incumbent House members have been reelected in every election. Few Americans can even name or intelligently discuss the challengers to these candidates (see Jacobson 1998). Since 1980, Senate incumbents have fared just as well. Even incumbent presidents, while not as overwhelmingly successful as members of Congress, have won more landslide victories in the previous five decades than ever before in American history. Presidential vote margins of 20 percent or more have become almost the norm in races featuring an incumbent, and only five presidents have been defeated in the nineteen presidential reelection bids in this century.[1]

The rise of the incumbency advantage in American elections poses a dilemma for those seeking to study ideological competition in elections. Many treatments of campaign competition derived from the rational choice or "median voter" approach to elections hold that incumbents should fare no better than their opponents if both understand voter preferences accurately. These candidates should take nearly identical positions and thus split the vote evenly. According to several of the more technical models of ideological competition, incumbents should, in fact, tend to lose their reelection bids (see, for instance, Tullock 1981; McKelvey and Ordeshook 1976).

This clearly is not happening in the United States. As a consequence, many students of electoral competition have turned to alternate theories that account for the incumbency advantage. In such retrospective voting models, voters first measure the incumbent's performance against their own personal standard—i.e., has the economy gotten better or worse during the tenure of the incumbent? Have their own economic circumstances improved or declined?—and only if they are dissatisfied with the incumbent's performance do they turn their attention to the challenger (Fiorina 1981). Such models have been highly successful at predicting voting at the presidential level and have also been useful for predicting voting in other types of elections (Rosenstone 1983; Tufte 1978; Kramer 1971).

Looking at election outcomes in this manner, however, tells us little about the behavior of those who challenge incumbent officeholders. Indeed, the best advice a potential challenger might gain from these studies is not to bother. Barring a sudden turn of events such as a scandal or an economic collapse, the challenger is unlikely to win no matter what ideological positions he or she takes. The centrist strategy of the median voter model would be unlikely to lead to victory. Yet in the vast majority of congressional elections, challengers do emerge, and they often run campaigns as spirited and vigorous as their meager campaign budgets allow.

Are these candidates, then, irrational? That is, is it irrational for them to run? Even if they have rational reasons for running, is it then irrational for them to follow any strategy other than a vote-maximizing, election-seeking strategy? The existing literature has a mixed record in answering these two questions. In their evaluation of George McGovern's failed 1972 presidential bid, Miller, Miller, Raine, and Brown (1976) argue that McGovern fundamentally misunderstood the preferences of American voters. They claim that he took positions that were clearly unpopular among a large majority of voters. The aforementioned retrospective voting models indicate, however, that whoever ran against Richard Nixon in that election was, regardless of the issue positions he or she took, doomed to lose by the same margin by which McGovern lost. This argument directly contradicts the Miller et al. argument—if McGovern knew he was certain to lose, did he really take his issue positions based upon erroneous information about what voters wanted? What did he stand to gain by taking more popular positions? Did his unpopular positions lead to his defeat, or did his likely defeat lead him to advocate positions quite different from those of his opponent? The same question might be asked of other candidates facing long odds. When we find other candidates making unorthodox, extreme, or quixotic policy statements, are these statements a harbinger of defeat, or are they a reaction to impending defeat?

Turning back to congressional elections, there has been a steady stream of literature analyzing why challengers to popular incumbents emerge and what reasons they have for running. Losing candidates, at any level of American politics, have held an intrinsic fascination for political scientists. Canon (1990, 1993), Huckshorn and Spencer (1971), Kazee (1980, 1994), Leuthold (1968), Kingdon (1966), Fishel (1973), and Maisel (1986) have all conducted analyses of congressional candidates, seeking to determine what motivates these candidates, and especially congressional challengers, to run for office. Some of these works have pointed out areas in which challengers are misinformed, deluded, or overly optimistic. There is a growing tendency in this literature, however, to refrain from deeming such candidates "irrational." Canon (1993, 1138) notes that many such candidates "do not think they have a realistic chance of winning. Instead, they run to air various issues, to advertise their business, or for other reasons, along with a modicum of office-seeking motivation. But their aggregate pattern of behavior reveals strategic and rational behavior among a group of challengers that has been largely ignored in the congressional elections literature."

The above quote notwithstanding, however, most of these studies have concentrated on *why* candidates emerge to challenge incumbents, particularly popular incumbents. Few political scientists have analyzed the logic of such campaigns—that is, there are few studies that investigate *how* such candidates approach ideological competition. If we are to refrain from judging such candidates to be irrational or misguided, then it is certainly difficult to claim in turn that their strategies of issue competition are misguided. The aim of this book is to provide insight into the way competition in most congressional elections now takes place—insight into how candidates run for office when their chances of winning are slim.

Much of the argument in this book consists of stories about how individual races for Congress in the 1990s were run. But there is also a theoretical point to these descriptions. I argue that the dominant theories of "rational" campaigning can and should be amended to account for the advantage incumbents hold in resources, visibility, and ability to gauge voter preferences. If we are to hold political competition to be a good thing, we ought not also to insult the candidates who attempt to bring competition to races, even at the expense of long campaigns that will almost certainly fail to yield the office they seek, by dubbing them irrational. Such candidates are not irrational, nor are they naive about their chances of winning. In this book I offer an alternative to the standard two-party or two-candidate ideological competition model. I contend that many political campaigns are best viewed as what I call "expressive campaigns," as means of voicing opposition to the status quo, even where such opposition will not yield victory. Such campaigns are frequently unencumbered by careful consideration of the median voter, for that voter is unlikely to pay attention to the challenger's campaign.

In chapter 1 of this book I briefly trace the simultaneous development of electoral competition models in political science and the decline of competition in American elections. Despite the technical sophistication of many explanations of candidate competition, the limited applicability of these explanations to more than a handful of elections has been part of a growing divide within political science between theorists and those who perform more descriptive or applied work. In this chapter I contend that greater attention to the role of ideological expression in congressional campaigns—expression which occurs primarily where one candidate is at a substantial disadvantage—can bring about a reconciliation between these strands of political science. In addition, a recognition of the importance of the articulation of political views in these campaigns highlights built-in channels for political dissent within our system of government.

Chapter 2 considers existing models of candidate competition on issues in greater detail. While I argue that the median voter conception still dominates our understanding of campaigns, this model has been improved upon and altered substantially since the 1950s. In addition to outlining in greater detail the context of this model, I also discuss other means of describing candidates' ideological positions. Several political scientists have pursued the implications of this model in greater mathematical detail than did its originator, Anthony Downs, and several of them have contradicted his findings. Others have taken issue with his assumptions and have developed similar models which stem from slightly altered assumptions. I explore literature in American politics and in comparative politics which has refined, disputed, or reinforced the median voter conception. I then propose a slight refinement or alteration which employs a sequential positioning framework—a scenario in which challenger positions are a reaction to the incumbent and the incumbent's popularity—and which allows for candidates' issue positions as a form of political expression. Such a scenario can bring about issue positions and outcomes quite different from those posited in most models. These are outcomes which still embody rational candidate behavior, but which do not feature the candidate convergence which is a hallmark of most two-candidate or two-party electoral competition models. Here, the campaign is, if not entirely an "end" in itself, not solely a means toward the end goal of winning election.

In the context of American elections, there is no better arena for exploring inequalities in electoral competition than in races for the House of Representatives. In chapter 3 I document the prevalence of expressive campaigning using data drawn from a 1996 survey by *Congressional Quarterly* and *Time* of all major-party House candidates. These data demonstrate that incumbents do act in a risk-averse manner; their positions on issues are highly correlated with the partisan allegiances of their constituents. The positions of challengers do correspond somewhat with district preferences, but to a much lesser degree than do those of incumbents. These data lend support to the notion that incumbents do have either better knowledge of voter preferences or more of an incentive to act upon those preferences. These data provide evidence, it would seem, that challengers are reacting to the incumbent and to the incumbent's positions and popularity. In this chapter I also provide an overview of my interview method and the candidates with whom I chose to speak.

In chapters 4 through 6 I turn my attention to a subset of nonincumbent candidates in the 1996 elections, and I present data drawn from open-ended interviews with these candidates. Chapter 4 considers candidates' assessments of public opinion. In this chapter I consider the information candidates have about voter preferences and about the probability they have of winning the election. I conclude that ideological divergence between incumbents and challengers does not arise because of a difference in information. Nonincumbents, regardless of their level of competitiveness, are not demonstrably less well informed about voter preferences, and they do make accurate assessments of their chances of victory. Nonincumbents are quite aware of instances where their issue positions diverge from voters' preferences, even without the means to conduct opinion polls or other rather scientific measurements of voter preferences. The idea that incumbents' financial advantage over challengers results in better information only holds if information is a costly quantity, as would be the case if opinion polls were seen by candidates as a superior means of information gathering. These interviews suggest that candidates do not see opinion polls either as a means of information gathering or as a particularly accurate means of gauging voter preferences. Instead, candidates gather their information on voter preferences in other, less expensive ways. They regard opinion polls as a means of campaigning, of persuading others to support one's campaign, not of gathering the information necessary to wage a campaign. If information, then, is not particularly costly, the incumbency advantage does not lie in superior knowledge of voter preferences.

In chapter 5 I turn to the issue positions themselves. I ask candidates why they took the positions they took in their campaigns, where they sought to diverge from their opponents, and where they sought to appear similar to their opponents. The candidates' responses indicate that candidates' beliefs about their own ability to win preceded their adoption of particular issue positions and issue emphases. Candidates sought to converge with their opponents where they believed their opponents' positions to be popular and to emphasize their opponents' unpopular positions only if they thought their chance of victory was good. If they did not believe they had a chance to win, they were reluctant to diverge from their own views about what policies were "right" and which policy positions to emphasize. This chapter provides further evidence that nonincumbents react to the incumbent's views when they have something to gain from doing so; where they do not, they seek to run their campaigns so as to emphasize their own views and the views of a distinct minority of constituents in their district, even at the cost of potentially losing extra votes.

In chapter 6 I explore the role of one potential external influence on candidate positions, the views of their political party. If nonincumbent candidates are indeed well informed about public opinion and yet they choose to diverge from the positions that would, all other things being equal, maximize public support, it does not automatically follow that they merely say and do what they want, that they fall back upon their own individual, noninstrumental belief about what issue positions are "right" and what issues are most important. Numerous other influences might influence their issue positions. I select out what I argue is potentially the most important of these influences, their political party, and investigate whether their party sought to encourage them to take particular positions. I conclude that political parties do indeed seek to sway candidates' views, but that, consistent with other literature on parties, such influence has a rather benign effect and does not even necessarily move candidates toward the party's own views, if indeed it has any. I separate party organizations in the states in which I conducted my interviews into strong and weak parties, based upon others' assessments of these parties, and I conclude that strong party organizations tended to allow candidates the latitude to define their own campaigns. These parties served primarily as financial supporters and information providers, seeking to help candidates determine where voter preferences lie in their district. Weaker parties, on the other hand, do try to influence candidates' positions in order to pull them away from positions favored by district voters and toward those preferred by party activists and leaders. Such efforts were viewed by candidates as a distraction to their campaigns rather than as a benefit. This chapter indicates that if a party's own issue positions are preeminent where a candidate cannot hope to win by following public opinion, it is at the expense of coercing reluctant candidates into taking positions they themselves do not prefer.

In chapter 7 I document trends in competition and in expressive campaigning since 1996. I discuss subsequent developments in the districts I studied in 1996 and I discuss a second set of interviews from the 2000 election which drew upon a different sample of candidates from four different states. In this chapter I discuss the generalizability of the findings in the previous chapters—for the most part, the patterns I discuss in chapters 4 through 6 can be generalized to explain campaigns in other states, in other election cycles. In addition, I demonstrate how redistricting cycles and changes in levels of competition over time can affect the frequency of expressive campaigning.

In chapter 8 I consider the normative implications of expressive politics for political scientists and for American politics. Throughout this book I note that both theorists of political behavior and candidates themselves are somewhat ambivalent about the merits of pursuing a median voter strategy as opposed to the merits of having two candidates who take principled and contrasting positions. The fact that in American politics we simultaneously seem to prefer candidates who represent public opinion yet also complain when there is not "a dime's worth of difference" between candidates is one reason why losing candidates receive so little attention in

American politics. In this chapter I explore the normative arguments for paying more attention to nonincumbent candidates and I describe means by which these candidates could also hope to receive more exposure to the public.

Here's to the Losers

One losing candidate asked me, after I had finished interviewing him and had filled him in on the nature of this project, "A lot of people aren't going to vote for you because you're just like him. If you're just like him, why vote for you?" This question might well serve as the epigram for this book. In a two-party system such as ours, the losing candidates comprise half of the names on the ballot by definition. We see their names when we go to the ballot box; in many cases this is the only time that we see their names. Frequently, the only news coverage a congressional challenger receives comes at the end of the race, when the local newspaper, in its endorsement of the incumbent, commends the challenger for raising issues and predicts a bright future for the challenger—either many years in the future, or in an arena other than Congress. Likewise, the incumbent, in thanking his supporters, will commend his opponent for running a campaign on the issues; he may even promise to work with him in the future on matters of mutual concern.

But are these editorials, or these incumbents, serious? Is there anything to be learned from challengers, or any benefit to having them run? Losing candidates are a frequent subject of fascination. Losing candidates in high-profile races, such as Barry Goldwater or George McGovern, are often studied for the lessons of their campaigns (see, for instance, Stone 1943; Thompson 1994). In the case of the congressional candidates considered here—most, but not all, of whom did lose their races—the lessons to be learned from their campaigns are less evident. Congressional candidates often trace a path, in the words of Sandy Maisel (1986), "from obscurity to oblivion." The landslide losers in presidential races often ran extreme campaigns despite counsel from party leaders, or often sought to run more centrist campaigns but could not overcome media depictions (Page 1978, 118–42). On the congressional level, there are often few advisers telling a candidate how to run, and there are frequently few in the party who have any significant investment in the race. In short, there is often no one that cares enough about challengers in House races.[2] On one level, this book is subject to the criticism that it focuses, at least in part, on individuals who run merely to take up space on the ballot. There are certainly a few such individuals in my interview sample. To put a more noble gloss on these candidates, there are some who run solely in order to prevent the incumbent from going unchallenged. There are, however, several candidates in this sample who did win election. There are others who would run again in 1998 or 2000 and win or come close to winning. There are still others whose campaigns appear to have forced their opponents to rethink what they had been doing in Congress or in their campaigns. Many of these candidates, however, would return to their private lives after the ballots were counted, never to be heard from again in the political arena.

Such candidates are, however, representatives themselves in one sense. They represent citizens whose views, if there were not a candidate other than the incumbent on the ballot, would go unregistered on election day. They send messages to members of Congress which help these members to assess how popular their actions are among their constituents. They provide at least a semblance of competition so that incumbents must constantly be somewhat concerned about reconciling their positions with their constituents' views. They provide an outlet for dissent. It is no accident that we often see arch-conservatives running in overwhelmingly liberal districts and vice versa, that the people who run against a Barney Frank or a Henry Hyde are people who would seem very unlikely ever to win the support of a majority in those districts whether or not Frank or Hyde were in the race. Those who could win a majority of the votes in an open-seat election in those districts have no reason to run; from an ideological standpoint, at least, they are satisfied with the incumbent.

In addition, these candidates can affect other candidates. They do this in three ways. First, they may help other candidates of their party by bringing voters to the polls—voters who will, in turn, vote for other candidates on the ballot. A challenger for Congress may boost the voting percentages of similar candidates for other offices. Second, they also may keep the incumbent in the district campaigning, preventing him from sharing his campaign war chest and his personal time with other candidates for office. And third, the issues these candidates raise may rub off on other candidates—they can raise issues that other candidates, be they of the incumbent's party or the challenger's party, might prefer to ignore.

Finally, these candidates do sometimes win. When they do, their victories may have profound policy implications. Candidates who do not expect to win, and whom observers, incumbents, and even voters do not expect to win, bring different views to Congress in the rare—but not nonexistent—cases where they do win. If these candidates did not campaign in a centrist style (relative to their district, of course), they may not wish, or may not know how, to change their strategies once elected. David Canon

(1990) has shown that political amateurs can dramatically change the behavior of Congress when they are elected. Others have argued that the Republican Party's unexpected victories in 1994, which won them control of the House of Representatives, brought about turmoil in Congress in large part because many of the victorious Republican challengers had not followed median voter strategies and did not necessarily wish to do so once elected (Rae 1998; Fenno 1997). While many of these victorious candidates have eventually reverted to more traditional campaigning and governing, or were defeated for failing to do so, they did have significant effects upon government.

In this book I seek to explain, in as objective a manner as possible, what these candidates were doing in their campaigns. Any true effect that these candidates have upon politics is, in effect, a bonus. There is intrinsic merit merely in explaining why these candidates act as they do, if only to demonstrate ways in which we can understand electoral competition. But these candidates also represent a large part of our political landscape, of the choices that we voters have, and it is important to understand why they exist, how their campaigns are run, and how they are encouraged by our current political system.

There is a tendency in the literature on congressional challengers to close with recommendations as to how their lot may be improved. I have consciously abstained from doing so in this book. A major premise of almost every theoretical treatment of elections is that we get the representation we deserve. Almost all of the candidates with whom I spoke were engaging, dynamic people. In many cases, they may well have made better members of Congress than the incumbents they sought to unseat. Had they all done so, however, significant majorities of the constituents of these districts would have been represented by someone whose policy views conflicted with their own. In addition, had all of the incumbents they ran against truly been vulnerable, many of these candidates never would have become their party's nominees to begin with. The passion and conviction many of these individuals brought to their campaigns made them ideal candidates for Congress, but these traits would not have made them good representatives.

It is impossible to measure the influence that these candidates truly did have on political events, but that is not necessarily the standard by which their campaigns should be judged. The fact that the competition for congressional seats features a truly high degree of diverse viewpoints should, at least, give comfort or pause to those who lament the lack of difference they see between political parties. Yet it should also be a reminder to any who hold that view that likely defeat is the primary reason for such divergence. It is not the result, but the cause. This is particularly important to remember at a time when it seems that fewer and fewer congressional seats are subject to real competition. The rewards of such campaigns are sparse; in the end, in order to either run such a campaign or support such a campaign, one must be an idealist. One must have the strength to find solace in claims such as that of historian Porter McKeever (1994, 126), who concluded his study of Adlai Stevenson's failed presidential campaigns by noting that "It is high time for us to reject the fantasy that ideas and ideals can't win and to recognize these qualities as essential characteristics for those we choose as leaders. Good ideas have a life of their own, and good candidates strengthen the fabric of our society whether or not they win."

CHAPTER 1

Parallel Histories: The Incumbency Advantage and Electoral Competition

Why is it that we know so little about congressional challengers, about what prompts them to run against seemingly insurmountable odds, or about what precisely they do during their campaigns? In part, we have so little understanding of their campaigns because we have never developed any particular expectations for them. In order to understand the predicament of today's congressional candidates, and the state of our knowledge of these candidates, two parallel histories are required. First, it is necessary to identify the root causes of the decline of closely contested elections in the United States and the rise of the incumbency advantage in House of Representatives elections. Second, it is necessary to look at the state of political scientists' theories of ideological competition in elections—theories, depending on one's point of view, of how candidates do compete in elections or of how rational candidates *should* compete if they aspire to win office.

These two somewhat parallel developments in the descriptive and theoretical political science literature have pulled the study of campaign behavior in opposite directions. Neither literature truly accounts for the political give and take of campaigns. In the first account, the political actions of the winner are virtually predetermined and those of the loser are irrelevant. In the second, the actions of both are predetermined. In neither case is there allowance for the conflict of ideas, for ideological argument, or for the sheer unpredictability that for many democratic theorists defines politics. Both accounts see candidates as responding in predictable ways to their political environment, but neither sees them shaping that environment. In this book I seek to define circumstances in which candidates for office can be expected to engage in political expression, to participate in politics out of ideological conviction rather than solely out of a desire to attain elected office. If they do not, in fact, shape their environment, at the least they attempt to do so. In short, I discuss circumstances where candidates are citizens engaging in a form of political participation. Before I do so, however, let us look more closely at political scientists' expectations about electoral competition.

The Growth of the Incumbency Advantage in Congressional Elections

First, let us consider a few facts about congressional elections. As figure 1.1 shows, incumbent candidates for the House tend to win over 90 percent of the time; notwithstanding such recent watershed years such as 1992 and 1994, only twice since 1948 have more than 10 percent of incumbents been defeated in the general election (Ornstein, Mann, and Malbin 2002, 69). Furthermore, incumbents do not just win reelection, they win comfortably; in 2000, fewer than forty House incumbents received less than 55 percent of the vote. Incumbents tend to represent districts that are drawn to their advantage—in every redistricting cycle, the "incumbent protection gerrymander" is common. They tend to outraise their opponents by tremendous margins—in 2000, the median incumbent outraised his opponent by a twelve-to-one margin ($618,718 to $51,418). Incumbents have numerous perks of office—free mailings, free news coverage, substantial office and travel budgets, to name a few—which enable them to help their constituents, to find out what beliefs voters have and what issues are important to them, and to shape the voters' perceptions of what incumbents have done to address these concerns. The incumbency advantage is the major obstacle to almost every aspiring member of Congress, and the incumbent's status, more than anything else, dictates how a congressional challenger will campaign.

All of these facts, however, say little about the content of campaigns—they say little about how the policy proposals and positions of either incumbents or challengers will be framed in a campaign. In order for incumbents to have an advantage in ideological or issue competition with their opponents, we might posit that incumbents must be as good as or better than their opponents at assessing voter preferences, communicating their issue positions to these voters, and assessing different outcome scenarios. The advantage incumbents hold in these areas may be simply described as an advantage in resources. They have the resources to find out what voters want—or, perhaps, to seek to persuade voters that the myriad

Figure 1.1.
Incumbents' Rate of Reelection and Rate of Comfortable Reelection, 1956–2000

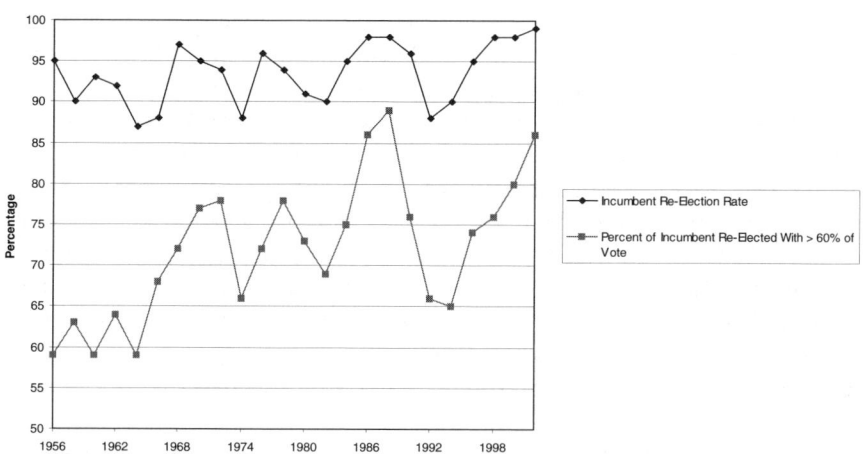

Source: Ornstein, Mann, and Malbin 2002, 69, 75; author's calculations. Incumbent vs. incumbent races in redistricting years excluded

votes they have taken in Congress do reflect the voters' somewhat amorphous views on what they want from government. These resources can be construed in a number of different ways—in terms of money, ability to secure benefits for the district, ability to communicate with voters, and so forth—but essentially, incumbents' resources are means of gathering information from voters and providing information to voters.

Political scientists have long debated the nature and extent of the incumbency advantage. Many of these studies have sought to isolate particular characteristics of this advantage. A very partial list of the different aspects of the incumbency advantage that have been studied includes consideration of changes in the size of the advantage over time (Erikson 1971; Fiorina 1989), its connection with positions (Erikson and Wright 1989), its connection with campaign communication (Coleman 2000), its relationship to fundraising and PACs (Ansolabehere and Snyder 2001; Alford and Brady 1989), its connection with voters' partisanship (Garand and Gross 1983; Coates 1995; King and Gelman 1991), and its relationship to the drawing of congressional districts (Cox and Katz 1996).

These studies have concurred on three issues. First, they agree that while the incumbency advantage has grown over the past three decades, the variability in incumbents' vote percentage has also increased. Thus, while the average incumbent may get a boost simply by virtue of incumbency, volatility in incumbents' vote margins ensures that incumbents ought not to think themselves safe. Second, following Mayhew's (1974, 5) "single-minded seeker of reelection" paradigm, we should expect incumbents to be risk-averse. There is little evidence that incumbents can systematically disguise unpopular positions, and therefore we should expect even the most secure incumbents to take positions preferred by the majority of voters. It is not competition that matters for these incumbents, it is the *implied threat* of competition. We cannot separate incumbents' advantage in resources from their selection of popular positions. And third, looking solely at incumbents' margins of reelection may lead us to underestimate the incumbency advantage because we cannot be certain that the same challengers would emerge in the absence of significant advantages in resources. The direct effects of incumbency create an indirect "scare-off" effect, where qualified potential opponents decide not to run, and weaker challengers result (see Jacobson 1997a, 1998).

The advantage incumbents hold is not necessarily a normative issue—none of the studies of the incumbency advantage have posited an optimal reelection rate. From a "good policy" perspective, it would not necessarily seem wrong for incumbents to be reelected if they do, in fact, accurately represent the views of their constituents.[1] Whether they do this or not is more difficult to demonstrate, but studies of congressional behavior have found few reasons why incumbents should not strive to represent the views of the voters. One component of the incumbency advantage, then, is that incumbents have the ability and the motivation to represent the views of their constituents. In the majority of races, we should see incumbents who know what the voters want and have sought to take positions that a majority of voters support.

What Is a Challenger to Do?

All of this research leaves us, however, with little understanding of challengers. As figure 1.2 shows, despite allegations of a growing incumbency advantage, challengers to most incumbents still emerge—in fact, the number of unopposed incumbents has declined in the past decade and reached a modern-day low in 1996. Faced with such an uphill climb to overcome the myriad advantages incumbents hold, what characteristics might we expect challengers, particularly long-shot challengers, to have? Should they be systematically different from incumbents? How should the incumbency

Figure 1.2. Percent of Uncontested Seats by Year, 1956–2000

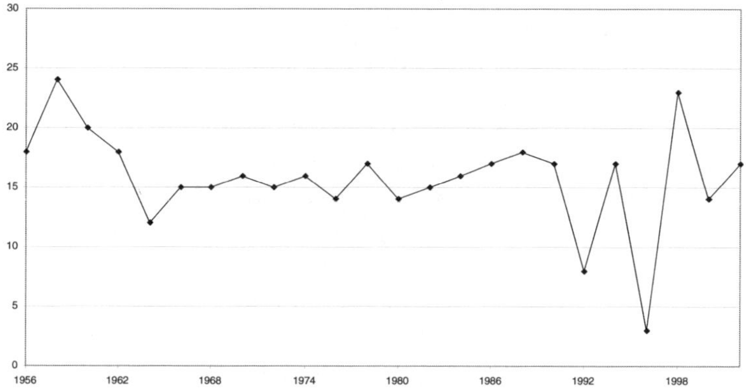

[Line chart showing percent of uncontested seats by year from 1956 to 2000, ranging roughly from near 0 to about 24 percent.]

Source: Jacobson 1990, 46–49; author's calculations. Louisiana elections excluded because of Louisiana's jungle primary.

advantage affect the issue positions and the ideological tendencies of nonincumbents?

Challengers are far more difficult to categorize than are incumbents. Incumbents are easily identifiable—a roster of members of Congress is all that is necessary—and in the American system it is a convenient assumption that in any given year most incumbents will seek reelection. They will seek to perform so as to keep their jobs. The universe of challengers, however, is somewhat more murky because one must consider not only those individuals who do run but allow for the fact that there are numerous potential challengers waiting in the wings. If a potential challenger chooses not to run for Congress, this decision is hard to study—we are not necessarily able to analyze the ways in which individual citizens assess their chances of winning an election were they to run, for the simple reason that we cannot identify all of these citizens. Stone, Maisel, and Maestas (1998) have begun a major systematic study of the variables which affect potential challengers' decisions to run or not to run. Such studies have also been conducted on a smaller scale by Kazee (1992) and Fowler and McClure (1989). A major fact that emerges in each of these studies, however, is that more politically experienced potential challengers tend to wait for elections where they do have a realistic chance of victory. The field is thus often left to individuals who are not professional politicians and who we should not expect to share the motivations of election-seeking politicians.[2] The task, then, is to discern what their motivations might be and how such motivations affect their position taking.

Many existing studies of challengers provide descriptive data on those who actually do run—their level of political experience; their age, income, gender, and so forth. They are about *who* runs, not *how* challengers run. Among the few studies that investigate the strategies of challengers, one of the earliest and best is John Kingdon's (1966) study of congressional and state legislative candidates in Wisconsin. Kingdon concludes that almost half (48 percent) of these candidates were certain of the outcome of their campaigns before Election Day (Kingdon 1966, 86–88). Among decisive winners and losers, 56 percent claimed to be certain of the outcome. Despite this finding, however, Kingdon spends much of his book analyzing misinformation that candidates received—he explores their tendency to rationalize election outcomes by arguing that voters did not absorb the message they attempted to send them. Kingdon also explores a "congratulation" effect, in which candidates rationalize their campaigns by reasoning that they had an effect upon the election insofar as they stimulated voter interest, raised important issues that would otherwise not have been brought up, and sent a message to the incumbent about the salience of these issues (Kingdon 1966, 23–25).

Most importantly for this study, Kingdon finds high percentages among both the most conservative (60 percent) and most liberal (42 percent) candidates who claim to have adopted their issue strategies out of concern only about the importance of those issues, independent of electoral concerns. Such a finding, while it still leaves out almost half of the candidates running, does indicate that significant percentages of nonincumbent candidates consciously stay away from the political center. Kingdon (1966, 133) does differentiate secure and "hopeless" candidates somewhat, noting that the long-shot candidates "tend to construct an undifferentiated appeal rather than an appeal to particular groups within their district. . . . The hopeless candidates, confident that they will lose, decide to 'speak their minds' instead of attempting to expand their base of support."

Subsequent studies, including those of Leuthold (1968), Huckshorn and Spencer (1971), Fishel (1973), and Hershey (1974, 1984) pick up more on Kingdon's analysis of candidates' sources of error and misinformation than they do on this latter assertion. In his study of candidates in ten San Francisco area districts in 1960 and 1962, Leuthold (1968, 60) notes that more competitive candidates spent more time acquiring information about public attitudes on particular issues than did less competitive ones, but he does not indicate whether this information led to different types of ideological appeals or whether it was merely a function of campaign resources. Huckshorn and Spencer's (1971) analysis of a written survey of 1962 challengers, aptly titled *The Politics of Defeat,* concludes that most candidates report that their issue positions made little difference in the election outcome. Perhaps as a result of this, Huckshorn and Spencer reiterate Kingdon's finding that those who believed they were likely to lose ran more issue-oriented campaigns than those who did not, and that candidates in more marginal districts underplayed ideology and instead emphasized experience and ability to help constituents in particular, narrow areas (Huckshorn and Spencer 1971, 208–12). And Maisel's (1986) study, which employs a written survey of congressional primary candidates, again focuses on the question of *why* people choose to run for Congress; he notes that the actual issue positions of candidates are deemed by the candidates not to matter in terms of the primary or general election outcome. He thus limits his consideration of issues to noting that challenges to incumbents are more issue-oriented than are open-seat campaigns (Maisel 1986, 84–85).

Maisel enumerates, however, what have come to be the standard reasons for candidate emergence—for why challengers run. In addition to the prospect of victory, where there is one, he notes that candidates frequently referred to providing an alternative to the incumbent, advancing their own careers through the visibility a congressional run would afford them, building a base for future campaigns, and having a platform to air their own political views (Maisel 1986, 24). Subsequent research, such as the case studies of Kazee (1994), Fowler (1993), and Fowler and McClure (1989), has built upon this typology. The study of 1964 candidates by Fishel (1973) and Kazee's (1980) study of twenty-five candidates in the 1978 elections have also contributed to identification of these factors as motivations for candidate emergence.

Within the scope of broader research on congressional candidates, Jacobson's (1990, 57–65) now familiar candidate quality measurements, which differentiate candidates by degree of past electoral experience, have become a standard means of gauging the degree of threat to incumbents, and they have also been used to explain incumbents' vote margins. Jacobson himself does not use his simple binary measure of whether a candidate has previously held elective office or not to distinguish types of challenger traits or strategies, yet others have begun to use his distinctions and to draw even further distinctions (see, for instance, Gerber 1998 on Senate challengers). Herrnson (2000) has conducted a thorough study of campaign strategy, finding no systematic difference in issue strategies according to candidates' prior experience, but he does reiterate the finding that challengers run more issue-oriented campaigns than do incumbents. This is, Herrnson argues, somewhat counterintuitive within an ideological competition framework because one might expect incumbents to have more resources at their disposal which can be used to speak authoritatively on policy issues (Herrnson 2000, 194–95). In other words, incumbents must be rationally steering the campaign away from substantive discussions of policy, while challengers are making an effort to learn enough about policy to argue with a reluctant incumbent.

By far the most systematic study of challengers' motivations for running, however, is that of Canon (1990, 1993). Canon subdivides political amateurs—challengers without prior legislative experience—into "ambitious" and "experience-seeking" amateurs. Canon further divides the experience-seeking amateurs into policy amateurs and hopeless amateurs (Canon 1990, 25–32). The bulk of his attention is devoted to what amateurs do when elected—do they adapt to the election-seeking environment of Congress, or do they maintain their outsider status? The resolution to this question depends upon the costs of their candidacy and the value they place upon maintaining their seat as opposed to advancing policy goals. This work contributes greatly toward illuminating the rational reasons candidates may have for running apart from an election-seeking orientation, and it identifies a class of candidates, and even of incumbents, who problematize the "single-minded seekers of election" paradigm.

The literature on the incumbency advantage and the literature on congressional challengers thus coexist with scarcely any mention of patterns of issue competition between incumbents and challengers. In virtually all literature on congressional challengers, the difficulty, even the futility, of challenging an incumbent is taken as a given. In the literature on the incumbency advantage, there is frequent discussion of the effects such an advantage has on the quality of the competition, yet there is little attention given to the ideological nature of the competition. The literature on congressional challengers provides some clues, most notably in the assertions of Kingdon, Huckshorn and Spencer, and Herrnson that noncentrist issue positions are taken more frequently by long-shot challengers than by more competitive candidates. Canon's typology of amateur candidates provides the groundwork for arguing that such positions are, in fact, rational responses to severely circumscribed chances of election.

Most studies of challengers, however, downplay the effect of campaign issues. It may well be true that, as the candidates interviewed by Maisel and by Huckshorn and Spencer argue, issue positions play a relatively minor role in determining these election outcomes. Yet issue positions clearly must be taken by these candidates. They will be asked in campaign appearances what they believe should be done about a particular policy problem, and they must have *something* to talk about in the campaign appearances they make. In addition, many of these candidates became involved in running uphill battles for Congress precisely because they have strong beliefs about issues which are not being addressed. It is difficult to argue that a substantial proportion of candidates are sufficiently motivated by their issue beliefs to run for office but that these issues beliefs eventually do not matter. These beliefs may not determine the outcome of the race, but they do determine the type of information voters receive about politics and the nature of the choices voters receive. To look for such beliefs, though, we must enter an entirely different realm of political theory, the realm of ideological competition and theories of rational issue positioning.

A Brief History of the Median Voter

In order to bring about a comparison between the actual ideological strategies of candidates and the idealized notion of issue competition in elections, it is necessary to consider the origins of rational choice theories of campaigning and their most prominent exemplar, the spatial theory or median voter model of competition. It is important to ask, that is, whether these models shed light upon congressional elections. And if so (or if not), why have they gained such prominence within political science? The limitations of these theories—and the reasons why they seem so inaccurate when applied to the vast majority of today's elections—are, I contend, rooted not in the idea of making issue competition intelligible but in a small number of the assumptions about issue competition that undergird these theories. Whereas the concepts behind these theories—their so-called scientific aspects—purport to stand apart from historical trends, I contend that it is the very rootedness of these theories in outdated assumptions about elections that make it necessary to amend them if they are to have any use for studying today's elections.

The rise of spatial models of party competition closed off an area of heated debate in the study of American political parties. Since the late nineteenth century, political science has been punctuated by periods of spirited debate about the nature of our two-party system. Much of this debate culminated in a 1950 report by the American Political Science Association (APSA) calling for a "more responsible two party system," one in which the two parties would offer coherent, yet divergent, packages of policy proposals to the public, which could then make an informed choice about the direction in which it wished American public policy to go.

Anthony Downs's *An Economic Theory of Democracy,* published in 1957, extended the concept of market competition to its logical political conclusion, and at the same time it exposed the inconsistency of pairing an economic conception of political parties with normative calls for the parties to espouse contrasting viewpoints and to design long-range plans that would "cope with the great problems of modern government" (American Political Science Association 1950). Employing Hotelling's (1929) theory of locational or spatial economic competition, Downs posited that a rational political party would, in two-party competition, seek out an ideological position at the middle of the electorate's preference distribution, just as competing entrepreneurs would, in Hotelling's argument, rationally seek to locate their businesses side-by-side. The two parties would then, under full information conditions, mimic each other, thus encouraging voters to make decisions not about policy, but about nonissue traits of the parties. Subsequent research has elaborated upon many of Downs's points, arguing that parties will be ambiguous about their positions on controversial issues (Shepsle 1972), will incorporate seemingly incompatible positions into their platforms (see Hinich and Munger 1994, 77–79), and will seek to avoid long-run solutions to problems in order to maximize their present electoral fortunes (Tufte 1978; Hibbs 1987). This economic conception rendered normative arguments such as those of the APSA report somewhat moot; the fault, if there was one, lay with the median voter himself, and no amount of exhortation by an elite cadre of political scientists would sway the parties from their course.

In a laudatory review of Downs's book in 1958, Charles Lindblom hailed the economic theory as a cure to what ailed political science:

> While economists have made the most of a seriously defective system, political scientists have permitted a kind of perfectionism to inhibit serious, explicit system-building. In talking with political scientists I am often struck by their dissatisfaction with theoretical proposals that do not promise a rough fit to the phenomena to be explained, while economists have happily elaborated, to take one example, a theory of the firm that is still a caricature of the phenomena described. (Lindblom 1958, 241)

The division between Lindblom's economists and political scientists still stands within the discipline. Rational choice modeling of electoral competition has, despite debate over its relevance to discussing actual elections, become an established part of political science and a standard shorthand for describing ideological conflict. The history of applications of these models to actual elections, however, is short, a circumstance which has been one of the chief complaints of Lindblom's political scientists. The median voter model is presently both one of the most widely accepted frameworks for inquiry among rational choice theorists and one of the most criticized by empirical scholars. The median voter model is under attack on three fronts. Outside the academy, "median voterism" is held in disdain by virtually all political observers and activists. Within political science, it is criticized for its "lack of fit to the phenomena to be explained," particularly in Green and Shapiro's (1994) broadside against rational choice theory. Among less quantitative social scientists, its assumption of a relatively atomized, self-interested public often draws fire. That is, it draws both normative criticism and two types of empirical criticism.

On a normative level, one need only open up a newspaper to sense the public dissatisfaction with the perceived ambiguity and lack of distance between America's two parties. From the right, one need only consider the attacks by the Club for Growth and other right-leaning groups on "RINOs" ("Republicans in Name Only"). From the left, liberal frustration with the Democratic Party is frequently in evidence, most recently in presidential candidate Howard Dean's claim to speak for "the Democratic wing of the Democratic Party." Such views may be commonplace among those with strong ideological views, but clearly they are a symptom of widespread sentiment among observers of politics that the two parties do not stand for anything, that they have abandoned their core beliefs, and that this abandonment is not beneficial to the nation. There continues to be conflict between the twin norms of representativeness and choice, but this conflict may have moved out of the academy. Public opinion polls seem to constantly top themselves in showing high levels of public disinterest in the issues of the day, public disgust with elected officials, and public cynicism about politics in general. If the median voter has triumphed within the public discourse, it has been at the expense of the public.

On a second, more applied level, quantitative political scientists have eschewed directly criticizing the median voter model's normative implications. The idea that politicians do behave instrumentally, at some minimal level, is fairly uncontroversial within political science, but why, the critics ask, have applications of economic models been so scarce? The median voter model was intended to be a general theory of elections, yet it has been successfully applied only to isolated, often anomalous elections, or to voting in elite bodies such as legislative committees. Despite the praise of those in political science who would be system builders, many contemporary researchers were skeptical. Stokes (1963) was among the first critics, arguing that candidates' issue positions play a relatively minor role in voter decisions. Other criticisms rooted in behavioral studies have been added since; the informational aspects of the model, the ideological mobility of parties, the unidimensionality of the model, and the lack of enforcement mechanisms are just a handful of the problems identified in Green and Shapiro's (1994) survey. Formal modelers have defended the theory by pointing to general studies such as Fenno (1978), Mayhew (1974), and Page (1978), but these studies, while they have been influential in guiding empirical research, are primarily qualitative, "soak and poke" research, not the highly mathematical papers at which the critics of spatial modeling have taken aim. Some formal theorists, most notably Sartori (1976) and Robertson (1976), have sought to correct some of the institutional factors in the Downs model, allowing for the uneven playing field to which I have referred, but their alternate proposals have, like the Downs model, suffered from limited empirical applications.

A third critique, one which blurs the lines between the descriptive and the normative, comes from theorists of political power. The median voter model rests upon assumptions about the nature of government and the nature of majority rule not particularly distant from the work of pluralist theorists such as Dahl (1961) and Lindblom (1977). As befits a model that aspires to a relatively uncomplicated assessment of the quest to capture majority preferences, the Downsian conception of majority rule is relatively straightforward: "Control over government decisions is shared so that the preferences of no one citizen are weighted more heavily than the preferences of any other one citizen" (Downs 1957, 32). Should this crucial presumption actually prove to be true, spatial modeling would be far more applicable to empirical reality than it has proven to be. Where this is not the case, however, numerous alternate candidate strategies and goals can be hypothesized.

This criticism challenges the very framework of the median-voter model in that it disputes the model's definition of the parties as office-seeking teams. In the economic model, the relationship between the parties is quite simple—one party has power, the other wants it. Bachrach and Baratz (1962) and Gaventa (1980) dispute this assertion. In a representative government, no party can be said to be completely without power. One party may hold more power than the other, but neither is completely without a voice. There may be a degree of collusion between the parties to keep certain issues, issues which fit into neither party's ideology, off of the agenda.[3] Or (a more mild formulation), because both parties are successful in some parts of the country, or with some constituencies, they may be sufficiently risk-averse to shy away from formulating new issues (Klingemann, Hofferbert, and Budge 1994, 11–12, 28). It is only the desperation of almost certain impending defeat, the chaos of social upheaval (see Page 1978, 62–107), or a lack of more risk-averse voices within the party that bring about new issue stances by parties. In comparison to these events, the pluralist approach comes off as particularly staid. In the pluralist one-dimensional approach, argues Gaventa, all grievances are recognized and acted upon, and all may participate in decision making. In this conception, even centrist voters may not be given choices which represent their "true" ideology. There is no vehicle for protest against the status quo.

These theoretical arguments about the assumptions of the median voter model ultimately have significant import for the study of ideological competition in elections. If one is to dispute the model on empirical grounds, one's argument must necessarily fall into one of two camps: first, that voters do not choose candidates as the model presumes them to, based upon their own ideological proximity to the candidates; or second, that candidates do not take the positions we would expect them to, based upon their knowledge of or beliefs about the electorate. It is difficult to disaggregate these arguments, and attempts to do so will inevitably take on a "chicken or the egg" quality: if voters do not vote ideologically, and candidates know this, candidates will not take the positions they would otherwise take. If candidates do not take these positions, however, it becomes difficult to ensure that voters are not choosing based upon ideological positions, because we do not have the convergence that would otherwise be predicted. What matters here is not how voters make their choices, but how candidates believe voters make their choices. Regardless of whether voters will consider ideology in making their voting choices, candidates must still take ideological positions. The relevant question, then, is whether candidates do have incentives to take a median position; and if not, what other incentives exist for the candidates. How do disparities in the electoral environment such as those I documented earlier in this chapter affect candidate incentives?

Are Candidates Rational Choice Theorists (Or, Again, What Is a Challenger to Do?)

The goal of this book, then, is to ask what a particular class of candidates for office—congressional challengers and nonincumbents—are thinking when they make strategic decisions regarding their ideological pronouncements or issue positions. On a basic level, the question is not whether candidates make mathematical calculations about where the median voter lies. The question is whether candidates are behaving "rationally," are making logical decisions given the various factors surrounding their campaigns that are out of their control. It would seem preposterous to argue that they are doing nothing of the sort, despite their often extreme or unusual issue positions. Many of the basic tenets of the theories we have about how ideological competition proceeds in elections seem logical, and the internal consistency of these theories has been worked out in great detail. Furthermore, the sheer comprehensiveness of these theories is unrivaled by any other theory of competition. Why is it, then, that the rough-and-tumble world of election politics seems so far removed from this stylized model? Are these two directions in our study of elections, the descriptive and the theoretical, mutually incompatible?

In the next chapter I argue that there is much we can learn from basic theoretical notions of issue competition that can shed light on the dynamics of issue competition in the context of congressional elections that betray a pronounced pro-incumbent bias. I argue that an overriding desire for political expression is the only explanation for the nature of ideological competition in such campaigns. In the remainder of this chapter, however, let us briefly try to assess why congressional challengers fall between the cracks of both of the streams of literature I have discussed here and why it is important to find a place for them within both literatures. In the introduction to this book, I argued that congressional challengers are an important subject of study because of what their campaigns can tell us about the state of American democracy. Here, since I have recapped the absence of serious analysis within political science of how congressional challengers campaign, let us briefly consider what a knowledge of the logic behind the challengers campaign can add to political science beyond merely filling a gap in our existing literature.

One crude, but enduring, distinction made in political science is between the study of political behavior and the study of governmental institutions. Elections are one of many areas in which citizens' political activities influence governing institutions, yet at times we are slow to incorporate concepts within the study of political behavior into our study of the actions of those who are part of, or who aspire to be part of, our government. The candidates I study here, precisely because of their low probability of victory, can thus be understood as being similar to other nongovernmental political activists and as representing something, even if what they represent is not the viewpoint of the majority.

If we concede that the majority of congressional challengers know, at a minimum, that they face extremely long odds against winning the elections in which they run, we are, in a sense, freeing them from the dictates of what we expect politicians to do. Most challengers have no political experience (if we define experience as having held office) prior to their campaigns, and most will have no such experience after their campaigns. Literature on political participation rarely lists running for office as a form of participation,[4] but surely few students of political participation would deny that running for office is on the same continuum of political participation as voting, working for someone else's campaign, contributing money to candidates, and so forth. Most importantly for the purposes of my argument here, however, few studies of political participation have limited their discussions of *why* people participate in politics to the likelihood of achieving one's preferred outcome. That is, citizens work toward a wide range of hopeless causes in part because they wish to express their own beliefs about what is right. A desire to express one's views has been held to be an important component of voting (see Schuessler 2000), contributing money to candidates (Brown, Powell, and Wilcox 1995, 45–48), running as an independent or minor-party candidate (Collet and Wattenberg 1999), and, in studies too numerous to mention, of more overtly expressive activities such as writing letters to members of Congress, participating in rallies, and so on. There is abundant evidence to suggest that such an expressive desire can take a backseat in the campaign behavior of elected officials, but there is no reason to exclude expressive behavior from studies of those who run for office as major-party candidates, particularly those who cannot realistically expect to win. And most importantly, one can agree with the findings of literature on congressional elections and one can agree with the basic tenets of rational choice theories of campaigning without denying the place of political expression within our system.

These candidates, then, can be seen as political participants. In addition, however, even if the candidates I study here are unlikely to ever become the elected representatives of their district, they are representatives in another sense. They do receive some votes, and thus the statements they make in their campaigns must be said to represent the views of some citizens. Above, I outlined one major criticism of the pluralist model of politics, a model from which, I contend, positive theories derive some inspiration. Critics of the pluralist conception of power have argued that ideas shared by significant minorities of the public tend to be left off of the agenda in American politics. Indeed, full candidate convergence would do just this; in a median voter scenario, it truly does not matter which party wins an election, or which voters—those on the left or those on the right—put the winning candidate in office. Policy views held by those on the extremes of the ideological spectrum tend to be left out of competitive campaigns. Again, rather paradoxically, the unbalanced nature of so many congressional campaigns means that those candidates who represent the preferences of particularly strong partisans are able to do so precisely because they have no rational expectation of attaining office.

In her study of conceptions of representation, Hanna Fenichel Pitkin describes just such a function. She notes that for Downs, representatives, in the elected sense, are, to quote Downs, "specialists in discovering, transmitting, and analyzing public opinion" (Pitkin 1967, 83, quoting Downs 1957, 89). She goes on, however, to note that for a government to be representative of the public, it must contain a representative of "every worthwhile opinion." The judgment of which opinions are "worthwhile" is, of course, subjective. The crucial distinction between elected representatives and others, those who are descriptively representative, is that elected representatives represent through activity. They deliberate over the enactment of laws, while descriptive representatives merely "stand for." Yet the representation that occurs in these elections, no matter how fleeting, provides a link between contemporary congressional elections and the normative calls by theorists such as Shklar (1991) and Fishkin (1997, 44) for the inclusion of as many views as possible in political discourse.

Finally, the broader scope of ideological conflict that can occur in such races—or at least, might occur were these candidates to receive a fuller airing of their views—can be exciting. For voters, it has been shown that campaign dialogue strengthens voters' sense of engagement in politics and increases their political knowledge (see Simon 2002). In addition, however, one should never underestimate the role of excitement or conflict even within dispassionate academic inquiry. Hannah Arendt's *The Human Condition*, published one year after *An Economic Theory of Democracy*, decried the absence of political speech from contemporary American life. For Arendt (1958, 5, 323–24), the entire enterprise of quantitative social science had begun to prosper precisely because mass human behavior had become so predictable—and for her, predictable behavior was antithetical to political expression. The presence of forms of political expression that are not solely aimed at achieving electoral office would seem to be a dose of unpredictability to our political system. As I argue in the following chapters, such expression may be doomed to reside at the fringes of our system, but the fact that it exists at all (and that such expression is hardly irrational for some political actors) may provide some consolation to the normative theorist.

In the next chapter I explore the place of political expression within rational choice theories of campaigning—that is, I establish theoretical reasons to look for such behavior. In the subsequent chapters I describe the forms in which such behavior does exist in American congressional elections.

CHAPTER 2

The Rational Candidate and the Hopeless Cause

Given the apparent incompatibility between theoretical treatments of "rational" candidate behavior and the reality of American congressional races, why should we turn to rational choice theory to provide guidance in understanding these races? One preliminary answer to this question comes from political theorist James Johnson. Rational choice theory, argues Johnson (1991, 117), is, or at least should be, a reconstructive theory. That is, "a presumption of rationality is a principle of charity. It mandates that when confronted with seemingly irrational action, the social theorist investigate the broader patterns of action, explore the social or political contexts, within which the perplexing action might be interpreted as rational." In other words, rational choice theory attempts to reconcile the unexpected with more understandable patterns of human behavior. In the previous chapter two potential charges of irrationality seem to emerge when we are discussing congressional challengers. First, the fact that they emerge at all might be considered irrational if they are solely seeking election. Second, given that they do emerge, the issue focus of their campaigns might be deemed irrational if they do not conform to the median voter paradigm.

In the next chapter I document the ways in which congressional challengers do deviate from this paradigm. For now, it is sufficient to note that few of them do run centrist campaigns—indeed, the lower their chance of winning, the less likely they are to run centrist campaigns. The very fact that they emerge, however, despite the advantage incumbents frequently have and despite the overwhelming odds against their victory, brings into question the relevance of applying a median voter framework to their campaigns. It would certainly be in accordance with what we know about congressional candidates to allege that candidate incentives are more varied than most spatial competition models suggest. Where alternate incentives exist, rational reasons for candidate divergence also exist. Can a theory of issue competition make sense of these reasons?

In this chapter I argue that merely identifying candidates who are not solely seeking election does not prove that the median voter model should be thoroughly rejected when studying elections featuring an incumbent. It also does not mean that we ought to circumscribe the model's predictions to cases where its predictions are fulfilled. As Martin Diamond (1959, 210) points out in his early review of Downs, a weakened median voter model is no model at all: "The revised 'fundamental hypothesis' would have to read: Some politicians formulate policy only for the rewards of office and some do not, and which behavior is decisive is a matter for study each time, all of which would leave political science in the difficult but fascinating position it was in before economic models were offered in succor."

Diamond is not entirely correct. He is correct, though uncharitable, in his "revised" hypothesis. If we are able to specify, however, precisely when candidates formulate policy positions in order to win election to office and when they do not, the model is richer and no less comprehensive than it was before his revision. His conclusion about the position in which we are left, therefore, seems overstated. I argue here that considering—as a precedent to candidate position taking—two variables, candidates' expected probability of winning and candidates' noninstrumental policy preferences, enables us to make this specification while retaining a basic issue competition framework.

The incorporation of both of these variables suggests the rejection of one crucial tenet of nearly all existing spatial models of candidate competition—the assumption of simultaneous or unrestricted movement.[1] The prediction of candidate convergence on policy is based in part upon candidates' certainty about voter preferences and their uncertainty about their opponent's ideological position. While it is true that in an election without a preexisting advantage for one candidate, an office-seeking candidate would choose to be at the electorate's median (or at least closer to the electorate's median than his opponent) even if he did know what his opponent's positions were, in a case where that opponent has taken a median position and has a preexisting, nonideological advantage this incentive disappears. If a candidate's maximum probability of winning is exogenously determined or truncated before he begins his campaign, his motivation to take a centrist position must also be reduced.

If this does occur then other incentives must enter into his calculation of which positions to take. It seems unreasonable to propose that candidates do not have any noninstrumental policy preferences at all; if our models require citizens to have such positions, surely we must extend the same prerogative to candidates. Mayhew's (1974) conception of members of Congress as individuals who are solely oriented toward reelection does not mean that they do not have opinions about what policies are best; instead, it means that they sublimate these views to their desire to win election. In cases where the possibility of election is limited or nonexistent, I argue that these opinions are more likely to guide policy positions and to bring about divergent candidate strategies than they are without circumscribed election prospects.

Making these adjustments amounts, in effect, to turning the traditional median voter model on its head—instead of having issue positions determine outcomes, expected outcomes *independent of the positions of one or both of the candidates* determine issue positions. As I seek to show, this does not happen in all situations, but it does happen in frequent and identifiable circumstances—namely, in challenges to incumbents. Ultimately, I argue, if the assumptions of a candidate competition model are specified such that distinct classes of candidates deviate from the median voter paradigm in rational ways, Diamond's trap is avoided. That is, certain classes of candidates—here, those who face a popular incumbent—can be predicted to be running for reasons other than seeking to win, and they can be expected to adopt issue positions that diverge not only from those of the incumbent, but also from those of the average voter in the district. In this chapter I outline three alternatives which illustrate the consequences of relaxing the median voter model's emphasis upon simultaneous position taking. The first alternative assumes simultaneity; as a result, candidate competition still reflects Downs's theory. The second and third alternatives assume sequential positioning. Here, I illustrate cases in which candidates' personal views play a role in dictating their positions and cases where the views of organizing forces such as political parties take up the slack left when election-oriented positions are less likely to actually result in election. The end result of presenting these alternatives is to make a case for what I call the "expressive campaign," the campaign designed to present an ideological agenda to the public even when such an agenda will not result in the defeat of the incumbent. Candidates who conduct expressive campaigns, are, as I show in the remainder of this book, rapidly becoming a majority among nonincumbent congressional candidates—if indeed they have not always been a majority.

Candidate Incentives: The Theoretical Context

Before setting forth the basic theoretical notions that underpin my argument, however, a review of some definitions is in order. In any model of ideological electoral competition, three variables are of primary interest: voter preferences, candidate positions, and outcomes. Voter preferences are simply the ideological positions voters prefer. In Downs's setup, preferences are conceived of as points on a single line—for instance, from most liberal to most conservative (Downs 1957, 115–17). Candidate positions are, likewise, positions on this same line—a very liberal position, a very conservative position, or anything in between. Finally, outcomes are the voting results of a given race, whether seen as the share of votes for each candidate or the winner and loser of the race.

The standard sequential means of ordering these variables would be to put them in just that order:

(1) Preferences ⟶ Positions ⟶ Outcome

Here, candidate positions are not differentiated from each other. They are taken simultaneously, and they jointly lead to the voting outcome. This is the classic median voter scenario. Downs contends that "parties in a two-party system deliberately change their platforms so that they resemble one another" (Downs 1957, 115). If parties have relatively complete information about voter preferences, their positions will both be taken at the median of the voters' preference distribution. For instance, if seven voters are arrayed along a line, the middle voter—voter number four moving in either direction—will dictate the winning position in this hypothetical election.

This conception holds that voter preferences are not malleable; voters know what they want from government, and they will evaluate candidates accordingly. Candidates cannot shift voter preferences to meet their own needs. If this were possible, scenarios such as the following might result:

(2) Positions ⟶ Preferences ⟶ Outcome

or

(3) $Preferences_1$ ⟶ Positions ⟶ $Preferences_2$ ⟶ Outcome

In scenario (2) here, candidates take positions which influence voter preferences and then lead to the voting outcome. In scenario (3), candidates assess voter preferences, take positions, and then seek to sway voters such that voters' preferences are more in accord with the candidates' positions. Why would candidates do this? A candidate with substantial power to sway the public—a candidate in office whose explanations of policy might influence voters, or a candidate with a substantial advantage over his opponent in the ability to advertise his positions and the reasoning behind those positions—might do so. This conception is not uncommon in comparative politics literature on governments with the power to set the public's agenda (Przeworski and Sprague 1986). It may even apply to a unitary actor such as the American president (Geer 1996) or to a party's leadership (Jacobs and Shapiro 2000). The problem with using this scenario in this book's empirical context, in looking at members of a large body such as the House of Representatives, is that citizens garner their political information from many sources. Any one candidate for office will have to compete with other candidates, with political elites not running for office, with the media, and with organized interests in communicating reasons for adopting any particular set of policy views. Even if one limits consideration solely to congressional persuasion, a collective action problem may result (Geer 1996, 21–22). This ought not to indicate that voter persuasion never happens, but the costs of successful persuasion may frequently be prohibitively expensive. Mayhew (1974, 32) notes in his discussion of marginal members of Congress—those who represent districts where both parties are competitive—that "There is after all the problem of generating collective action . . . the rational way for marginal congressmen to deal with national trends is to ignore them, to treat them as acts of God over which they can exercise no control." This is not to say that members of Congress will not react to trends in public opinion; indeed, we know that they do act in responsive ways. They do not, however, act to change these trends themselves. It seems far more cost-effective to merely shift one's positions in response to shifts in public opinion than it would be to attempt to move public opinion back to one's own *ex ante* positions.

In simply looking at these three variables, of course, other plausible arrangements of these variables remain. One could, for instance, order these variables such that the outcome may be known before positions are taken:

(4) Preferences ⟶ Outcome ⟶ Positions

This proposition may seem absurd on its face, as the outcome of any election necessarily comes after candidates have taken positions. Candidates may have information about the likely outcome of an election, however, which affect their decisions. A candidate may reason that "this district has overwhelmingly voted for Democrats, and it will continue to do so." An incumbent may look back at previous vote margins and reason that "this district has always voted overwhelmingly for me in the past, and it is likely to continue to do so." These assessments may not be certain, but they may influence candidate behavior. Of course, this argument is somewhat circular, in that previous voting is still based upon previous candidate positions.

Such previous voting seems likely to benefit an incumbent candidate more than a nonincumbent candidate. Mayhew also posits, however, that members of Congress are risk-averse: "What characterizes 'safe' congressmen is not that they are beyond electoral reach, but that their efforts are likely to bring them uninterrupted electoral success" (Mayhew 1974, 37). Incumbents, in addition, operate under conditions of uncertainty about their opponents; they can try to stave off a difficult challenge, but they cannot be certain that such a challenge will not take place. They have no incentive, even if they do have reasonably accurate guesses about what the election's outcome will be, to deviate from that position which will maximize votes. Thus, to place their positions after their beliefs about the outcome seems unrealistic.

What of nonincumbents, however? A candidate who challenges an incumbent enters a race with knowledge of who the incumbent is, what positions he has taken in the past, and how he has fared in the past. At the very least, the challenger is taking positions after the incumbent has already established positions:

(5) Preferences⟶Position$_{(Incumbent)}$⟶Position$_{(Challenger)}$⟶Outcome

Here, the incumbent takes positions under conditions of uncertainty—not uncertainty about voter preferences, which I shall consider in a moment, but uncertainty about the challenger's positions. The incumbent necessarily acts in accordance with the median voter theory. The challenger, on the other hand, knows where the incumbent stands. If the incumbent has inadvertently taken positions which do not guarantee at least a split of the vote—if the incumbent is mistaken about the median of the electorate's preference distribution and has taken a position away from the median—the challenger has an opportunity to defeat the incumbent. If, on the other hand, the incumbent has correctly gauged the median, and has adopted that position as his own, the challenger must reason that he has at best a

50 percent chance of victory—at best, he can ape the incumbent's position and split the vote.

Can he really do this, however? If the challenger does have this information, then the proper sequencing of these variables should be

(6) Preferences ⟶ Position $_{(Incumbent)}$ ⟶ Outcome$_1$ ⟶ Position$_{(Challenger)}$ ⟶ Outcome$_2$

where the first outcome is the challenger's assessment of the likely election outcome (or range of outcomes), and the second outcome is the actual result.

The relationship between this first outcome variable—the expected range of outcomes for the challenger—and the challenger's position is the subject of inquiry for the remainder of this chapter. If the incumbent does take a position first, it stands to reason that the probability of victory for the incumbent is unbounded before that position has been taken; the incumbent has some control over the lower bound of this probability, but not of the upper bound. That is, if the incumbent correctly takes a median position, he has at least a 50 percent chance of victory, depending upon what the challenger does. A rational incumbent's chance of winning will be bounded between 50 and 100 percent. The challenger, in turn, can have no better than a 50 percent chance of victory if the incumbent has adopted a median position.

This scenario presupposes no advantage to incumbency other than the fact that the incumbent chooses a position before the challenger does. This is a best-case scenario for sequential positioning. If the incumbent has further advantages, the bounds of the challenger's probability of winning will be further circumscribed. To this theoretical construct one might add the empirical conclusion that over the past fifty years, the upper boundary on challengers' probability of winning has been far less than 50 percent when they face an incumbent who is properly informed about voter preferences. In many cases, then, the challenger may enter a race knowing that his chance of winning is, for all practical purposes, zero. Theoretically, what this means is that the median voter, confronted with two candidates with identical positions, goes with the incumbent, the known quantity.

In any such situation, voter preferences play a very small role in determining a challenger's ideological positions. If adopting positions favored by the voters will not improve one's chance of victory, the incentive to do so declines. According to many, the entire rationale for running for office disappears. I argue in this book that such a rationale does not disappear, but that candidates are subject to different incentives when their probability of winning is so severely bounded. The candidates who emerge will not be regarded as "serious" by their parties, by the incumbent, or by much of the public, and as a result they may serve to give voice to the "nonissues" or the ignored issues of which Bachrach and Baratz and Gaventa speak.

More specifically, I argue that three general types of campaigns are made possible. These types are consistent with the median voter framework to an extent; that is, they retain the notion that candidates and voters take positions that fall somewhere on a continuum from liberal to conservative, and they retain the notion that voters select the candidate they believe is closest to them on this continuum. In other words, the median voter remains pivotal. These types differ from the strict median voter model, however, in that they allow candidates to take positions sequentially rather than simultaneously and in that they posit a "first-mover advantage," in which the first mover—the incumbent—wins if he successfully identifies the median of voter preferences and stakes out a position at the median.

This sequential positioning alternative leaves the challenger, or second mover, three options. First, the challenger can still pursue a vote-maximizing strategy and adopt a position only slightly different from that of the incumbent. In this scenario, the challenger's motivations are scarcely different from those of the incumbent. Second, the challenger may adopt a position that accords with his "expressive preferences." That is, he can adopt a position that most closely accords with the policy views he, as an individual, holds. This position is neither a vote-maximizing position nor a winning position, but where no position is a winning position he can maximize his own personal satisfaction with the way he has campaigned. He can further the cause of what he believes is "right." Third, the challenger may be influenced by other actors who seek to draw him to their preferred position. Certainly the leading contender for this role is his party. If parties hold distinct noninstrumental policy views—views that they hold independently of concern for winning—they have no incentive to deviate from such positions where deviation will not yield electoral advantage. If, to take the obvious example from American politics, one party is somewhat left-of-center and one is somewhat right-of-center, the candidate will be a faithful messenger for his party's platform, even where advocating such a platform will not help him get elected.

In the remainder of this book I test each of these alternatives on the 1996 and 2000 House of Representatives candidates. Before doing so, however, I briefly provide further details on each of these alternatives. On a purely descriptive note, it may seem obvious to the reader that the second of these alternatives seems most plausible. That is, given my argument about losing candidacies such as those of McGovern and Goldwater, it would seem that candidates with a slim chance of victory do not, in fact, ape their opponents. Likewise, the weakness and ideological heterogeneity of political parties has become a staple of American politics literature, so we would hardly expect American parties to dictate positions to their candidates. These alternatives have several more subtle differences in the way we study candidates who challenge incumbents, and they comprise a field of possible theoretical treatments of political ideology that requires some discussion of each. The remainder of this chapter is devoted to that discussion.

Options for Candidate Competition

To recap the setup thus far, let us reconsider the quantities in which we are interested. Above, I outlined several plausible arrangements of three basic variables: voter preferences or positions on the issues of the day; candidates' positions on those same issues, and outcomes (or candidates' expectations about likely outcomes given any particular position). For the sake of argument here, voters' *actual* preferences are irrelevant; what matters are candidates' *beliefs* about voter preferences. The proof of the accuracy of candidates' beliefs about the voters is, as they say, in the pudding. That is, a candidate can be mistaken without meaning that the candidate is behaving irrationally. The outcome of any race can, of course, be known after the fact, and if candidates are honest in their accounting of their campaigns, we can also assess candidates' beliefs about the outcome. Likewise, we might imagine a means of scaling candidate positions or we might depend on candidates, again, to tell us where they stand on issues. These quantities, then, are somewhat measurable if we talk with candidates.

To these quantities let us add a few definitions of secondary variables. First, it is clear here that when we discuss candidates' beliefs, we are talking about information that they have gathered about their own circumstances. *Information,* then, has a dual meaning. All candidates seek to gain information, and reduce their uncertainty, over both the distribution of voters' preferences (and the voting decisions that these preferences imply) and the positions that have been or will be taken by their opponent. Candidates would certainly like to know what their opponents are doing in order to better understand how these positions affect their own chances. In the case of a challenger, information about unpopular positions on the part of the incumbent may imply an opportunity to defeat the incumbent, while information indicating that the incumbent has not made blunders on the issues implies the equally valuable (yet less heartening) conclusion that the incumbent is unlikely to be defeated no matter what the challenger does.

Second, the careful reader of Downs and other works in the candidate competition literature will note that while Downs and some of his successors present models with political parties as the actors, others refer to candidates in constructing their models. In this book, I have referred frequently to candidates' ideological strategies, not parties. I do this because in this context candidates and parties are two distinct entities. It is true that virtually all successful candidates in American politics belong to one of the two political parties. Yet these candidates are not equivalent to the parties. For the most part, issue competition models can speak in terms of either one without confusion. Yet in practical terms, they are not the same. Downs refers to parties as "unified teams," yet where parties must adopt different strategies in different constituencies in order to win elections, it becomes difficult to sustain this assumption. In other words, a Georgia Democrat is not the same as a Massachusetts Democrat, nor would the Democratic Party wish them to be if it is to win congressional seats. These candidates run before different constituencies, yet they must legislate, if elected, within one political system. In such a case, it makes sense to conceive of parties as a force exogenous to the candidates themselves—an entity that may have a rough ideological stance, but which allows considerable flexibility for its members to define themselves. Thus, I speak primarily here of candidate positioning, but I shall return to the role of parties, in the sense of organizations that can seek to shape the positions of their candidates but often do not do so, later in this chapter.

Third, it should be clear from the above discussion that I am also discussing two distinct quantities that candidates seek to maximize. Either they are trying to maximize their *probability of winning* or they are trying to maximize their *vote share*. The distinction here requires some explanation. A common early line of criticism of the median voter model is that the market analogy, in which candidates compete for votes much as businesses compete for customers, has limited utility in describing politics precisely because candidates gain little by winning by overwhelming majorities or in losing close elections. Barry (1970) and Przeworski and Sprague (1971) point out that in market competition, a firm always benefits from greater sales or more market share, while a party does not necessarily benefit from votes beyond a narrow majority or plurality. This argument is systematized by Riker and Ordeshook (1973), who substitute benefit maximization for vote maximization; in such an alternative, a party seeks to ensure victory and thus might prefer to seek as many votes as possible only where the preferences of voters are somewhat uncertain.[2]

Given that we cannot seriously expect candidates to be able to calculate outcomes down precisely to the median voter—the vote that provides the magic 50 percent plus—one share—it can be difficult to disentangle a candidate maximizing vote share from a candidate maximizing his chance of winning. And in practical terms, increasing one's chance of winning would seem to be the same as increasing the number of votes one receives. When we turn this statement around, however, it becomes apparent that increasing the votes one is likely to receive may not increase one's chance of winning. That is, the value added in moving from 49 to 51 percent of the votes is obvious, but the value added in moving from 20 to 25 percent of the votes is not. In the latter case, our candidate still has been resoundingly defeated. There may be some fringe benefits that accrue from a respectable, but unsuccessful, campaign, just as there may be some fringe benefits that accrue from a landslide victory as opposed to a narrow victory. Yet there are trade-offs inherent here, and it seems somewhat sweeping to say that candidates always seek to gain as many votes as they can, insofar as these candidates may have to water down their message, to compromise the positions they have taken. Which of these quantities candidates seek to maximize, then, is an open question that I consider in this book.

Fourth, the discussion thus far in this chapter has considered only one set of preferences—those of the voters. Yet voters certainly are not the only actors in this game with policy preferences. Candidates certainly have them as well. Yet candidates have two different types of preferences. *Instrumental preferences* are preferences for a position that will enable a candidate to win office. A candidate may have beliefs about the positions he must take in order to win office that conflict with that candidate's actual beliefs about what is right. These latter beliefs, which in game theoretic literature are often called *sincere preferences,* I here describe merely as *noninstrumental* or *expressive preferences.* That is, these are issue positions that candidates believe in independent of their utility in winning an election or gaining votes. All politicians have both types of preferences; it is the trade-off between the two that varies from one politician to the next. On occasion, we do hear stories of politicians who have "fallen on their swords," who have taken unpopular positions because they sincerely believe that their conscience will not allow them to advocate something they do not think is right. Likewise, we also hear stories of politicians "selling out" what they believe in, making compromises in search of votes. For each politician—as, perhaps, for any human being—there is a trade-off here.

For the sake of my argument here, I propose that instrumental preferences dominate noninstrumental preferences where they increase a candidate's chance of victory. That is, the candidate may well reason that some compromises in order to attain victory will surely be worthwhile, for once he has been elected to office he will still do a better job than his opponent. Given, however, two different winning positions, it seems logical to assume that the candidate will then maximize his own personal satisfaction on this secondary dimension, by taking that position among those two that is most in line with what he truly believes. The converse of this argument, of course, is that where a candidate can take no position that is a winning position—where, for instance, he is hopelessly outmatched by his opponent on nonpolicy grounds—there is little rationale in taking any position other than one he truly believes is the "right" one irrespective of whether it is popular.

Fifth, and finally, it is necessary to specify the order in which candidates take positions. If nothing else, the description in chapter 1 of the incumbency advantage certainly indicates that incumbents adopt positions before their challengers. They are in office, they have made issue statements in previous campaigns, and they have a track record of voting on all matters of policy. Empirically, it seems obvious that incumbents position themselves first. Their challengers, then, respond to the incumbents' positions, using easily available information about where the incumbent stands in order to form their own issue positions. Thus, in a challenge to an incumbent, *sequential positioning* is occurring.

With these definitions established, let us return to the options I discussed above. Table 2.1 lists four potential scenarios (the three I have already mentioned, plus a null hypothesis) for groups of elections in which party influence over candidates is either present or absent, and in which probability of winning for the second candidate is either known or unknown. Where *ex ante* probability of winning is known, a two-stage game results; I assume that incumbents cannot know with certainty their probability of winning because they cannot know, when establishing positions in office, who their future opponent will be or what that opponent will do. Incumbents and open-seat candidates always operate under conditions of uncertainty about their opponent's strategy; challengers operate with certainty about the position their opponent has taken and potentially, but not necessarily, about the incumbent's (and hence their own) probability of winning.

As I describe each alternative below, I shall provide hypothetical scatterplots. These scatterplots are not intended as testable hypotheses; rather, they represent plausible arrangements of often unmeasurable variables. In each of these alternatives the primary subject of concern is the positions of challengers, not incumbents. In what follows, I assume incumbents to (a)

Table 2.1. Candidate Competition Theories Compared

Level of Party Influence on Candidates	Simultaneous Positioning (Probability of Winning Unknown)	Sequential Positioning (Probability of Winning Known)
	Median Voter Model	*Party-Based Campaigning*
High	Convergence for all pairs of competing candidates regardless of whether incumbency advantage exists or not. Party serves as information provider.	High correlation between challenger positions within each party where incumbency advantage is present; convergence where incumbency advantage is absent. Party coerces position taking.
	Null Hypothesis	*Expressive Campaigning*
Low	Random spread for challenger positions regardless of whether incumbency advantage exists or not. Candidates may still sort by party (i.e. challenger position for left-party candidates will still be to left of incumbent).	Random spread for challenger positions where probability of winning is low; convergence where incumbency advantage is absent. Candidates may still sort by party (i.e. challenger position for left-party candidates will still be to left of incumbent).

have knowledge greater than or equal to that of their opponents about voter preferences, and (b) to seek to maximize probability of winning, following Mayhew (1974).

Each of these options may be construed to contain candidates with a primary preference for maximizing probability of winning and a secondary preference for maximizing proximity to their noninstrumental ideal point. As I illustrate each of these alternatives, it is important to note the difficulty of assessing the trade-offs for candidates who believe their campaigns are neither hopeless, completely up in the air, or assured of victory before taking positions. Here, there is a trade-off between instrumental and noninstrumental position taking. In chapters 4 through 7 I discuss the ways in which candidates make this trade-off. For the purposes of illustration, however, I consider only candidates with a probability of winning of 0, .5, or 1, since the differences in the behavior of such candidates are of the greatest importance in distinguishing between the alternatives I discuss. In each of the graphs that follow I also presume the existence of a left party and a right party; for the sake of illustration, the challenger is always of one party. That is, if we assume an ideological dimension running from 0 to 100, where 100 is the most liberal position and 0 is the most conservative, the graphs depict a challenger from the liberal party opposing an incumbent of the conservative party.

Let us move through these options, beginning with the common median voter model, and then considering the expressive campaign and other alternatives.

The Median Voter Model Reconsidered

As articulated by Downs (1957, 114–41), candidate convergence is predicated upon seven claims about party and voter behavior:

1. Each candidate takes policy positions as a means toward gaining office.
2. Voters judge candidates based upon the proximity of the candidates on policy issues to the voters' own preferred position. Voter preferences can be reduced to a unidimensional policy space. They are single-peaked and monotonically declining from the voter's ideal point. Voters prefer the candidate closest to them, the candidate who maximizes their utility (or minimizes their disutility) in this function. Voter preferences are exogenous to the actions of candidates.
3. All potential voters vote; there are no abstentions.
4. Candidates have full information regarding the distribution of voter preferences.
5. Candidates are free to position themselves at any point along the preference distribution.
6. Candidates choose positions simultaneously. One candidate cannot know *ex ante* where the other candidate will position himself, although following assumption 1, each candidate should presume the other to take positions rationally.
7. Candidates' utilities are defined by the number of votes they receive; they are vote maximizers.

Given these seven assumptions, the result in a two-candidate election will be convergence at the median of the distribution of voter preferences.

Figures 2.1 and 2.2 merely apply the median voter logic to multiple races. The median voter model contains no provision for any sort of *ex ante* probability of winning; here, I hypothesize a range of probabilities of winning which are either unknown or irrelevant to candidates in their choice of issue positions. If both candidates choose positions simultaneously, neither candidate knows his true probability of winning at any position because neither knows the strategy of his opponent. The intuition of this model is that if candidates have no knowledge of each other's posi-

Figure 2.1. Candidate Positions for Multiple Races, Median Voter Model

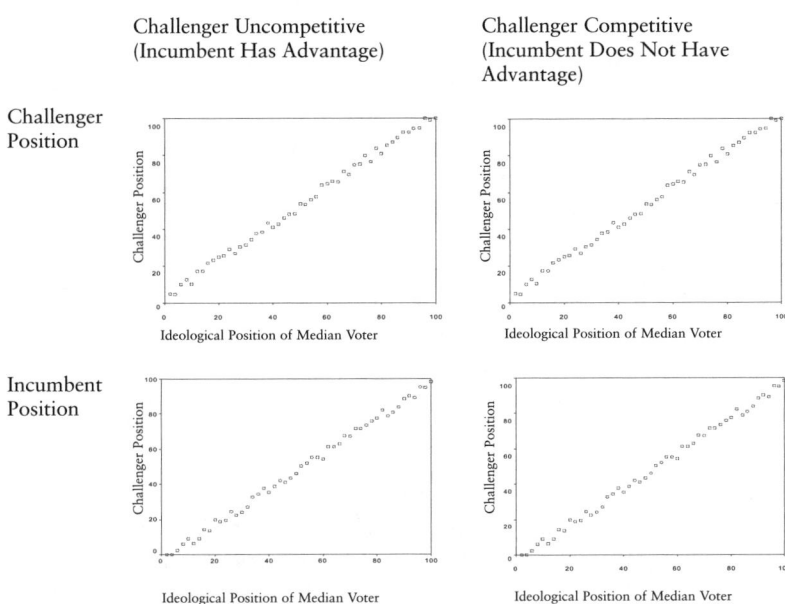

tions, they can be certain of no more than a split of the vote, a .5 chance of winning, at any position. There should thus be minimal distance between the candidates. Regardless of the actual (unknown) probability of winning, candidates will be clustered around the median of their preference distributions, as shown in figure 2.2.

The median voter model does not allow for motivations other than winning the election at hand. Victory is held here to be attainable for any candidate who chooses the correct policy positions. There is thus no range of winning positions; only one position can maximize probability of winning. If there is a personal advantage which accrues to one candidate, it is also not known. The only known quantity here is the distribution of voter preferences. Party control here can thus be construed as the ability to ensure that candidates have information about voters' preferences.

For a particular group of elections, then, we would expect from the median voter model that ideological distance between candidates will be

Figure 2.2. Candidate Distance in Median Voter Model

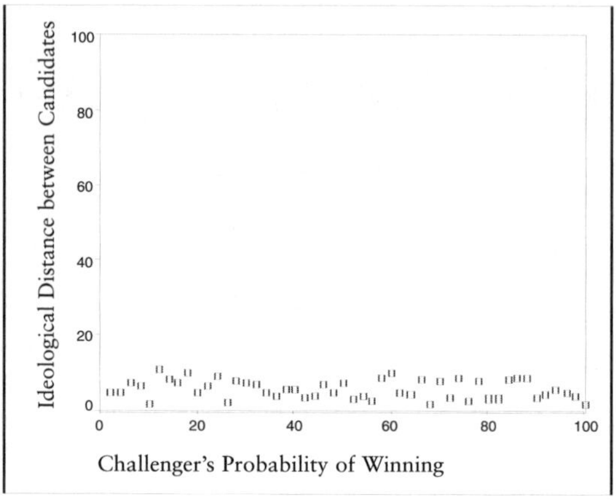

[Graph: Ideological Distance between Candidates (y-axis, 0-100) vs. Challenger's Probability of Winning (x-axis, 0-100)]

small for each candidate pairing, and it will be independent of any nonpolicy factors that influence candidates' chance of victory. We will be able to gauge nothing about candidates' noninstrumental preferences. We will be able to identify no concerns on the part of candidates other than winning office or gaining as many votes as possible. These results remain faithful to Downs's logic with the very slight exception of the allowance for *a priori* probability of winning to be established; in other words, the convergence prediction implies Downsian candidates in a game which is not necessarily as abstract as that of Downs.

One crucial extension of this set of hypotheses is that if we assume candidates to be vote maximizers, even the presence of an incumbency advantage, and therefore a sequential setup, has virtually infinitesimal influence on the positions candidates take. If the incumbent wins by taking a median position, a vote-maximizing challenger merely slides one slot to the left or the right, drawing an extremely slight contrast between himself and the incumbent. The logic of the median voter model still holds; candidates will differentiate themselves, but by as little as possible.

Many of Downs's assumptions have struck observers as unrealistic. As Johnson (1991) notes, however, empirical evidence indicating that Downs's model does not accurately explain political phenomena is not in itself a refutation of the internal logic of the median voter model; it only suggests that certain assumptions do not hold in the real world. Nonetheless, much of the work done in the area of spatial modeling since Downs (e.g., Hinich and Munger 1994; Enelow and Hinich 1984 for lengthier treatments) has been devoted either to formalizing his propositions or to relaxing the above assumptions in order to increase empirical support for an economic model of candidate competition. It is certainly possible to construct an elegant rational choice model based upon unrealistic or erroneous premises, but such a model would have very limited utility to political science. Thus, empirical questions about each of the above assumptions have preceded theoretical work on the effects of alternate assumptions. In explaining the next three alternatives, I note areas in which I have incorporated criticisms of each of Downs's individual assumptions.

Challenging an Incumbent: Expressive Campaigning and Party-Based Campaigning

Both of the alternatives on the right-hand side in table 2.1 rely upon discarding the simultaneity and vote maximization assumptions of Downs's theory. Where sequential positioning occurs, and where candidates in fact choose to maximize probability of winning, not votes, candidate divergence may be rational. Where candidates take positions simultaneously, and are thus unaware of each other's positions, maximizing probability of winning and maximizing vote share are equivalent. If one candidate can observe that another candidate has chosen positions first and has a nonissue advantage, the election is in effect over if the first candidate has taken his position rationally. In such circumstances, maximizing votes will have few benefits for a losing candidate.

In one sense, the simultaneity assumption can be relaxed without altering the outcome of the model. Simultaneous positioning necessarily implies a lack of information about one's opponent's position; hence, each candidate must follow a minimax strategy and assume his opponent to be rational. This ensures that each candidate will seek a median position regardless of the other candidate's position. As Riker and Ordeshook (1973) show, however, simultaneity is a necessary assumption for a median voter outcome where candidates are vote maximizers. It is not a necessary assumption where candidates merely seek to win a bare majority. In the latter circumstance, a rational candidate should seek a median position even if that candidate has knowledge that his opponent has failed to take such a position. Whatever benefits accrue from winning a supermajority may be outweighed by the downsides of taking positions that may leave one vulnerable in a future election.

This seems like a rather rare defect to the model, however; this instance only occurs in cases where one candidate is irrational or misinformed and the other candidate knows the first to be irrational or misinformed. Where both candidates are rational and informed, and where one candidate has a first-mover advantage, the second mover can neither win a supermajority nor seek a split of the vote by aping the other candidate. The candidate who has moved first has "captured" a position.

This is not an entirely novel conception in candidate competition models. Other models have sought to account for incumbents' advantage, but they have not done so in the explicit context of a sequential movement framework. Feld and Grofman (1991; also Grofman 1993 and Merrill and Grofman 1997) have developed a theory of "incumbent hegemony" in which incumbents have a "benefit of the doubt" zone, a zone of invulnerability around their spatial position. Here, voters give the incumbent the benefit of the doubt if the incumbent's positions seem relatively close to theirs because of nonpolicy attributes of the incumbent. If this zone includes the electorate's median, the incumbent cannot be defeated. They extend this model beyond the unidimensional framework to argue that where it exists, the two-dimensional instability described by McKelvey and Ordeshook (1976) does not exist. In this alternative, the incumbent need not be precisely at the electorate's median, only somewhat close to it. Thus, an incumbent might also be able to maximize utility in regard to secondary, non-vote-maximizing goals.

The Feld and Grofman model assumes simultaneity, but it hints at a two or more stage process. They demonstrate that, where this benefit of the doubt accrues to incumbents, "certain centrally located points will defeat any challenger by a substantial margin" (Feld and Grofman 1991, 117). Should a potential challenger suspect that this will transpire, competition and candidate entry will be deterred. Thus, a sort of two-stage process transpires where an incumbent establishes a central position and a potential challenger decides whether or not to run.

Groseclose (2001) does not make direct reference to Feld and Grofman, but his model of two-candidate competition where one candidate has a personal advantage is quite reconcilable with Feld and Grofman. Groseclose notes that any personal advantage, no matter how small, causes the Downsian equilibrium to disappear. Again, candidates choose positions simultaneously, but the advantage held by one candidate is exogenous and is known. Should this transpire, candidates know that if indeed they do converge, the candidate with the personal advantage will be the unanimous winner. Groseclose assumes "non-policy triviality"—that is, that the personal advantage is not so large that there is no pair of positions where the disadvantaged candidate wins. Given this, the disadvantaged candidate will gain votes by moving away from the center if the advantaged candidate is at the center, and by moving toward the center if the advantaged candidate moves away from it. There is thus substantial allowance for candidate divergence. Groseclose closes by arguing that as the personal advantage of one candidate grows, the disadvantaged candidate adopts a more and more extreme position. This alternative is equivalent to Feld and Grofman's benefit-of-the-doubt scenario.

Each of these models, as well as the incumbent hegemony model of Snyder (1994), assumes the establishment of a nonideological advantage but simultaneous establishment of positions. Retrospective voting, however, a factor which has been acknowledged as rational behavior by spatial theorists at least as far back as Downs (1957, 41), must be considered at least in part to be retrospective evaluation of the ideological pronouncements of a candidate. As such, it is difficult to imagine the establishment of a personal advantage on the part of an incumbent which is completely devoid of issue positioning. The incumbent must take positions while in office and before the true extent of his "benefit of the doubt" or personal advantage is known; a vote-maximizing incumbent thus has an incentive to adopt a median position as early as possible—before competition arises.

If simultaneity is not assumed, and where there are exogenous factors such as an incumbency advantage, information costs should decline for the second mover—this advantage should be observable. Divergence, then, becomes difficult to attribute to error or uncertainty.[3] If we then allow for deliberate divergence, two different circumstances may occur. First, an advantaged candidate may have a range of winning positions. Second, a disadvantaged candidate may have no winning position. In the first circumstance, a candidate with a benefit-of-the-doubt zone and full information about voter preferences can take any position within that zone. In the second, a candidate with knowledge that his opponent has taken a winning position has a choice of many positions, all of whose probability of winning is zero. Where candidates position themselves sequentially, the candidate that chooses a position second may have a range of winning positions if the first mover has taken a suboptimal position, or he may be able to adopt any position without affecting his probability of winning (because he has no chance of winning) if the first mover has an advantage and has taken a position rationally.

These may seem to be relatively extreme circumstances, but they do necessitate the introduction of secondary goals for candidates if we are to make any claims at all about rational position taking. Even if the extreme nature of the above is reduced somewhat—where the probability of winning is not one or zero, but is highly restricted and there are secondary concerns, a candidate's decision-making calculus may be affected. This begs the question of what these secondary concerns might be.

Where vote maximization is posited, there is always a trade-off between votes and noninstrumental policy concerns; even where one candidate has a significant advantage, there are votes to be gained or lost through movement within the ideological space. Several formal modelers (Groseclose 2001; Wittman 1973, 1977, 1983; Chappell and Keech 1986; Schlesinger 1975, 1994; Roemer 2001) have sought to model the trade-off between the two, assigning weights to each concern and constructing a utility measurement which accounts for both concerns. If probability of winning is posited as the dominant concern, however, a deterministic, sequential, and full-information model throws such secondary incentives into sharp relief—there is nothing else to guide candidate position taking across a range of positions where probability of winning is equivalent.

Secondary utility concerns have been inserted into hypothetical models, most notably in the work of Wittman and Chappell and Keech. These concerns are not directly measurable because they are idiosyncratic characteristics of each candidate. We cannot measure the actual preferences of candidates; even if we could ask them what they "truly" believe about policy issues, it seems unlikely that they would claim to be advocating policies which deviate from their *ex ante* beliefs for the sake of being elected or gaining votes. As Canon (1990, 27–30) notes, however, a candidate who truly believes he has little chance of winning has less incentive to compromise his positions; the very fact that he has chosen to run indicates that he is guided by his devotion to a cause, his desire to bring greater attention to his own *ex ante* preferences, or his desire to induce his opponent to address these issues. He will only make himself—and his fellow partisans—unhappy by deviating from such positions. Should this candidate find himself able to win, however, he may reason that even should he compromise his positions he will still be no worse in regard to these issues than his opponent.

Economist Albert Hirschman (1970) has noted that rational choice theory has not been able to successfully incorporate the twin phenomena of "exit" and "voice"—the fact that given a set of options, some citizens will decline to choose at all, to exit, while others will derive substantial value in making their dissatisfaction at the options they have been presented known—at seeking to change the rules of the game, in the long run, through voicing their own views. The exercise of voice seems to adequately describe the relatively powerless position of the long-shot candidate or party.

The primary testable question of this theory, then, is whose voice is being exercised. Two alternatives will be entertained here: first, that it is the voice of the candidate alone, or of some idiosyncratic group the candidate seeks to represent; and second, that the voice is that of the party, stripped of instrumental vote-maximizing or probability of winning concerns. As I shall discuss shortly, this is a useful test of the nature of parties—that is, not only of whether they can be seen as teams, but of whether they are indeed *unified* teams across different elections. A unified party could be presumed to hold all candidates who have little or no chance of victory to a common platform, while a party that exerts little control over candidates should produce candidates whose issue positions have little in common. As I conceptualize it here, we therefore have two options for defining rational position taking on the part of challengers: the expressive campaign and the party-based campaign.

The Expressive Campaign

In what I term the "expressive campaign," probability of winning can be known by candidates, and there are no efforts to coerce position taking, by the candidate's party or anyone else. Whatever utility candidates gain from their campaign derives from the satisfaction they receive from stating their views, educating the voters, or expressing their own ideas. We still have candidates seeking to maximize probability of winning, but with a secondary concern for maximizing proximity to their own *ex ante* or noninstrumental preferred position. This theory necessarily relies on sequential positioning insofar as the challenger chooses whether to advocate views that diverge from those of the incumbent or to move toward the district's median based upon his assessment of whether the race is winnable.

Where the incumbent holds a personal advantage and has successfully identified and taken the median position, all positions for the challenger yield a probability of winning of zero. Where the incumbent has not taken a median position or where he is at a personal or nonpolicy disadvantage, the challenger may have a range of winning positions. We might posit that the former type of candidate would resemble the "policy amateurs" described by Canon—there is a selection mechanism operating here in which election-oriented candidates choose not to run, and the field is filled by candidates motivated by ideological or expressive concerns.

Note that this alternative does not preclude long-shot candidates from adopting positions close to the median. Candidates are assumed to vary in their noninstrumental preferences, much as do voters. A candidate would

Figure 2.3. Candidate Positions for Multiple Races, Expressive Campaigning Alternative

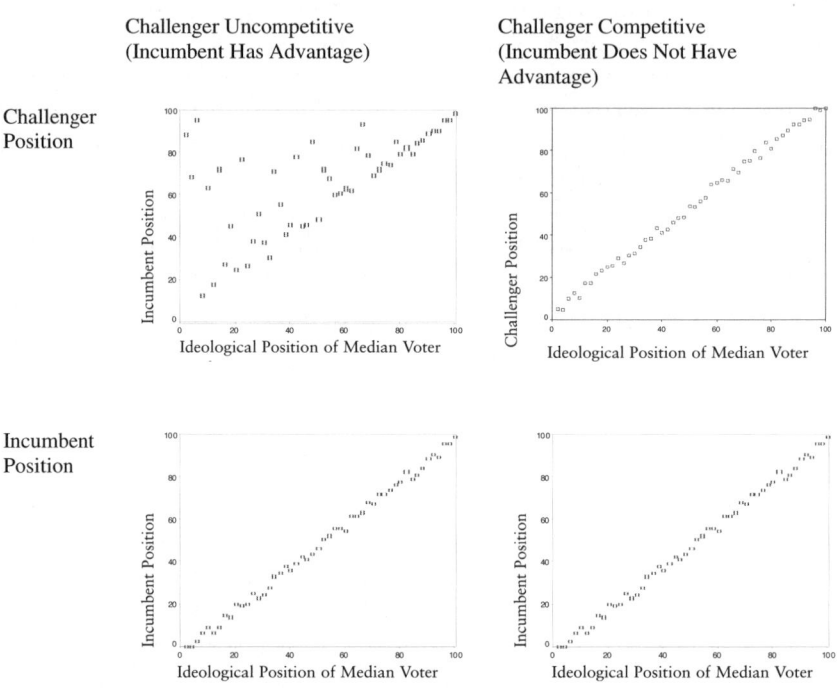

appear to have less reason to challenge an opponent whose positions are similar to his if his chances of winning are negligible, but, as much of the research discussed in chapter 1 shows, challenges need not be based solely upon policy grounds. We would thus expect, as figure 2.3 shows, that candidate positions will be randomly distributed for long shots (on the left of the figure), but where probability of winning is high for the challenger, candidates converge. There should be no correlation among the positions of uncompetitive challengers save for a slight correlation imposed by my sorting of candidates into left and right parties. In between these extremes, candidates balance a desire to maximize probability of winning with a desire to remain close to their ideal points.

If candidates are waging expressive campaigns, we would expect several things. First, ideological distance between competing candidates will vary less as the probability of winning for the disadvantaged candidate increases. Issue distance will be lower across districts where candidates approach equal probabilities of winning than it will be across districts where one candidate holds a significant advantage. Second, the lower a candidate's chance of winning, the more apparent that candidate's noninstrumental preferred position becomes. Third, although far less common, we may also observe attempts to maximize proximity to a noninstrumental ideal point by challengers who have a very high probability of winning. These candidates will move away from the median only to the degree that their probability of winning is not diminished.

This alternative seems also to be the most cost-effective strategy for both parties (at least in the short run) and candidates. Parties do not expend energy or resources seeking to choose candidates or coerce candidates into adopting a particular set of positions; likewise, candidates need not actually assess voter preferences unless they have a substantial probability of winning. This informational condition is perhaps the most important implication of this alternative. Candidates do need to be aware of whether they have a chance of winning. Where they do not have a chance, or where they have a fairly minimal chance, they do not have to gather information on where the median voter stands. If information about voter preferences is costly and it is not possible or worthwhile for candidates to gather this information—to conduct opinion polls, for instance—a general knowledge of their disadvantage is all the information it is necessary for candidates to have.

In addition, the option of expressive campaigning accords with the growing turn from exclusive attention to outcome-oriented behavior in rational choice theory. That is, in an expressive campaign, it is the campaign itself that is of value to the candidate, not the electoral outcome. In much of the terminology I use here to describe expressive campaigning, I rely on Schuessler (2000), whose theory of expressive choice by voters also emphasizes the noninstrumental benefits that accrue immediately from participation in political activities. In his theory, as in mine, the outcomes of this participation are of distinctly secondary importance in explaining the content of the participatory act or the decision to act at all. For Schuessler (2000, 5, 51), however, an "expressive campaign" is one aimed at fostering a sense of "expressive attachment" among voters, so that a vote is an expression for the voters of their identity. As such, expression can be entirely divorced from ideology or issue positions (Schuessler 2000, 59).

In the expressive campaign as I term it, it is the expression of the candidate, not the voters, that is of importance, and this expression is primarily defined through issue positions. That is, our theories share the turn away from exclusively outcome-oriented approaches, while differing in our expectations of candidate behavior and the role that the candidate's audience (i.e., the voters) plays in expression. For Schuessler, voters, and their attachment to candidates' expressive statements, drive strategies, while in my own conception of expressive campaigning, candidate expression exists entirely independently of voters' attitudes toward it. Candidates are, in his words, "producers of participation" (Schuessler 2000, 63), while in my theory candidates themselves are the participants of interest. The two theories are not at odds, but they seek to describe different political acts using a common rational choice conception of motivations and benefits.

In the chapters to follow I explore the existence of expressive campaigning in American congressional elections by describing my conversations with congressional candidates, some of whom engaged in expressive campaigns, some of whom did not, and some of whom were torn over whether to seek to take winning positions or to speak their minds regardless of the consequences. Above, however, I have merely sought to establish the plausibility and the rationality of the expressive campaign given particular assumptions about candidate competition. Before looking for empirical support, however, there are certainly other plausible and rational alternative theories of candidate competition to explore.

The Party-Based Campaign

Expressive campaigning is a consequence of unbalanced electoral competition and of benign neglect by the parties. This can, as I have noted, be cost-effective for the parties because they need not expend resources on candidates who are unlikely to win election. Yet parties, insofar as they may have ideological beliefs of their own, may nonetheless wish to maintain a party image or proclaim a party message in races where they cannot win. I noted above that while parties and candidates are often considered to be the same for the purposes of theorizing ideological competition, it makes sense in a context such as American congressional elections to conceive of them as two separate entities. Parties certainly may, and do, find advantage in encouraging party members who are running for office to break with the party on some issues where it will improve their probabilities of winning. As is the case for candidates, the grounding for this in the case of parties is simply that parties would assume that their members would be at least slightly closer to the party's preferred position than would candidates of the other party. In the congressional case, having officeholders who vote with the party on procedural votes, to elect the congressional leadership and the like, clearly outweighs these members' divergence on policy issues.

Figure 2.4. Candidate Positions for Multiple Races, Party-Based Campaigning Alternative

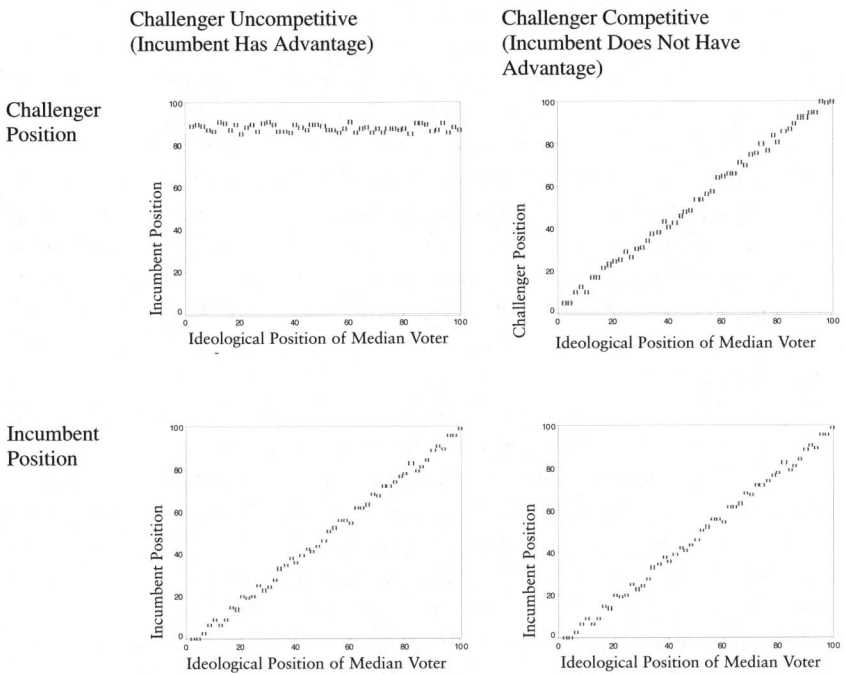

But what of the case where having candidates break with the party does not improve those candidates' chance of victory? What of the longshot challenger to an entrenched incumbent? The candidate clearly has little to gain in terms of probability of winning from breaking with the party, nor does the party gain from having this candidate do so. In fact, it may dishearten the party faithful in the district to have a candidate who does not share most party members' views. There are many valid reasons to expect parties to seek to encourage candidates to wave the party flag, even if in a losing cause.

In figure 2.4, parties are able to enforce their *ex ante* preferred positions upon their candidates. Should parties be able to field strong challengers to the incumbent, they can then choose to lessen their enforcement of policy positions, as reflected by the deviations on the part of competitive challengers from any established party position (the upper right-hand graph in the figure). Parties, however, may not necessarily need to encourage too much compromise here, insofar as an increased chance of winning the election may reflect greater proximity of the median voter to the party's most preferred position.

A party-based theory would presume party unity in cases where candidates' probability of winning is low. This alternative must be one with sequential positioning because parties must have several types of information. They must have information not only about the preferences of voters but also about the advantage the opposing candidate has, the position of that candidate, and the probability of winning in a campaign against that candidate. With such information, they are able to determine which candidates to exercise coercion upon to enforce a party position and which candidates to provide information aimed at allowing these candidates to deviate from the party's platform in order to maximize probability of winning.

In this alternative, then, the "true" voice of the party emerges among candidates with a low probability of winning. This alternative says nothing about the strategies of candidates with a high probability of winning, although one might assume that they are relatively close to the party's median as well, insofar as they did get nominated as the party's standard-bearers. Because convergence here is dependent upon incumbents, however, it must be assumed that they do have some freedom of movement, or else all candidates would be polarized and each party's probability of winning would be solely dependent upon the position of each constituency's median voter. The hallmark of the party-based campaign is thus the similarity between candidate positions on the upper left-hand side of figure 2.4, where probability of winning is at its lowest. Similar positions for different candidates in this area of the graph indicate a level of party coercion or unity, while a range of positions for such candidates indicates a lack of unity which cannot be explained by concern for maximizing probability of winning under conditions of full information and sequential movement.

The plausibility of the party-based campaign in practice depends on the finitude of party resources. Can parties really pay attention to all of their candidates? If so, what types of party organizations are we talking about—the congressional campaign committees? State or local parties? Party officeholders? This alternative's plausibility also depends on evidence about the ability of parties to choose their own candidates. There is scant evidence that parties can effectively tie their candidates to a set of positions, and most students of the congressional campaign committees agree that those committees concentrate only on viable candidates. As I explore later in this book, however, local party organizations do work to assist candidates or steer them in particular directions, whether toward party positions or toward vote-maximizing positions. Empirically, we have little reason to believe that party-based campaigning of the sort I have described is widespread in congressional elections, but this should not stop us from evaluating the ways in which congressional candidates, particularly those who are not particularly likely to win, interact with the different types of party organizations. I explore these issues later in this book as I distinguish between expressive campaigning and party-based campaigning.

What If There Is No Pattern?

Finally, we are left with one other option in our table, shown graphically in figure 2.5. What if there is no pattern at all for challengers? What if we have a large number of idiosyncratic challengers, ignorant of their chance of victory, running all manner of odd campaigns? If this is the case, we might say that these candidates have not, in fact, drawn any conclusions about the incumbent or the district's preferences save for the information necessary to counter the incumbent from their party's side (again, in my hypothetical graphs, to the incumbent's left). As I note above, incorrect or incomplete information gathered by candidates does not serve to refute the notion that candidates are behaving in a rational manner—one can make errors yet still be acting rationally. Let us, however, briefly consider another option—that campaigns are not, in fact, the sequential procedure that I have outlined in the previous two alternatives, that candidates are still acting more or less simultaneously. Simultaneous movement without some type of information, whether provided by parties or anyone else, is effectively no model at all. Here, there is little to guide candidate position taking save for their own assessments of voter preferences. If information about voter preferences is a function of resources, we can expect that the quantity or quality of resources will vary dramatically, and party provision of resources and information will not be present.

Such an argument depends upon alteration of as many as three of Downs's assumptions: it must either posit that voter preferences are not single-peaked, and thus are difficult for candidates to respond to; that potential voters may abstain or threaten to abstain from voting, thus making measurement of the expected vote or probability of winning at any position difficult and of an idiosyncratic nature for candidates; and/or that candidates cannot gain relatively complete or accurate information about voter preferences. Let us entertain each of these objections in turn.

First, one could certainly posit "all or nothing" situations when voters

Figure 2.5. Candidate Positions for Multiple Races, Null Hypothesis

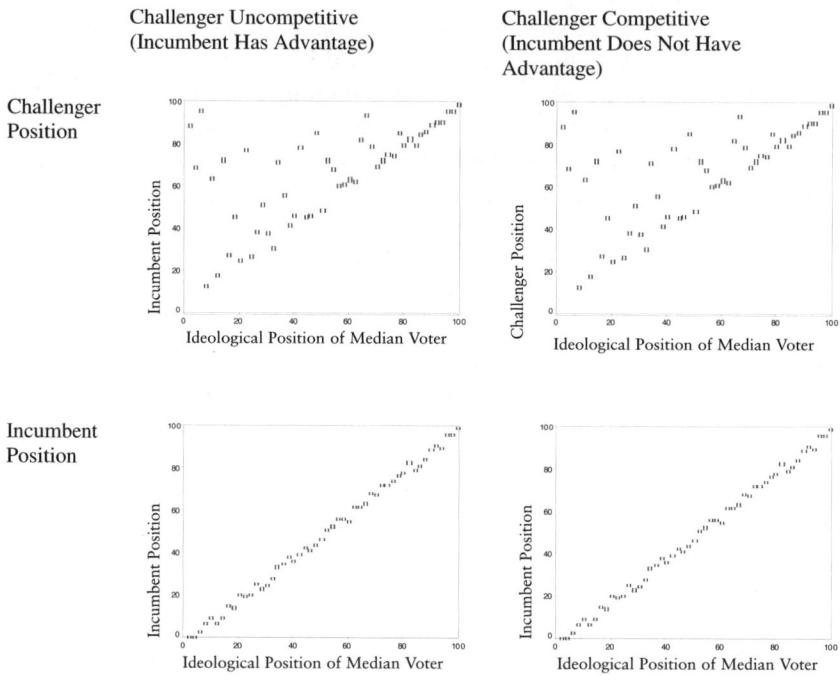

choose, for instance, to spend no money at all on missile defense, but prefer a substantial amount—enough to "do it right"—as a second choice. On particular issues, single-peakedness may not apply, and were such issues our sole area of consideration we could indeed question the spatial ordering of preferences. Where we aggregate issues into the type of liberal/conservative dimension used here, however, a situation that departs from unidimensionality becomes less easy to imagine. Alternate theories to that of Downs—most notably, the directional voting model of Rabinowitz and MacDonald (Rabinowitz and MacDonald 1989; MacDonald and Rabinowitz 1993a, 1993b, 1998)—have sought to dispense entirely with the median voter framework, but have retained the basic dimensionality approach and much of the discussion here would still seem relevant under their model. And multidimensional models have also been proposed to extend the median voter framework beyond the simple line discussed here. As Ferejohn (1993) argues, however, unidimensionality may still remain the most accurate way of depicting candidate strategies, and at least in the American case, a basic liberal/conservative organization of views seems the most inclusive of the various models of voter choice.

Second, abstentions would seem unlikely to affect candidates' perceptions unless it is expected that the abstainers will come disproportionately from one side (see Adams and Merrill 2003). "Selective mobilization" remains a much-trumpeted candidate strategy—witness the Republican "silent majority" of the 1960s—yet in practice the results seem mixed (see Wolfinger and Rosenstone 1980). In the case of the challenger to an incumbent, at any rate, it seems unlikely that a resource-poor challenger could realistically expect to mobilize enough potential abstainers, or cause enough of his opponent's likely supporters to abstain, to make a difference in the election outcome. Furthermore, a belief that there are abstainers who might be convinced to vote, or voters who might be convinced to abstain, is actually a belief about where the "true" median lies. Again, mistaken beliefs on the part of either candidate about the location of the median—a class to which the abstention issue belongs—do not invalidate these basic precepts about what candidates are *trying* to do in their campaigns.

Third, as noted above, we can certainly envision underinformed or misinformed candidates making unwise decisions about policy positions. This may, in fact, happen, but such an occurrence does nothing to undermine the alternatives I have discussed above. Again, insofar as my aim here is to document what candidates are *trying* to do, they can make mistakes without behaving irrationally. In regards to underinformed candidates, however, it is plausible that incumbents, or candidates with greater resources, can purchase better information (see Ferejohn and Noll 1978). However, as I document later in this book, even the most obscure congressional candidates are generally better informed than we often give them credit for being. That is, whether information is costly is more of an empirical question than a theoretical one. Our concern here is candidates' beliefs and intentions, not the results of their strategies, so we cannot attribute a lack of any pattern in candidate competition to misinformation and thereby also conclude that the median voter model or the two sequential setups I have explained are not in play.

Figure 2.5, which depicts an absence of any type of pattern in challengers' positions (save for the existence of a left and right party), is a null hypothesis, however one might seek to put a theoretical gloss upon it. Yet it must be built upon one or more of the above three assumptions. Two of these assumptions—that voter preferences are not single-peaked or unidimensional and that potential abstentions may alter a candidate's strategy—are at least as questionable as the Downsian assumptions which they seek to replace in the case of mass elections. The third, that candidates may lack complete information, also seems to have shaky support and in itself does not refute any of the above theories. This final option, then, merely states that candidates make mistakes; it does not assess what they are trying to do.

The prediction of this null hypothesis, then, as shown in figure 2.5, is a random distribution of differences between candidates (save, again, for party sorting). There would be no systematic differences between candidate positions across different levels of actual probability of winning for either candidate. Positions that embody noninstrumental preferences of the candidates cannot be distinguished from positions intended to maximize probability of winning but taken based upon inaccurate or incomplete information about voter preferences. And the noninstrumental preferred positions of parties likewise cannot be distinguished from the noninstrumental preferred positions of candidates. This null hypothesis remains a potential rejoinder to Downs, but it is still somewhat atheoretical and also seems rather unlikely.

Building a Case for the Expressive Campaign

The median voter model has often been reduced to a mere caricature in political science literature—not necessarily by spatial modelers, but by those who seek an offhand means of explaining the inevitable outcome of policy debates. There is widespread empirical debate, however, about whether it fulfills its most basic function, that of describing electoral outcomes. The sequential positioning alternatives I outline above provide an explanation for why its predictions so seldom come to pass, and they do so without disputing the internal logic of the model or the empirical fact that successful politicians do appear to capture a centrist position.

The median voter model has also been bedeviled by the accusation that it provides few incentives for those on the extremes of political debate to become active in politics at all—despite empirical evidence that they frequently do become involved, and often shape, policy debates. As Jane Mansbridge (1986, 3) notes, it is impossible "to dispense with 'ideology' in favor of practical political reasoning when the actors in the drama give their energies voluntarily, without pay or other material incentives." Considering expected electoral outcome as a determinant of candidate strategy allows ideology to be reinserted into a median voter paradigm in its most pure form. It also allows candidates to be treated as political actors who share with voters, political activists, or interest-group members (see Salisbury 1970) a desire or ability to procure expressive benefits from activities that might not seem at first glance to be in their self-interest.

Considering candidates in this manner, however, brings about a rather discomforting scenario for those who would advocate "choices" rather than "echoes." The sequential positioning alternatives suggest that we are given a choice precisely where having a choice matters the least—where the actual choices of voters are already preordained. We can expect divergence only where the stakes in taking a divergent position are relatively low. There are many candidates who would seem of interest to Diamond. They do not, however, win elections; if they were elected, they would no longer be of interest to him, and they exist, or at least they adopt divergent campaign positions, precisely because they are unlikely to win election.

Of these alternatives, the expressive campaign seems not only to have the most empirical backing, given what we know about American political parties and American elections; it also would seem to grow as a phenomenon in American politics with increases in the incumbency advantage, and it has substantial consequences for the choices voters are given by candidates. In the next four chapters I subject the above alternatives to both quantitative and qualitative testing. Because the actual estimates candidates make of their probability of winning are subjective, it is impossible to conclusively identify candidates' motivations from replication of the hypothetical scatterplots shown in the figures in this chapter. Seeking to replicate these graphs does, however, enable us to test (and, as I show, to discard) the median voter conception and the null hypothesis for elections featuring an incumbent and a challenger. In chapter 3 I utilize scaled issue position data for 1996 House of Representatives candidates to assess the degree of responsive position taking (or election-seeking behavior) in these campaigns. In the following chapters I present qualitative evidence drawn from interviews with over sixty congressional candidates to gauge the degree of information, strategic behavior, and party influence in these campaigns. These interviews form the core of my argument for the prevalence of expressive campaigning in congressional campaigns. The discussion in this chapter provides the theoretical backing for seeking to understand the expressive campaign. Once we have studied its existence in American politics, as I seek to do in the subsequent chapters of this book, we can begin to assess the practical and normative implications of the fact that ideology becomes prominent only in losing causes. In doing so, we are able to identify implications of this type of campaigning for both the formal study of elections and for the study of congressional candidates.

CHAPTER 3

Incumbents and Challengers Compared

In order to provide evidence for the expressive campaigning theory outlined in chapter 2, it is necessary to demonstrate four things:

1. Challengers and incumbents employ different strategies in choosing issue positions. Throughout chapter 2 I assume that incumbents seek a median position. Only in the median voter theory, however, do all challengers seek a median position. In each of the others, challengers employ other strategies.
2. Challengers know where the electorate's median is, where the incumbent stands, and what their probability of winning is. That is, challengers have information about voter preferences or, at a minimum, they could have access to this information if they chose to seek it. Information about voter preferences is not prohibitively costly for challengers. A finding in support of this proposition, in conjunction with evidence that challengers do take positions according to a different logic than incumbents, would establish the plausibility of a claim that challengers take positions out of a desire to maximize their own, or their party's, expressive utility rather than taking positions they erroneously believe will help them win or get as many votes as possible.
3. Candidates with a low probability of winning adopt noncentrist positions for their expressive value. That is, they take positions based on their beliefs about what is right rather than based on what they think voters want. Support for this argument would provide positive support for the expressive campaigning theory, instead of merely disproving other alternatives.
4. Political parties either do not or cannot compel position taking. That is, we need evidence that candidates are taking positions that they, as individuals, feel are right rather than adopting the party's message.

The first of these propositions can be demonstrated in a relatively straightforward manner using data on the positions of candidates in different types of districts and races. The second, third, and fourth propositions depend more heavily on candidates' subjective assessments of their strategic choices, and therefore these propositions must be demonstrated in a more qualitative, interview-based manner. In this chapter I provide evidence in support of the proposition that incumbents and challengers differ in their position-taking strategies, and I then outline the design of the research I conducted to establish the second, third, and fourth of these propositions. Each of the subsequent three chapters is concerned with one of the remaining propositions.

Measuring Candidates' Issue Positions

In order to test candidates' responsiveness to voter preferences, it is necessary to develop proxy measurements for candidates' policy positions and their beliefs about their probability of winning. That is, it is necessary to look at measurable outputs of incumbent and nonincumbent candidates' campaigns before we explore their campaigns in detail. In this chapter I regress a scaled measure of self-reported candidate issue positions for all major-party 1996 U.S. House of Representatives candidates on past presidential vote share for each candidate's party in the district. These data demonstrate that a majority of incumbents follow a median voter strategy, while nonincumbent candidates are much less likely to tailor their issue positions to the voting habits of their district. The data also demonstrate that there are significant differences in the issue positioning strategies of incumbents and nonincumbents within each party—differences that are due in large part to a lack of responsive positions on the part of the 1994 freshman Republicans.

Both of these measures are proxies for candidates' overall ideological stance and candidates' probability of winning. These proxies enable us to use commonly available information to address the behavior of congressional candidates as a group. They do not establish any causal mechanism—that is, they do not allow us to discern *why* candidates took any particular positions—but they do provide a starting point for exploring candidates' reasons and motives in taking positions in their campaigns.

Studies of nonincumbent candidates' issue positions have been handicapped in the past by the lack of a uniform measurement device. The most common means of placing incumbents on a liberal/conservative scale is an index of their voting records. Such scales range from the relatively straightforward addition of votes conducted by interest groups to DW-NOMINATE and other more complicated devices created by political scientists. Any scale of this sort will not truly be a means of measuring positions, however, since it does not account for intensity of preferences and, especially in the case of interest group ratings, because it may not consider a representative sample of members' votes. Several of these scales, particularly the ratings of ideological groups, as opposed to groups with a single issue focus or a limited range of concerns, do provide a means of comparing incumbent members to each other on a left-right continuum. Americans for Democratic Action (ADA) ratings are perhaps the scaling devices most commonly used by political scientists, although they are at times problematic.[1]

Because they have no voting record, however, no such easily accessible scaling device exists for nonincumbents. The closest we can come to approximating such ideological scales, then, is to survey the candidates. For issue position data in this chapter I have used the 1996 *Time/Congressional Quarterly* Candidate Survey.[2] In this survey, the text of which is provided in the appendix to this chapter, candidates were asked to respond to thirteen yes/no questions about their views on legislation considered by the 104th Congress.[3] Responses to these questions can be scored in a manner similar to the scoring of interest groups. For questions on this survey which showed a liberal/conservative split—that is, a majority of Democrats were on one side and a majority of Republicans were on the other—I coded each response 1 (a "liberal" response) if it was the answer given by the majority of Democrats and 0 if it was the answer given by the majority of Republicans. As I further explain later in this chapter, eleven of the thirteen survey questions could be coded in this manner.

To compute individual candidates' scores, I divided the number of "liberal" responses by the total number of responses to devise a "liberalism quotient" (LQ) which ranges from 0 for the most conservative set of responses to 1 for the most liberal set of responses. The LQ scores for incumbent candidates are highly correlated with the incumbents' 1995 ADA scores ($R^2 = .955$; $N = 377$). To compute distances between candidates within districts, I constructed a "liberalism quotient differential" (LQD) by calculating the absolute value of the difference between the two candidates' scores, excluding questions which were not answered by both candidates. Use of the LQD helps to skirt the thorny issue of computing a median position for the district. It is, I argue, a safe assumption that where the LQD is low, both candidates are moving toward the district's median, however liberal or conservative the district may be.

There are problems to confront, however, in interpreting these scores. Most importantly, it is not possible to be certain that the scoring accurately reflects the image the candidates choose to present to the voters or the perception that voters have of the candidates. A sample I have collected of the nonincumbent candidates' campaign literature concentrates on very few of the issues raised in the *Time/Congressional Quarterly* questions, and several issues not addressed at all in the survey receive substantial attention in the candidates' literature. The inability of these data to address the issues candidates choose to present is an important failing, which I shall consider later in this chapter. Failure to address voter perceptions is somewhat less relevant. It is the candidates' perceptions of what they should emphasize and how they should campaign that matter in my theory, not what part of the message voters receive. The fact that most nonincumbents' positions are less well known than those of the incumbent and the possibility that incumbents can often distort the public's beliefs about their challengers actually illustrate the first-mover advantage so many incumbents have.

In addition, not all candidates responded to all of the survey questions. Some failed to do so because they were not asked all of the questions; four separate versions of the survey exist, in which either eight, ten, twelve, or thirteen of the thirteen questions were asked. Other candidates chose not to respond to the survey at all (N = 73, 8.4 percent) while still others responded to some questions and failed to respond to others. I excluded questions to which candidates did not respond. The LQ and LQD indexes were constructed by dividing by the number of responses given, not the number of questions asked, leaving out those four candidates who had responded to less than half of the questions.

To measure probability of winning I use the percentage of the two-party presidential vote won in the district by the presidential nominee of the candidate's party in the most recent election, with the intuition that a district evenly split in presidential voting should be evenly split in congressional voting. This is, of course, often not the case, but I use this measure because it is one of the few pieces of information that is easily available to candidates of all resource levels and across all districts before they begin their campaigns.

There are other alternatives for measuring probability of winning, but each is lacking. Any measure used here must be available before the campaign begins; hence, commonly used estimates made during the campaign, such as the *Cook Report* or *Congressional Quarterly* competitiveness ratings, are not applicable. Other measures do not exist for all districts. Opinion polls might be obtainable for some districts, but clearly not for all. We can acquire campaign finance data for all candidates, but there is no clear relationship between candidate spending and probability of winning, nor does fundraising precede assessments of viability (see Herrnson 2000, 229).

All candidates, however, can be presumed to have access to records of past voting in their districts. Even the poorest challenger can easily find out the incumbent's previous margins of victory and district trends in voting in presidential, senatorial, and gubernatorial elections. There are certainly other, more idiosyncratic means that candidates use to gauge their chances, yet previous vote margins are pieces of information that all candidates can obtain easily, and they are the only probability of winning variables that are easily generalizable and quantifiable. Of these measures, presidential voting is the only measure available for all districts (it solves the problem of interpreting uncontested incumbents in previous elections) and easily interpreted by candidates. Because I consider the 1996 House races in this chapter, I use both the most recent election—that of 1992—and, because of problems interpreting the effects of Ross Perot's third-party candidacy, I also use the 1988 presidential vote in the district (adjusted for redistricting).

With these two measures, the LQ index as a measurement of issue positions and past presidential voting as a proxy for candidates' (subjective) probability of winning, we can thus proceed to looking at trends in the ideological positions of House candidates from 1996.

Differences between Incumbents and Challengers

The first, most basic distinction to be made in looking at these data is between incumbents and nonincumbents. Note that I include open-seat candidates here, insofar as open-seat candidates can be construed as also evaluating their chance of winning using the variables noted above. Although the competitiveness of open-seat races varies, of course, the equal footing and simultaneous position taking in open-seat races should lead open-seat candidates to be as responsive to voter preferences, if not more so, than challengers, if the sequential positioning alternatives of chapter 2 are to hold.

Before analyzing the scaled data, however, it is worthwhile to look at the individual questions in the *Time/Congressional Quarterly* survey. As table 3.1 shows, each of the survey questions identifies an issue on which the parties are polarized; there is significant difference in party means ($p < .001$) on all questions except the question of gays in the military. There are also, however, significant differences between incumbents and nonincumbents of the same party on many of these issues. These differences enable

Table 3.1. Candidate Issue Positions in the 1996 House Elections

	Democrats				Republicans				All	R^2 with LQ Index
	Incumbent	Challenger	Open Seat	All	Incumbent	Challenger	Open Seat	All		
Clinton Budget	98.8 (163)	96.6 (172)	100 (42)	97.9 (377)	0.9 (2)	5.0 (7)	5.3 (2)	2.8 (11)	50.1 (389)	.880
Medicare	99.4 (166)	99.4 (178)	97.7 (43)	99.2 (387)	1.9 (4)	13.6 (18)	6.1 (2)	6.3 (24)	53.6 (412)	.873
Welfare	97.6 (160)	73.0 (127) **	69.4 (25)	83.4 (312)	3.3 (7)	0.0 (0)	4.9 (2)	2.3 (9) ? ?	41.7 (322)	.827
FMLA	95.6 (151)	100 (184) **	100 (42)	98.2 (377)	27.6 (42)	38.8 (54) *	40.0 (16)	34.1 (112)	68.1 (486)	.777
Partial-birth Abortion	65.1 (108)	75.7 (128) **	61.5 (24)	69.5 (260)	6.6 (14)	9.4 (13)	4.9 (2)	7.4 (29)	37.9 (290)	.738
Bosnia	90.4 (150)	89.6 (163)	83.7 (36)	89.3 (349)	18.1 (38)	28.8 (40) *	29.7 (11)	23.1 (89)	56.4 (439)	.725
Brady Bill	75.9 (120)	85.1 (154)	77.5 (31) ?	80.5 (305)	32.5 (49)	25.5 (36)	14.3 (6)	27.2 (91)	55.5 (396)	.697
Term Limits	83.6 (133)	46.2 (79) **	52.6 (20)	63.0 (232)	17.1 (35)	11.3 (15)	8.3 (3)	14.2 (53)	38.5 (286)	.623
B-2 Bomber	68.5 (111)	79.8 (142)	76.3 (29)	74.6 (282)	36.2 (76)	37.4 (49)	30.6 (11)	36.1 (136)	55.4 (419)	.506
Aid to Russia	84.2 (128)	78.0 (124) **	50.0 (19) ? ?	77.7 (271)	27.6 (42)	32.3 (41) **	37.5 (12)	44.7 (134)	62.3 (405)	.504
EPA	87.3 (131)	8.0 (9) **	3.3 (1)	48.1 (141)	25.1 (51)	58.5 (38) **	70.6 (12)	35.4 (101)	42.0 (243)	.401
NAFTA	70.7 (111)	55.0 (93) *	64.1 (25)	62.7 (229)	25.3 (38)	41.6 (57) *	33.3 (13)	32.8 (108)	49.3 (342)	.321
Gays in Military	53.5 (84)	29.5 (51) **	47.5 (19)	41.6 (154)	11.3 (17)	59.3 (80) **	56.1 (23)	36.8 (120)	39.5 (275)	.249

Source: 1996 Time/Congressional Quarterly Congressional Candidate Survey. Percentages shown are "liberal" responses to each question; for coding and question texts, see appendix.
*chi-square test for mean challenger score = mean incumbent score p<.05
**p<.001
t chi-square test for mean challenger score = mean open-seat candidate score p<.05
tt p<.001

us to see whether challengers adopt more centrist strategies on the whole than do incumbents, and they also enable us to see where—on which issues—such moderation is taking place. On two issues, gays in the military and EPA restrictions, the differences are so sharp that I have excluded the questions from the overall index, thus constructing an LQ index with a maximum of eleven questions, guided by the hypothesis that incumbents and nonincumbents understood the questions differently.[4] The far-right column of table 3.1 also lists correlations between the individual question responses and candidates' LQ scores, and it further shows that these two question responses are atypical. Although the NAFTA question also exhibits a somewhat low correlation with candidates' overall average, responses to that question do break down in the expected partisan fashion, so I have kept that question in the revised LQ index.

In table 3.1 we do see preliminary evidence that some challengers are behaving responsively. Insofar as Republican nonincumbents tend to be running in more liberal districts than their incumbent fellow partisans, and vice versa, it is to be expected that nonincumbents as a whole will take more moderate positions than will incumbents. The fact that incumbents represent these districts to begin with means that the median will be closer to their positions than to those of nonincumbents; in other words, there is a sorting mechanism in these districts, either on the part of the voters, who chose the candidate closest to their views when they first elected the incumbent, or on the part of the candidates, who choose to run as the candidate of the party which captures their views most closely. Nonincumbents should, in more cases than not, have further to move to capture the median than should incumbents.

On three issues, NAFTA, aid to Russia, and welfare reform, Democratic nonincumbents as a group were significantly ($p < .05$) more conservative than were Democratic incumbents. Republican nonincumbents as a group were more liberal than were Republican incumbents on Medicare, Bosnia, the Family and Medical Leave Act, and NAFTA. Given the prominence of many of these issues in the presidential campaign and in the national media, these results are as an observer might predict—nonincumbents might be expected to compromise on high-salience issues more readily than on low-salience issues. Less intuitively, however, Democratic nonincumbents were more liberal than were Democratic incumbents on the Family and Medical Leave Act, and Republican nonincumbents were more conservative than Republican incumbents on gun control and aid to Russia. Finally, nonincumbents of both parties were, unsurprisingly, more in favor of term limits than were incumbents.

Figures 3.1a and b show the relationship between incumbent and nonincumbent candidates' LQ scores and these candidates' parties' presidential vote in the district in 1992 and 1988. As suggested by ADA scores for the years surrounding the 1996 elections, the parties are highly polarized; there are relatively few candidates in the middle of the distribution. There

Figure 3.1a. Candidate Ideology by 1988 Party Presidential Vote

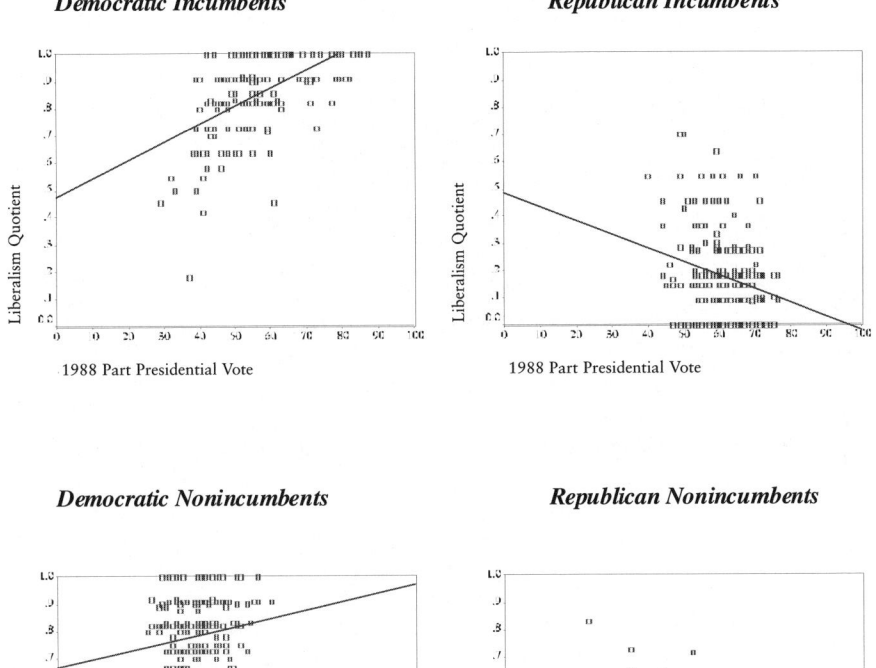

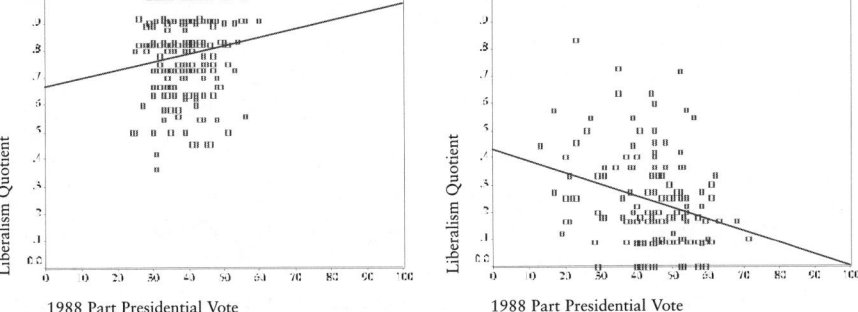

is little overlap between Democrats and Republicans, and there is even less overlap between Democratic and Republican incumbents. In fact, there was only one House race in the nation in 1996 where the candidates actually converged on the LQD index.[5] This polarization certainly indicates that candidates do not actually converge, but it is still possible to note movement by the candidates in accordance with district partisanship; candidates can fail to actually converge while still seeking to compromise on selected issues (see Wright and Berkman 1986 for a similar argument regarding Senate candidates).

Figure 3.1b. Candidate Ideology by 1992 Party Presidential Vote

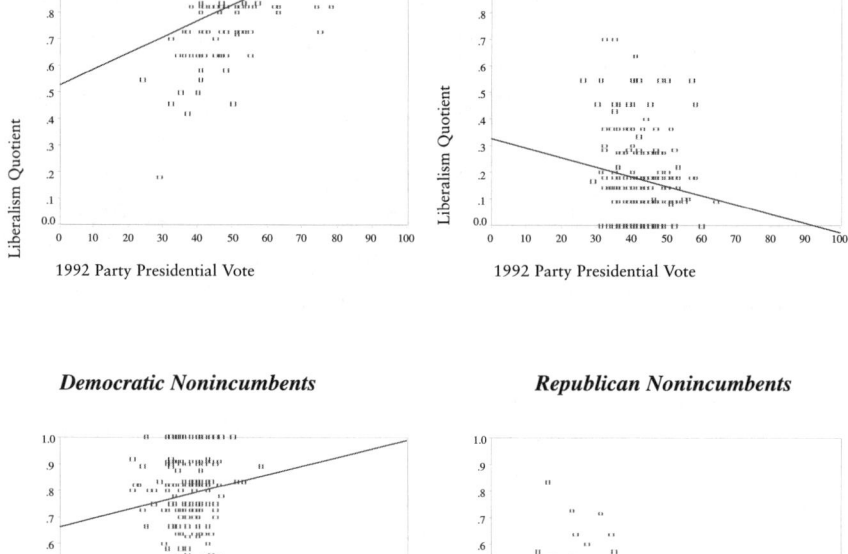

In this figure, strategic differences between nonincumbents and incumbents are evident, as are differences in strategic behavior between the parties. We should expect incumbents to become more conservative as their districts become more conservative if incumbents are seeking out a median position for their district. Democratic incumbents clearly are doing this. Whether Republican incumbents are doing so is less evident. For both parties' incumbents, the outliers are important; at a minimum, the small number of points at the upper end of the distribution of LQ scores for Republicans and the points at the lower end of the LQ score distribution for Democrats all are for incumbents who represent districts where their party's presidential candidate performed poorly.

Nonincumbents, however, are only expected to behave responsively as a group in the median voter model. The lack of a pattern for nonincum-

Table 3.2. Tobit Estimates of LQ Scores by 1988 and 1992 District Presidential Vote

	All Democrats	Democratic Incumbent	Democratic Nonincumbent	All Republicans	Republican Incumbent	Republican Nonincumbent
1988 Party						
Presidential	.0061 **	.0099 **	.0032 *	-.0045 **	-.0053 **	-.0038 **
Vote	(.0007)	(.0011)	(.0014)	(.0007)	(.0018)	(.0010)
Constant	.537 **	.373 **	.663 **	.436 **	.477 **	.407 **
	(.034)	(.061)	(.057)	(.041)	(.112)	(.050)
Mean X	46.84	55.30	40.66	53.92	60.76	46.31
LL Ratio	66.86	26.58	46.00	40.73	-2.33	-44.02
1992 Party						
Presidential	.0060 **	.0082 **	.0026	-.0052 **	-.0031	-.0053 **
Vote	(.0007)	(.0010)	(.0014)	(.0009)	(.0020)	(.0014)
Constant	.558 **	.438 **	.690 **	.388 **	.286 **	.397 **
	(.032)	(.053)	(.056)	(038)	(.088)	(.047)
Mean X	44.41	52.80	38.28	37.64	42.71	31.99
LL Ratio	66.63	26.74	46.00	36.88	5.29	44.04
N	393	166	227	397	209	188

**p < .01 *p < .05
Presidential vote is measured on a 0<->100 scale for each party. Standard errors are in parentheses.

bents here does not establish any particular set of strategic choices for this group of candidates, but it does indicate that incumbents are far more concerned with reflecting their constituents' preferences than are nonincumbents. I did generate scatterplots for the LQD scores for each district, but few of these show any pattern, further indicating a lack of vote seeking or election seeking on the part of most challengers. The majority of races with an LQD of .20 or less occur in districts without strong partisan leanings, yet it is hard to draw any conclusion from the remainder of the observations.

In figure 3.1 I provide OLS regression lines for reference. As is evident in the plots, however, regressions for both parties will be biased and inconsistent because each party's distribution of LQ scores is censored. Because the LQ scores range from 0 to 1, the Democratic scores will have upper censoring at 1, while the Republican scores will have lower censoring at 0. That is, we should see a large number of particularly extreme LQ scores for incumbents in safe seats for their party. Accordingly, in table 3.2 I present bivariate tobit results measuring the impact of 1992 and 1988 district presidential vote for each of the classes of candidates. The reader should note, however, that any linear equations here will be at the mercy of the outliers. That is, the phenomenon of "clumping" in the middle will give the small number of outliers on either side tremendous leverage in any equation.

Here again, there clearly is a significant relationship between LQ scores and district presidential voting in this table, but the differences between types are instructive. Just as our scatterplots, when looked at individually, show a strong trend on the part of incumbents (particularly Democratic incumbents) and a seemingly random spread for nonincumbents, so in the equations do we see substantial differences between incumbents and nonincumbents. In both parties, incumbents take positions with more regard to voter preferences than do challengers, particularly in the Democratic case. Democratic incumbents and Republican challengers show some convergence as districts become more conservative, but this is due to the responsiveness of Democratic incumbents to district preferences, not to compromise by their Republican challengers. Republican nonincumbents also shift their positions according to the presidential voting in their district, but they do so far less rapidly than do their incumbent foes. Democratic nonincumbents are barely taking positions responsively at all when we consider the 1988 vote, and their coefficient for 1992 presidential vote is not significant. Republican nonincumbents show slightly more responsiveness to district preferences than do Democratic nonincumbents.

One striking finding in this table, however, is the lack of responsiveness on the part of Republican incumbents to presidential voting in their districts. The outliers for Republicans in figure 3.1 do show that the most liberal Republican incumbents do represent districts that are less than 50 percent Republican. True to their reputation, first-term Republicans (the class of 1994) are driving this difference. Figure 3.2 demonstrates that much of the apparent randomness in district comparisons for Democrats challenging Republicans occurred because members of the freshman Republican class were on average more conservative than the districts they represented. Challenges to nonfreshman Republicans follow a path in which candidates move closer to each other as the partisanship of the district tightens. An analogous tobit estimate to those above for nonfreshman Republicans (not shown) shows a coefficient of -.0110 for 1988 party presidential vote and -.0075 for 1992, both significant at $p<.01$ and both larger than that of Democratic incumbents. The coefficient for freshman Republicans was insignificant. Districts held by nonfreshman Republicans that are closest in terms of presidential voting are also among the districts featuring the closest set of issue positions between the candidates; they are the only districts where there appears to be a pattern to the LQD scores,

Figure 3.2. Candidate Ideology and Ideology Differentials for First-Term and More Senior Republicans

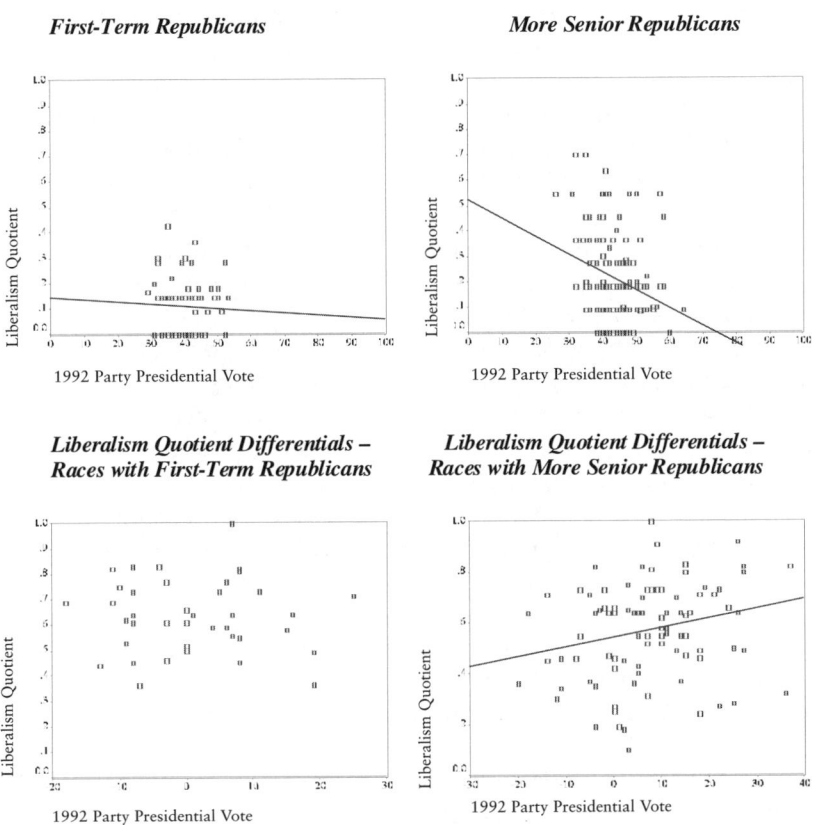

although the convergence here is driven more by incumbents than by challengers.

This lack of responsiveness on the part of many first-term Republicans is important for assessing challenger strategies. It means that many of the more competitive Democratic challengers for 1996 may not need to ape their opponents' positions to do well. They may be among the fortunate few in the sequential positioning alternatives who have a range of winning positions among which to choose. In any year, there may be a crop of challengers who have this option, and so it is important to note that while convergence is possible in competitive races, races can be competitive without requiring convergence.

Talking to the Candidates

These data are a means of assessing outcomes, not incentives; that is, they enable us to identify patterns in the positions candidates take, but they provide no direct insight into why candidates took the positions they staked out. Nonetheless, they do provide a preliminary answer to the question of whether there is a rational choice logic to candidate position taking. They enable us to make some basic determinations about the accuracy of the argument I presented in chapter 2.

Most obviously, these data do provide evidence of responsiveness to voter preferences on the part of incumbents. Not only is this unsurprising, but it accords with each of the alternatives I discussed. The only particularly surprising feature of incumbent position taking was that there was an identifiable class among incumbents—namely, first-term Republicans—who did not follow this strategy. The real test of the theory, however, is in the positions of the challengers. Here, we find scant support for a median voter strategy among challengers in the aggregate.

Nonincumbents do sway somewhat with the partisanship of their districts, yet not nearly to the degree that incumbents do. The only way that we could reconcile the median voter model with the data would be to assert that challengers, on average, have extraordinarily incomplete or inaccurate information about voter preferences, that they are, to put it bluntly, quite wrong about what voters want. For some candidates this may be true, but this seems like an unrealistic claim based upon the easily accessible voting histories of each district. The small sample of open-seat races, in which more of the candidates should have relatively high, and equal, levels of information, does little to confirm the median voter model.

The two sequential positioning alternatives provide reasons for nonincumbent candidates to take positions different from those predicted by the median voter model. If candidates are seeking to be reliable messengers of their party, one would expect that in races featuring an incumbent, the ideological distance between candidates would decrease as the challenger's *a priori* probability of winning increases; where the challenger faces a low probability of winning, challengers will adhere to the preferred positions of their party. The most important candidates to investigate here are those who are running long-shot campaigns. Are long-shot candidates more ideologically coherent than more serious challengers? In the aggregate, the answer appears to be no. There is certainly consistent polarization in all races, but if long shots were consistently adopting their party's preferred positions, the slope of the regression lines in figure 3.1 and the estimates in table 3.2 would actually be the reverse of what they are—that is, Republican nonincumbents would actually become more liberal as their districts grew more conservative, and the converse would be true for Democrats. There is no evidence for this in the data.

In the case of the expressive campaign, issue distance should decrease as *a priori* probability of winning increases for the challenger, but attempts to draw a neat regression line will be complicated by the lack of order to long-shot candidates' campaigns. That is, the variance for uncompetitive races should be much greater than for the more competitive ones. Here, we would expect that candidates who are unlikely to win run for a plethora of reasons and espouse a variety of ideological positions, while candidates who believe they have a good chance of winning are more often than not seasoned politicians who are accustomed to tailoring their positions to make this belief a reality. The unsystematic nature of challenger positions lends some support to this notion, but the question in distinguishing between this alternative and the others is where to draw the line between adherence to party positions and individually chosen expressive positions on the one hand, and between expressive positions and random variation on the other. The fact that challengers are less likely to adopt moderate positions than are incumbents does indicate that either challengers do not have the information necessary to make informed decisions about voter preferences, or that they are more inclined to let their own personal views stand in the way of changing positions than are incumbents. If the latter holds true, the expressive campaigning theory provides a rational choice articulation for this finding.

The data presented here are meant to demonstrate the plausibility of different theoretical conceptions of why candidates run for office and how they view their issue competition with their opponent. Ultimately, however, there is no substitute for exploring the actual decisions made within the campaigns of different types of candidates. Many candidates with whom I have spoken characterized themselves in a far different way than one might characterize them after reading a summary of the positions they took in the *Time/Congressional Quarterly* Candidate Survey,[6] and many also had assessments of their opponents' strengths and weaknesses that went far beyond what presidential vote totals for the district might suggest. As one candidate told me,

> You miss a lot of things in those statistics. There are more than two sides to most of those issues. NAFTA, for example, is more complicated than "are you for or against it?" And some of those issues just aren't relevant—I mean, how many candidates really cared that much one way or the other about aid to Russia, unless you were running in a district with a

lot of Russian immigrants. You pick the two or three issues you think are going to matter in the election, but the others, you just say what you think when people ask you and don't bring them up the rest of the time.

The candidate in question here was indeed a strong candidate, as election results showed; he was the beneficiary of a substantial independent advocacy campaign, but he was unsuccessful in defeating an incumbent who, despite his conservative voting record, had successfully cultivated an image as a moderate, responsive candidate in a district that leaned Democratic (in his opponent's words, voters viewed him "more like a city councilman than a congressman"). We might develop our own means of categorizing this election, and the strategies of the candidates in it, just as we might do so for any individual election in which we could talk extensively with the candidates and others involved in each race. Needless to say, such categorizations would sometimes be at odds with the conclusions we might draw about the same elections from the data I have just reviewed.

In order to build upon the above findings, however, while still keeping in mind the skepticism of this candidate, I conducted a series of interviews with nonincumbent candidates from the 1996 elections. I spoke with these candidates about their assessment of voter preferences, their issue strategies, and their relationships with their parties. Before I turn to these interviews, I summarize the interview process below.

The Candidates

During the summer of 1996 I contacted fifty-seven nonincumbent House candidates. I sent letters to all major-party challengers and open-seat candidates in Illinois, Minnesota, Ohio, and Wisconsin informing them of my study and requesting their cooperation. After the election, I waited three weeks for the candidates' lives to calm down, and I then began my interviews. Between November 1996 and July 1997, I interviewed forty-nine of these candidates in person and another three by telephone. Only five of the original fifty-seven candidates that I sought to contact could not be located or declined to be interviewed. These five candidates are relatively similar to the candidates who were interviewed; the fifty-two candidates interviewed provide a relatively complete picture of the political circumstances of their respective states. These candidates are drawn from fifty-six districts; there were four open seats and three incumbents without major-party opposition in these states in 1996. A full list of candidates interviewed is provided at the end of this book.

Seven candidates, including all six victorious ones, referred me to their campaign directors for my interviews. While speaking to the campaign directors may obscure some of the candidates' subjective appraisals of their campaigns, in many cases these interviews may have provided me with more information about strategic decisions and the work that went on in the campaign than talking to the candidates would have. I have treated campaign directors' comments with caution, but I have retained these for analysis in the subsequent chapters.

Waiting until after the election poses some validity problems, as candidates may revise their beliefs about what their chances of winning were and why they made particular strategic decisions. John Kingdon (1966, 23) refers to a "congratulation/rationalization effect," in which candidates adjust their thinking after the election in often unrealistic ways. I felt that, because most of these candidates were bound to lose, they would be far more candid with me after the election than during their campaigns, and that I myself would ultimately be the judge of whether candidates were being unrealistic in their judgments on their campaigns. Although many candidates appeared to have taken their losses quite hard, and a few had indeed developed means of rationalizing the election outcomes, I detected very few comments that seemed an obvious attempt to rearrange the facts.

Virtually all of these candidates were extremely forthcoming. Following the recommendations of literature on elite interviewing (see Converse and Schuman 1974; Fenno 1990; Jones 1962; Robinson 1960) I administered a relatively open-ended questionnaire, and I did not adhere rigorously to a questionnaire text. Interviews ranged from half an hour to over two hours.

Representativeness of the Candidates

For analytical convenience, my discussion of these interviews in the following chapters breaks the candidates up into three types. Of these fifty-two candidates, only six were elected to Congress, four of whom were open-seat candidates. This is typical of 1996 House campaigns, in which there was a 94.5 percent incumbent reelection rate. Along with these six, I term another eight candidates "very competitive" candidates. These are candidates who either garnered above 45 percent of the vote or were targeted for extensive support by their national party congressional organizations. Throughout my analysis, I consider both the winners and the narrow losers in the "very competitive" category. Twenty-one candidates ran what I term "somewhat competitive" races, in which they either received between 35 and 45 percent of the vote or, failing to do that, raised and spent over $100,000. An additional seventeen candidates ran relatively underfinanced, long-shot campaigns which resulted in less than 35 percent of the votes and less than $100,000 raised. In each of these cases, the candidates are relatively evenly distributed among the four states; Minnesota is the only state of the four whose congressional delegation did not change in 1996.

These competitiveness distinctions break with the party presidential vote indicator I have used thus far in this chapter, in part because that is a somewhat unsatisfactory indicator of competitiveness and in part because the use of these three broad categories makes comparison of candidates in a group of this size more meaningful.[7] While the categories provide a convenient means of analyzing different classes of candidates, the divisions between them may appear somewhat arbitrary to some. As I seek to show in the subsequent chapters, however, these three categories do quite accurately capture different types of candidacies in terms of ability to acquire information, beliefs about the likely outcome of the election, and the involvement of party organizations in the campaigns.[8] These distinctions are also important insofar as we have built-in comparisons or controls. That is, although the focus of this book is on expressive campaigning, a phenomenon most prevalent in races where one candidate has a low chance of winning, it is important to have candidates who we would *not* expect to be conducting expressive campaigns—candidates who can reasonably expect to win—among the interviewees in order to serve as a control group.

These are also admittedly *ex post facto* definitions of candidate types; that is, implicit in them is the assumption that the competitiveness of a candidate was a determinant, not a result, of candidate finances or of the individual viewpoints recounted below. To support this assumption, I refer the reader to the very high correlation of .875 between incumbent vote share in 1994 and incumbent vote share in 1996. Incumbent vote share in past races, as I have already argued, is not in itself an accurate means of measuring challengers' subjective beliefs about victory, but surely the range in which those numbers fall is a more relevant concern of candidates than other candidates' vote share. The categories I have chosen allow for variance which might be attributed to the candidates' actual campaigning skills, yet this variance is assumed to be, in most cases, rather small. These categories are based upon the notion that there is some satisfying mechanism in congressional voting; where an incumbent has received, for example, over 65 percent of the vote in the past election, this vote share

Table 3.3. Comparisons of Candidates Interviewed with All Nonincumbent 1996 Candidates

	Democrats	Republicans	Winners	Long-Shots[a]	Somewhat Competitive[a]	Very Competitive[a]	Median Receipts[b]	Median LQ Score
All Races (N = 469)	54.4% (255)	45.6% (214)	15.5% (72)	34.3% (161)	39.9% (187)	25.8% (121)	$201,710	.580
Candidates Interviewed (N = 52)	57.7 (30)	42.3 (22)	11.5 (6)	36.5 (17)	38.5 (21)	26.9 (14)	180,310	.640

(a) Competitiveness is measured as defined above--long-shot candidates received less than 35% of the vote and raised under $100,000; somewhat competitive candidates either received 35% to 45% of the vote or, failing to reach this mark, raised over $100,000; very competitive candidates received over 45% of the vote.
(b) Figures are taken from the 1996 year-end FEC reports. Candidates who raise less than $5,000 are not required to report; any unreported campaign figures were thus coded as $5,000. Three of the 33 nonreporters were among the candidates interviewed.

indicates satisfaction of the voters with their member of Congress and a reluctance to consider a challengers' positions no matter how skillfully the challenger, or the challenger's party, runs a campaign. Given not only the high correlation between incumbent vote shares from one election to the next, but also the reluctance of the national parties to pour resources into campaigns against popular incumbents, this seems a reasonable assumption, or at least an assumption that the behavior of the parties is unlikely to disprove.

As table 3.3 demonstrates, the group of candidates with whom I spoke roughly reflects national patterns. These candidates raised, on average, less money than did other nonincumbent candidates, yet they were comparable in terms of their ideology, their party affiliation, their vote percentage, and the competitiveness of their elections. The candidates I interviewed were somewhat more liberal, on average, than were other candidates. This is partially a function of the larger proportion of Democrats among my interviewees, and it may be partially a function of the more liberal politics of the four states in which I chose to conduct interviews.

In part because I define competitiveness using financial resources, differences between categories in financial expenditures are quite large. Among all candidates, the average amount spent by long shots was $27,975; for somewhat competitive candidates, $371,317; and among very competitive candidates, $729,169. Among the candidates I interviewed, the corresponding figures were $26,042 for long shots, $267,091 for somewhat competitive candidates, and $608,488 for very competitive candidates. The means for very competitive candidates are lower among the candidates interviewed because of differences at the very top of the spending hierarchy; only one of the candidates I interviewed spent over $1 million, while twenty-seven nonincumbent candidates nationwide did so, with two spending over $2.5 million.

The 1996 Elections in Context

One area in which the selection of candidates is not representative, of course, is timing. Ideally, a thorough test of candidate strategy would include a truly random cross-sectional sample of candidates drawn from several different election periods. In chapter 7 I discuss similarities between a selection of candidates from the 2000 races from several different states and the 1996 candidates considered in the next three chapters. For the time being, however, a brief consideration of some of the potential peculiarities of the 1996 candidates is in order.

First, one might argue that 1996 is anomalous, that the congressional candidates of 1996 were different from the average candidate in another year. While certainly every set of elections is unique, 1996 is in many ways typical of congressional elections of the past twenty years. It was certainly not as anomalous as was 1994.

As is the norm in presidential election years, the party of the victorious presidential candidate gained seats in the House. The Democrats gained only nine House seats, however, and they remained in the minority. As was the case in 1984 and 1972, one might contend that the incumbent president had some effect on congressional races, but this effect was nowhere near as great as the effects of presidential coattails had been in the past. The average Republican incumbent outspent the average Democratic incumbent, and challengers were outspent by approximately a seven-to-one ratio. According to FEC year-end reports, the median incumbent spent $538,845 to the median challenger's $77,978. The 94.5 percent incumbent reelection rate for 1996, then, is hardly surprising. In this respect, 1996 was not by any means an unusual election, and its candidates can be assumed to have behaved similarly to House candidates in other recent elections.

One way in which the candidates of 1996 were unusual is that there were more of them, and they may have garnered more attention than the average crop of congressional candidates. Nineteen ninety-six was a year of particularly heated competition in several ways. As the first year in which the new Republican majority had to defend its seats, both parties felt they had a good chance of holding majority status in the House following the election. Certainly it had been many years since both parties had been uncertain who would organize the chamber following the election. Early in the campaign, the Democratic Party and the AFL-CIO identified several vulnerable Republicans against whom to concentrate their efforts. The lion's share of media attention in 1996 went to the AFL-CIO's advertising campaign. Jacobson (1999) has argued that the AFL-CIO campaign had little effect on the overall outcome of the race; he attributes this not to flaws of the AFL-CIO's strategy but to a lack of quality candidates put forward by the Democrats; only 22.1 percent of Democratic challengers had prior political experience, as compared to the postwar average of 25.3 percent.

Despite this low number of experienced candidates, however, it appears that the parties did place a premium on fielding candidates in as many districts as possible. In 1996, 3.2 percent of House seats were uncontested, a decline from 17.4 percent in 1994 and a low in the post–World War II years (see table 1.2). Nineteen ninety-two was the only other election in which the percentage of uncontested seats fell below 10 percent. Because we know that challengers did not fare better than usual, the only conclusions one can draw from this fact are that there are likely to have been a higher number of long-shot candidates and perhaps a higher number of recruited candidates than normal.

Thus, 1996 has some unique features, but it seems that these features are likely to have played a role in only a small number of elections. It is a year in which competition was in some regards more heated than it had been in previous elections, but this fact actually makes 1996 an appealing year to study rather than a particularly poor case from which to generalize. In the subsequent chapters I note unusual features of the election, but these seem few enough that they do not pose a significant problem for generalization.

State Political Culture and Historical Background

A second area in which these candidates are not representative is, of course, geography. I found that in order to conduct successful interviews, I needed to have relatively extensive background knowledge about local politics. By choosing four neighboring states, I was able to follow candidates when they made comparisons to other candidates, or when they discussed local politicians and events. By choosing to interview all candidates in these states, I was able to gain an understanding of how the parties operated in each state and how geographical considerations determined campaign strategies. In chapter 7 I compare candidates in these states with candidates from four other states, and I find few ways in which my choice of states appears to affect my overall conclusions about expressive campaigning.

Within these four states, however, there is a great deal of variation. When put together, these states represent a microcosm of the nation both politically and demographically. All are large states with a rich political history. In terms of politics, the relatively balanced party competition in these states ensures that both parties are represented adequately in the study. Each state displays a level of volatility in elections great enough to qualify it as a relatively competitive two-party state, in each state both parties have shown in recent years that they can win at the state level, and voting in each state has generally followed national trends in presidential voting. Wright, Erikson, and McIver (1985) also demonstrate that these four states are all close to the mean in terms of voter ideology and partisanship.

Most importantly, it is clear that these states have a relative balance of power in their congressional delegations. There is within them, however, some volatility. "Safe" Republican districts in Minnesota, such as the Second and the Seventh Districts, had fallen into Democratic hands at the time of my 1996 study, although the Second is now Republican again. Minnesota actually had three of its eight districts change party hands in the 1990s. Likewise, in Wisconsin Republicans have proven competitive in Democratic areas such as the Second District, where Madison is located, which was held by a Republican from 1990 to 1998. Ohio shows a slow trend toward the Republicans, although this may be due in part to the 1992 redistricting, which prompted the defeat of one relocated Democrat and the retirements of four others in the more Democratic, northeastern part of the state. Illinois is the most consistent of the four states; redistricting in both 1992 and 2002 seems to have affected both parties equally, and the only unusual change in district control is that of the Fifth District, formerly held by Dan Rostenkowski but temporarily in Republican hands as of the time of this study. Only in Wisconsin has one party maintained control of both Senate seats for the past decade, and only in Ohio has the governorship remained in one party's hands.

Presidential voting in the four states is also not strikingly far from the national average. Illinois has opted for the winning candidate in nine of the past eleven elections, Ohio has missed only one, and Wisconsin has missed only four. Only Minnesota consistently runs more than three points away from the average; Minnesotans have voted more Democratic in general, but some of this disparity may be accounted for by the presence of

Minnesotans on the Democratic presidential ticket in five of the past ten elections.

As I show in chapter 6, the four states also allow us to analyze variations in party strength. Mayhew (1986, 66–77, 159–64) and Fenton (1966, 44–54, 194–218) concur about the strength of the political parties in the states considered here. Fenton divides the four states into issue-oriented (Minnesota and Wisconsin) and patronage-oriented (Ohio and Illinois) states. In his ratings of party strength by state, Mayhew rates Ohio and Illinois as strong-party states, while he classifies Wisconsin and Minnesota as weak-party states. Minnesota, it should be added, is the only one of the four states to have a relatively unconventional manner of nominating candidates. Party caucuses convene to endorse candidates, after which the party's endorsed candidates must run in a primary; those candidates formally endorsed by the party may not wind up being the nominee of the party. The other state parties I consider here refrain from endorsing candidates until after the primary.

There is also significant demographic variation within each state and between the states. Each of these states is characterized by a push and pull between urban, suburban, and rural areas. The Illinois population is roughly evenly split between Chicago, the Chicago suburbs, and the more rural downstate area; the Democratic Chicago machine that once controlled Illinois politics no longer exerts much power over the rest of the state. Chicago continues to be among the most Democratic cities in the United States, while the Chicago suburbs continue to be among the most Republican regions of the country. The rural, "downstate" region is thus a battleground in state races. With the exception of the very southern tip of the state, which includes strongly Democratic cities such as Decatur, Cairo, and East St. Louis, in the remainder of Illinois both parties exhibit equal strength.

Ohio, which was strongly Republican early in the century, but which has at times had strong Democratic bases in rust-belt cities such as Cleveland, Akron, Canton, Youngstown, and Toledo, has also been characterized by urban/rural conflict. Twenty-six percent of the Ohio population lives in rural areas, but all of the major cities except for Columbus have shrunken dramatically over the past few decades as the steel industry and other manufacturing industries have declined (see Duncan and Nutting 1999, 1043; Barone, Cohen, and Ujifusa 2001, 1184). For most of the postwar years, Ohio had a predominantly Republican congressional delegation, with the few consistently Democratic seats located in the major industrial cities and in the primarily industrial counties of the north and northeast. Cincinnati and Columbus have during this time distinguished themselves as two of the most conservative of major American cities. The

Ohio delegation actual tilted toward the Democrats for a time in the 1970s and 1980s, but recent Republican gains have brought Ohio's partisan balance back toward the Republican advantage of the 1950s and 1960s (see Diemer 1994).

Minnesota and Wisconsin are both more rural states than Ohio and Illinois. The population of the Minneapolis and St. Paul region is easily several times larger than any other city in the state, but there is somewhat less of a disparity in politics between the urban, suburban, and rural areas, in part because Minneapolis has never been the industrial center that Chicago and the larger Ohio cities are or once were, and in part for distinctive cultural reasons. The Twin Cities area and the northern part of Minnesota are strongly Democratic; the Twin Cities suburbs are somewhat more Republican; and the three southern Minnesota districts are, and have traditionally been, very conservative, primarily agricultural areas. These differences have often been attributed to Minnesota's immigration patterns; much of northern Minnesota was originally settled by Scandinavian immigrants, while the southern part of the state was originally settled by German immigrants.

Wisconsin is the most rural of the four states. Although it does have one major industrial city, Milwaukee, the Milwaukee area has never had the size to be a focal point of state politics. The Republican Party has played a major role in Wisconsin politics since its first meeting in Ripon, Wisconsin. However, the policies advocated by Republicans in Wisconsin have at times been to the left even of most Democratic initiatives during the twentieth century.

For each of the quotes I use in subsequent chapters, I have appended the state name so that the reader may identify peculiarities of the individual state the respondent is from. With the exception of chapter 6, in which I explicitly consider party strength, I do not explicitly draw out state differences. In the cases of information acquisition and issue strategies, there should be little reason to suppose these candidates to be particularly unrepresentative. In the area of party activities, I have sought to emphasize differences between the states, in the hope that the findings might be extrapolated to states with similar political cultures.

Listening to the Candidates

The primary goal in my interviews, and in my discussion of the interviews, is to let the candidates speak for themselves. In presenting their comments on their campaigns and their campaign strategies, I do briefly note any methodological issues present in formulating questions or interpreting candidates' comments. I have sought wherever possible, however, to put matters in the candidates' words rather than in my own.

The candidates' comments, as well as several representative case studies, are arranged so as to draw finer and finer distinctions between the theoretical options I have outlined. In chapter 2 I presented a two-by-two table that I seek to address through the candidates' comments. Earlier in this chapter I addressed the differences between incumbents and challengers and established the viability of exploring a campaign strategy and an issue strategy for nonincumbents that departs from what we know about incumbents' campaigns. In chapter 4 I address the problem of information acquisition. I explore candidates' use of public opinion data, voting trends, and other measures candidates might use to inform themselves of what their chances of victory were in their campaigns. In chapter 5 I explore the issue positions of the candidates and the reasons why they chose these positions. In this chapter the candidates frequently refer to a desire to diverge from the positions of their opponent even where doing so seems unlikely to improve their chances of victory. It is in this chapter that candidates' forceful statements of their own policy beliefs and their separation of these beliefs from electoral calculations establish the prevalence of expressive campaigning in many of these races. Finally, in chapter 6 I present candidates' comments on the role of their party—be it the national congressional campaign committee, the state party, the local party, or prominent leaders and party office-holders—in their campaigns. This chapter provides a qualification to my theory of expressive campaigning. It shows that political parties can encourage expressive campaigning, or they can exert pressure upon candidates either to take positions more akin to those of mainstream party members or to take election-oriented positions. That is, expressive campaigning takes root where parties practice a form of benign neglect in regard to many of their candidates. When parties take an interest in a campaign, election-oriented intervention is often unnecessary, insofar as candidates themselves recognize the value of election-oriented positions. Meanwhile, intervention aimed at producing a party-based campaign can often hurt candidates, or at least leave them unhappy with the results of their campaigns. In short, this chapter establishes the push-and-pull of the two sequential positioning alternatives, the expressive campaign and the party-based campaign.

We shall revisit the theoretical implications of these distinctions at the close of this book. Until then, let us turn to our nonincumbent candidates' views on what they did in their campaigns and why they did what they did.

Appendix to Chapter 3: *Time/Congressional Quarterly* 1996 Congressional Candidate Survey

Questions and Coding

Clinton Budget: Would you have voted for the budget-reconciliation bill aimed at balancing the federal budget by fiscal year 2002? The bill had provisions reducing expected federal spending $894 billion over seven years, including major restraints on Medicare, Medicaid and welfare spending, and cutting expected tax revenue $245 billion. (1 = NO)

Medicare: Would you have voted for the bill to reduce expected Medicare spending $270 billion over seven years? (1 = NO)

B-2 Bomber: Would you have voted for the amendment to cut $493 million provided for continued production of the B-2 Stealth bombers? (1 = YES)

Term Limits: Would you have voted for the "term limits" constitutional amendment imposing a twelve-year lifetime limit on congressional tenure in either the House or the Senate? (1 = NO)

Partial-Birth Abortion: Would you have voted for the bill to ban so-called partial-birth abortions, in which the doctor removes the fetus's brain tissue after bringing the fetus into the birth canal? Under the bill, doctors who perform the procedure could be subject to criminal and civil penalties. (1 = NO)

EPA: Would you have voted for the amendment striking seventeen provisions from a fiscal 1996 spending bill that funds the Environmental Protection Agency? The provisions would limit the EPA's enforcement of certain environmental regulations. (1 = YES)

FMLA: Would you have voted for the Family and Medical Leave Act, which requires many businesses to provide workers up to twelve weeks of unpaid leave for the birth or adoption of a child or a medical emergency? (1 = YES)

Brady Bill: Would you have voted for the "Brady Bill," which requires each would-be purchaser of a handgun to wait five days while local law-enforcement officials conduct a personal background check on the purchaser? (1 = YES)

Gays in the Military: Would you have voted for the amendment to allow the Pentagon to implement its "don't ask, don't tell" policy, continuing the existing ban on known homosexuals in the military, but preventing military officials from asking about service members' sexual orientation? (1 = NO)

Bosnia: Would you have voted for a bill to bar the use of federal money for the deployment of U.S. troops in Bosnia-Herzegovina? (1 = NO)

NAFTA: Would you have voted for legislation to implement the North American Free Trade Agreement, which links the United States, Canada, and Mexico in a free-trade zone and requires each country to eliminate numerous tariffs and trade barriers? (1 = NO)

Aid to Russia: Would you have voted for the foreign-spending bill that included $2.5 billion in direct aid for Russia and other former republics of the Soviet Union? (1 = YES)

Welfare: Would you have voted for the bill overhauling the federal welfare system, ending welfare as an entitlement, turning it into a block-grant program to be run by states and placing certain work and behavioral requirements on welfare recipients? (1 = NO)

(c) 1996 TIME Inc., reprinted by permission.

CHAPTER 4

"It's Not Like Rocket Science": How Candidates Understand Public Opinion

As I outlined in the previous chapter, the second condition in my argument for the prevalence of expressive campaigning in congressional races is that challengers have, or at least are able to acquire, two different types of information. First of all, probability of winning is presumed to be a quantity that can be estimated relatively accurately by candidates. If the long-shot candidate does not know that he is a long shot, if he dramatically overestimates his chance of winning, we would expect him to take positions instrumentally, to adopt a median voter strategy which will have little observable effect upon his actual chance of winning. Conversely, if the very competitive candidate is unaware that he is in a position to win his election, he may not take the strategic positions that will help him to do so, and he may diminish his chance of winning. In each case, candidates are presumed to want to know which candidate the median voter prefers, and to what extent this preference is based upon nonpolicy characteristics of the incumbent.

Second, even if candidates do make accurate assessments of their probability of winning, they may still be mistaken about the policy preferences of voters. A challenger may be aware that the incumbent is vulnerable or unpopular, yet still err in his or her assessment of why the incumbent is vulnerable. Where candidates are able to estimate probability of winning, and where probability of winning is high enough to encourage candidates to follow a median voter strategy, they must then gauge where the median voter stands on the major policy issues. Thus, the second type of information of relevance is information about voter preferences on policy. If probability of winning is low enough that candidates decide they will not benefit from following a median voter strategy, this information is irrelevant to them. It is only where candidates deem winning the election to be within the range of possibilities that they will even have use for this information.

Information, in both of these senses, is frequently regarded by social scientists as a quantity that can be easily obtained through careful analysis of survey data. Politicians' means of gauging public opinion, however, are hardly limited to social scientific techniques. Most politicians take pride in their intuitive understanding of what voters want, just as many citizens surely feel that they gather some information about their neighbors and fellow citizens through conversations, through reading the newspaper, and through other unscientific, informal techniques (Geer 1996, 4; Herbst 1993, 99). In the interviews I discuss in this chapter, I therefore do not limit my definition of "information" to the results of opinion polls. The candidates with whom I spoke made assertions about public opinion far more frequently than they referred to opinion polls. The impressions they had about their chances of winning and about voter preferences on policy were often based upon a complex mix of information sources. These sources were certainly as influential in their campaigns, if not more so, than were opinion polls.

In this chapter I attempt to sift through the various types of information candidates have in order to pass some judgment upon the accuracy or utility of that information. Did the candidates with whom I spoke realistically assess their chance of winning? If so, and if they did deem winning the election to be within the realm of possibility, were they able to identify the preferences of voters? How did they do so?

In answering these questions, I aim to make a very simple point—that the type of information relevant to most congressional candidates is not particularly costly and that few nonincumbents make substantial errors in their measurement of voter preferences. To put this claim in the context of the alternatives in chapter 2, it presents evidence against the null hypothesis, the argument that there is no pattern to candidate competition in these races. Furthermore, insofar as nonincumbents derive cues about voter preferences from the incumbent and we know from chapter 3 that substantial divergence in these races does exist, it also casts doubt upon the median voter model.

Few would argue that opinion polls or other sophisticated measurement techniques are the one true way to measure voter sentiment. My intention in beginning my analysis with consideration of information, and of opinion polls, is not to argue against such a straw man. Rather, the interviews I describe here show the diversity of ways in which candidates gather information for their campaigns and the way in which opinion polls and other information-gathering mechanisms fit into candidates' strategies. I focus for much of the chapter on opinion polls because it can be easy for the casual observer to mistake polls for information-gathering devices when in many cases they are not used to acquire information at all.

Probability of winning, the first informational variable candidates must study, is not particularly difficult to gauge. Few candidates with whom I spoke were significantly in error about what their chances of winning were. The candidates who did have a good chance of winning did not necessarily learn their status from a poll; they did, however, have the resources to conduct polls, and many of them found polling helpful for other reasons. These candidates may have gained some information from their polls but most of these candidates did not believe that polling results changed their strategy. Instead, candidates viewed polling results as a persuasive tool; polling results could be selectively disclosed to campaign contributors or to the news media as a means of generating attention or of creating a bandwagon effect. The degree of cynicism about polling that I discovered among these candidates certainly indicates that they did not limit their definition of public opinion to what they were told in polls, nor did they necessarily view polls as a part of their information-gathering strategy. Polls were simply one more persuasive tool to be deployed in the campaign. As a result, the actual information contained in polls was only helpful insofar as it showed the candidate in the best possible light.

If opinion polls do not serve an informational function, this does not mean that candidates who conduct polls are still not somehow "better" than less competitive candidates at articulating public desires. There are certainly differences in candidate quality, but these differences have nothing to do with how well informed a candidate is. Knowing what the public prefers is one thing; using that knowledge to guide one's campaign is another. In this chapter I demonstrate that opinion polls are (predictably) conducted by more competitive candidates more frequently than they are conducted by less competitive candidates; however, there is little difference across candidate types in the degree to which opinion polls are employed to determine policy positions. Consequently, the accuracy of public opinion measurement techniques does not necessarily improve as one moves from less competitive to more competitive candidates. Many candidates, incumbents and nonincumbents alike, rely in large part upon heuristics such as voter contact, interest groups, or the media to gauge public preferences. These candidates' understandings of voter sentiment are often just as sophisticated or nuanced as are the understandings of candidates who poll extensively.

One note of caution in these findings is in order, however. The majority of these candidates lost; if they did hire highly paid pollsters and consultants, they are likely to believe that these advisors failed them. In an era where even an inexpensive campaign poll costs $10,000 to $20,000, many candidates cannot afford to conduct opinion polls and thus must rely exclusively upon other means of gaining information. Many of these candidates may be guilty of disparaging polls that they could not have afforded anyway. I did not find, however, that cynicism about polls was a function of near losses, or of a lack of resources. Some candidates did make extensive informational use of polling data, and some candidates were very enthusiastic about the ability of survey data to guide their campaigns. Yet I was pointed to so many other sources of information—the incumbent's past record, cues from the presidential campaign, literature from interest groups, anecdotes from voters, articles in newspapers or magazines—that it is difficult to identify many cases where polling data would have been helpful to candidates to whom it was not available. This chapter does not seek to explain how candidates use information they have gathered to campaign (that is the aim of the next chapter); its modest aim is to ascertain that candidates know what they are doing and that those candidates who run against incumbents are able to base their information-gathering strategies upon the incumbent's positions and popularity.

The Role of Information in Three Campaigns

To explore the types of variations in campaign information, let us consider the perspectives of the candidates in three of the races I studied in 1996. The first, Betty Hull, technically qualifies as a "somewhat competitive" candidate under my definitions because of her ultimate vote share, but she raised little money, received scant media coverage, and was considered a long shot by campaign watchers. Because Hull was not able to poll, I contrast her campaign with that of Ken Blair, who fared as well as Hull yet did conduct polls which he seemed rather disgusted with. Finally, I look at the use of polls in an open-seat race, the race between Jay Hoffman and John Shimkus in southern Illinois, where polls were a major campaign resource and were used both as information and as rhetorical weapons. Together, these candidates show that opinion polls have value, and can provide some information, but many candidates, especially long-shot candidates, can easily do without them. Those who rely too heavily on polling can easily become frustrated; and those who use polls best use them both to reinforce other types of information and to deploy as a campaign tool in their own right.

Campaigning without Polls

Illinois's Eighth District is one of seven predominantly Republican districts that cover Chicago's suburbs. According to *Politics in America* (Duncan and Nutting 1999, 444), it is the most conservative district in Illinois, although residents of neighboring districts might argue this point. Former presidential candidate Phil Crane has represented the district since 1969; in that time he has had more competition for the Republican primary nomination than he has in the general election. He was not regarded as vulnerable by either national or local Democrats in 1996. In fact, the Democratic Party had trouble finding a challenger for him. The only Democrat who filed in the primary was eventually forced off the ballot, and Elizabeth Hull, an English professor at a local college, was recruited by the party to run. Hull raised slightly over $30,000 in her campaign and finished with 36 percent of the vote.

Hull did no polling during her campaign, and she remarked in her interview that she might have benefited from having poll results: "I didn't pay for any polls, but maybe I should have, because everybody who was interested in giving money, they asked 'What do your polls show?' And I'd say that I hadn't done any. That's a very expensive process. It costs thousands of dollars, and for thousands of dollars you can do a lot of printing."

The issues Hull presented in her campaign did not seem dramatically different from those of other Democratic challengers in the region. Hull gave no indication that opinion poll results would have changed her perception of voter preferences in the region. She recognized that the Eighth is one of the more conservative districts in the state, but she argued that she had a fairly good sense for the district: "You know, I didn't do any push-polling or anything like that. Twenty-five years of living here and listening to my students, I get a really representative sample of the community."

Hull was also provided information on the district and on issues to use against Crane by several previous challengers. She also cited the media as a major source of information for her campaign. During our interview she showed me extensive notes she had taken on Crane's voting record. She also claimed that she was able to infer the direction of the campaign from Crane's demeanor and his treatment of her. She confessed that she was uncertain about whether Crane had conducted polls; if he had, he had found little to worry about: "I kept hoping that Philip Crane would do some polling and would be so smug about the results that he would announce them, but apparently he either never did them or he didn't like the results. I think it was most likely that he didn't bother doing them. Why should he?"

As a recruit, Hull was not necessarily expected by her party to perform well. In the scant news coverage of her campaign, party officials were quoted pointing out the reasons why it was important not to allow Crane to go unchallenged (Talbott 1996). Hull still insisted that she could have won, given more time and money, but she also noted that from the beginning of the campaign she was "prepared to lose." Hull's campaign actually seems to have exceeded the expectations of those who persuaded her to run; she herself was quite proud of her showing. She would have been happy to have opinion polls, but not for the information; she seemed confident that she knew the views of her would-be constituents and that she knew the issues. Had she spent campaign money on polls, she might have had a different perspective on them, as the next case demonstrates.

A Campaign with Minimal Polling

In Ohio's Thirteenth District, third-term Democrat Sherrod Brown won by almost as comfortable a margin as Crane, dispatching his Republican rival, trucking company owner Ken Blair, by a 60 to 36 percent margin. The Thirteenth, however, was drawn to be a competitive district. Bill Clinton won it very narrowly in 1992, and Ross Perot has fared quite well here, gaining 27 percent in 1992 and 14 percent in 1996. The Thirteenth includes several Cleveland suburbs and satellite cities; satellite cities such as Lorain and Elyria provide strong Democratic support, while some of the eastern Cleveland exurbs lean Republican. Brown had faced stiff competition in 1994, and had won that race by a mere seven thousand votes. His well-publicized fundraising following that scare may have scared off some Republicans. Blair, his eventual opponent, won a four-candidate Republican primary to face Brown but was only able to raise $54,000 to Brown's $600,000.

When I spoke with Blair, he mentioned that he was still paying off campaign debts because of his polling: "I ran one poll. That's why I still owe some money. I knew pretty well where everybody stood. Pretty much everything flowed the way I felt it would, so I didn't do any more polls. It's pretty much a waste of money."

Blair claimed that he received most of his information about the district through his business and through research on the district. His relationship with Brown, in fact, goes back several years; Blair has been such a frequent letter writer and critic of Brown that, he says, the congressman has a staff person assigned to respond to his letters, and Brown himself had called Blair a few times prior to the campaign to address his complaints. Blair thus seemed to be a candidate whose policy views would not have changed regardless of the findings of polls. He noted that his polls were conducted in order to have something to show contributors, and that he views the polls now as a net loss: "Our consultant said we needed to do a poll, which they charged me $8,200 for. Now I find out that I could get almost the same identical poll done for about $1,800 or $1,900 by a credible pollster. You know, those doggone polls are only as good as your questions. The only thing that's different is how the questions are asked. You point your questions in the direction you want to go, and you've got five or six to corroborate each issue."

Blair was somewhat detached from the actual mechanics of the poll; he received data analysis of the survey results, but felt he was paying too much for consulting when "really, the computer does the work." Eighty-two hundred dollars is actually relatively inexpensive for a campaign poll, so the polling done for him may have been of lower quality than that done for some of the other candidates. Like many candidates who ran respectable campaigns yet never came close enough to winning to garner major attention or contributions, Blair did not note any informational uses of his polling; he appears to have had all of the information he required to run his campaign.

A Heated Campaign: Polls as Information and as Persuasion

Illinois's Twentieth District is the only district among those I consider here that changed from Democratic to Republican hands in 1996.[1] The contest in the Twentieth was one of the closest in the country. The district had been held without serious difficulty by Democrat Richard Durbin since 1982, but Durbin left the seat in 1996 to run for the Senate. Both the Democrats and Republicans poured money into the district; the end result was a 1,200 vote (0.4 percent) victory for Republican John Shimkus over Democrat Jay Hoffman. This contest also may have been the closest to a median voter scenario of the districts I studied. While the Springfield newspaper, the *State Journal-Register,* claimed in its endorsement of Shimkus that the two candidates held "widely divergent views of the role of federal government" (*State Journal-Register* 1996), the paper's main political correspondent wrote the same day on the candidates' similarities: "The new U.S. representative, who lives in Collinsville, will have spent some years in parochial school, favors gun-owners' rights, is pro-life and was a high school jock. . . . All of those things describe both the Republican candidate and the Democratic candidate" (Schoenberg 1996b).

Prior to running for Congress, Hoffman had served in the state legislature and Shimkus had been a county treasurer. Shimkus had also run for Congress against Durbin in 1992, garnering a respectable 43 percent. Both candidates were relatively well known for nonincumbents, so much of the campaign debate revolved around the candidates' past records. The two candidates also amassed large campaign treasuries; Shimkus spent $647,796 and Hoffman spent $812,397 (Duncan and Lawrence 1997, 501). Both had the resources to conduct extensive campaign polls, and the results of several of these polls were discussed in the Springfield and St. Louis newspapers. Clearly, Hoffman and Shimkus were playing a different game than were the other candidates I have discussed here.

According to Shimkus's campaign manager (and, after that, congressional chief of staff) Craig Roberts, Shimkus had a benchmark poll done by the Wirthlin Group in January, while he was still in the midst of a seven-candidate primary. He then commissioned another large poll in May, pairing him and Hoffman, and his campaign continued to conduct tracking polls throughout the course of the general election campaign. Hoffman, who faced less serious primary competition than did Shimkus, did not take a benchmark until May. He then had the Feldman Group conduct another four-hundred-respondent survey in October. Both candidates found each other's polls scientifically sound, and they had few differences in their interpretations of each other's polling strategy. For both candidates, poll results were used as a persuasive tool. Shimkus's May poll showed him with a 50 to 39 percent lead over Hoffman, with a name recognition edge of 77 percent to 56 percent. Roberts stressed in media coverage that this result came before any push questions about Shimkus or Hoffman were asked (Schoenberg 1996a). When I spoke with Hoffman, he did not dispute Shimkus's early advantage, but he noted that "It was entirely a function of name recognition. I don't know about his poll. I don't know how much of it is true. But the question is, once you start asking other questions, whether it tightens up. This is a fifty-fifty district. . . . Our May poll showed that he had greater name recognition; it didn't show an eleven point gap. I don't know what it was—maybe seven, eight, or nine percent. I can't remember. But towards the end our poll showed it was a dead heat."

Roberts agreed with Hoffman's assessment of the district:

> Our district, even when Durbin was here, is probably the closest swing district that's out there. Every poll that we had done, when we just asked Republican versus Democrat in this race without names attached to it, at any point during the campaign it was almost always even. . . . Even in

that poll, there was no question that Hoffman was going to regain the base. That was what the poll reflected, was that John had already locked in the Republican base for himself. Hoffman was still needing to pull his base in. Eventually he did. In that poll, too, it was consistent throughout—if you asked just the generic ballot test, Republican versus Democrat, it was even. Then what mattered was the name ID, and that was John's biggest advantage.

Hoffman had conducted a poll by the time Shimkus's poll was made public, but he did not release the results. Instead, he merely noted in a June 13 *State Journal-Register* article that it was his policy not to release poll results, but that his own polls "show we're right where we want to be" (Schoenberg 1996a).

Certainly it was to Shimkus's advantage to release his benchmark results, while it was not to Hoffman's advantage to do so. Shimkus was able to present a straightforward candidate-choice question, while Hoffman was not. Roberts admitted as much: "One of the biggest problems you'll have is that you'll hear about that ballot test—'Oh, he's at 48, I'm at 37'—and you'll think it's over. As the campaign manager, I don't care about the ballot test. That's the last thing I focus on. If that didn't even get reported on, I don't care. Well, that isn't entirely true, I do care. If John is running ahead then you want to release it to the media. That bolsters your support and diminishes your opponent's."

The Shimkus campaign used this poll to maximum advantage. In a June 5 *St. Louis Post-Dispatch* article, Shimkus responded to Hoffman's challenge to a series of debates by insinuating that Hoffman's desire for numerous debates was an indication that he was trailing in the polls (Sievers 1996). Hoffman responded shortly before the election by releasing a poll that showed the candidates tied at 43 percent, with 14 percent undecided (Schoenberg 1996c). His press release pointed to Hoffman's gains since May by pointing out that as his name recognition increased, so did voters' preference for him. The press release argued that he would thus continue to gain: "Momentum is on his side. He has the advantage among undecided voters and the political atmosphere favors Democrats" (Schoenberg 1996c). Hoffman argued that Shimkus's polls were attaining similar responses: "Our poll showed it was a dead heat, and I got 49.8 percent of the vote. So the poll was right. The only one that Shimkus released was the one showing him eleven points up, which was very early. Towards the end he wouldn't release his poll results, because I assume it tightened up in his polls, too."

Roberts did not dispute this. He argued that spending money to do polls cannot be justified if poll results cannot be used to persuade: "What a lot of people don't realize is that if they go out and spend ten or fifteen thousand dollars on a poll, then what do they do with that poll? You do the polling, you get the data, now you've got to do something with it. If you can't mold the message you get out to the media from poll results, then you've really got to question why you did the poll in the first place."

Roberts did note, however, that the polls Shimkus had done provided important information to the campaign. He cited the campaign's emphasis on taxes as a decision influenced by poll results, and he pointed to Shimkus's 1992 emphasis upon congressional ethics as another decision based in part on polls. Roberts claims that the greatest informational benefit of an opinion poll, however, is in targeting: "The value of a poll is not the ballot test, it's the crosstabs. Who is out there supporting us? Who is not? Who is neutral? That's what the value of that poll is. You see a lot of candidates who do the poll, and they look at the ballot test and they toss it aside. It's no good use of your time to do that, and certainly no good use of your money."

Hoffman agreed that polls were useful in targeting voters but claimed that his polls had little impact upon the issues he discussed during the campaign. He stated that this was a result both of his political instincts and his record as a state legislator: "We ran on issues that I believed in and on issues I thought were important to working families. We didn't do that based on a poll. That's what I ran on before, and that's what I campaigned on in the primary. The same message that I delivered when I announced was the same message that I was delivering in November, more than a year later. What I was saying back then wasn't based on a poll because we hadn't done one yet."

Both Hoffman and Shimkus used opinion polls with more facility than did most other candidates. The availability of veteran Washington pollsters enabled them to make informational use of their survey data, but it also provided them with a strong persuasive strategy. The Twentieth District was clearly a toss-up in 1996, and opinion polls may well have been useful in determining how to sway a few thousand votes. They could not, however, have made the difference in a campaign such as Betty Hull's or Ken Blair's. Neither Hoffman nor Shimkus seems to have made significant accommodation for polls in their issue approaches, primarily because there was no need to make such adjustments. These candidates showed an appreciation of the resources campaign polls could provide them, but they regarded them as a limited tool and an imprecise indicator of public opinion.

Contemporary Campaign Polling Techniques: Information or Persuasion?

These candidates' comments reinforce much of what is already known about information acquisition, but their comments also enable us to put together different types of research so that we can have a broader picture of nonincumbent candidates' strategies. As I argue below, these candidates, despite their differing electoral fortunes, are in fact each making rational political decisions. And each of these candidates' information-gathering strategies is driven by what they need and what the costs of different alternatives are. Before fitting these case studies in with the rest of my interviews, however, let us consider existing research on information acquisition, and particularly public opinion polling, in congressional campaigns.

How pervasive is polling in congressional elections? And what other sources are there? Herrnson (2000, 186) reports that approximately 75 percent of House candidates used some form of polls; furthermore, when asked to rank different types of information sources, the candidates surveyed by Herrnson ranked opinion polling behind only voter contact in terms of importance. In Herrnson's survey, the relative importance of polls is also consistent across parties and several other different candidate types. The only major difference is one of resources—uncompetitive candidates ranked polling third, behind voter contact and behind newspapers, television, and radio.

Since the beginning of the 1980s, political polling has become relatively standardized. Costs of polling have declined as centralized phone banking has become easier and more affordable, and as statistical programs have also become more accessible. By the 1980s, the national congressional campaign committees had begun to encourage, even to require, candidates in search of party assistance to supply them with the results of benchmark polls (Hamilton 1995). A benchmark poll can run anywhere from $10,000 to $25,000, and is generally the single most expensive component of a candidate's polling (see Herrnson 2000, 102). The benchmark features a fairly large sample size, four hundred to five hundred respondents, and can run as long as one hundred questions (Hamilton 1995, 172–73). As one would expect with a survey of this size, it takes a bit of a kitchen sink approach, including open-ended questions, questions on voter mood, different framing devices for campaign issues, the positives and negatives of the relevant candidates, paired heats between candidates, probing of the incumbent's potential liabilities, and name-identification questions (Hamilton 1995, 173; Asher 2001, 117–20). Unless the benchmark yields surprisingly good numbers for a candidate, it is generally limited to internal consumption by the candidate and the party campaign committee. In the case of nonincumbent candidates, the probability of high numbers for name recognition is quite low. The benchmark, then, is not exclusively informational—disclosure does occur (as the Shimkus case shows), and experiments in question framing may stray far from voters' actual policy preferences—but it is the most informational of the polls conducted by congressional candidates.

Given the high cost of the benchmark and the exhortation of Hamilton (1995, 170) that congressional candidates should spend between 5 and 10 percent of their campaign budget on polling, it seems that only the wealthier, more competitive candidates could afford more than a benchmark. For a candidate to take even a low-end benchmark and remain within Hamilton's range requires raising at least $100,000. As I showed in the previous chapter, a sizeable minority of congressional candidates (41 percent of 1996 nonincumbents) do not raise this much. The party committees expect candidates to conduct a benchmark as both a demonstration of their prospects for winning and as a demonstration that they can raise the money necessary to poll (see Herrnson 2000, 91). After this hurdle is leaped, however, the party committees have shown more of a propensity to assist with polling.

The major polling activity after the benchmark is the tracking poll, which features a rolling sample, with a smaller sample size, over several days (Herrnson 2000, 187). The tracking poll is aimed at capturing change in voter preference and generally features only questions about voting preference. Some candidates also conduct focus groups to test issue approaches. According to Hamilton (1995, 174–75), 25 to 30 percent of House candidates use some sort of focus group; among the candidates I interviewed the numbers are lower, no doubt because I limit my inquiry to nonincumbents. Both types of methods are less statistically sound than the benchmark, and tracking polls are less informational. A candidate faced with numbers only on voting preference must make substantial inferences about which of her own campaign activities, be they spending, issue messages, advertising, or other strategic actions, have caused fluctuations in vote choice. Tracking polls serve more of a persuasive function than an informational one; disclosure of favorable tracking poll results is a common strategic tactic.

Cantril (1991, 226) has described these two functions of polls as the "town crier" function and the "political intelligence" function. His discussion of political intelligence is in part drawn from Gallup (see Gallup and Rae 1940) and Bruner's (1944) early hopes that public opinion surveys would bring about more democratic government—that they would allow politicians to assess the will of the public directly, as opposed to using the filter of pressure groups. Both Cantril and Crespi (1989) have catalogued the potential uses of polls above and beyond this standard social scientific function of learning about the public; these uses all fall within the "town crier" function of polling. That is, the poll is more valuable for what it can do for the candidate than for what it says to the candidate.

Cantril (1991, 215) also points out the value of polls in creating a "bandwagon" effect, wherein favorable poll results will encourage voters, the media, or interest groups to look more favorably upon a candidate, or at least to pay more attention to a candidate. He also emphasizes the value of opinion polls in raising campaign contributions; here, good polling numbers are a signal to potential contributors that a candidate is viable and is worthy of a contribution. While DeClercq(1978) downplays this function, the mentions of this phenomenon in numerous polling articles and the financial and polling expectations of the parties' congressional campaign committees indicate that it is an important concern. Asher (2001) notes that strategic release of polling numbers also can maximize attention and contributions. Bradburn and Sudman (1989, 64) note that even when campaign polling results are "buried," or kept from the public, they can play an important role in boosting the morale of campaign staff (or even of the candidate himself). In each of these cases, the accuracy of the poll results is of secondary importance. The DCCC and NRCC have restrictions for their candidates in defining which pollsters' results will be deemed legitimate, but there are no similar safeguards for the public. There is still significant leeway in this regard, as candidates may time polls or frame questions to maximize favorable responses.

It is no wonder, then, that candidates often take a particularly instrumental approach to polling. Several studies have uncovered critical attitudes of candidates toward polls. Karlyn Keene, herself an influential pollster in Washington, has described a "Washington bias" in polling that diminishes the relevance of poll results for congressional candidates (cited in Cantril 1991, 207). Because of the emphasis on "established" polling companies, Keene argues, poll questions often do not address issues of particular relevance or salience to many congressional districts; this can, in effect, keep those issues off of the campaign agenda. Candidates are also aware of the numerous "town crier" functions of polls and are reluctant to place significant stock in poll results.

This reluctance may be partially normative; there has always been some stigma for many politicians in actually admitting that they are guided by polls. As Herbst (1998, 51) notes, politicians may feel insulted if their own political judgment is contradicted by polls. Herbst's interviews of state legislative staffers uncovered a disdain for opinion polls based not only upon the interviewees' faith in their own political instincts, but also upon their belief that polls are used strategically to support legislative purposes. Polls are a useful communications or legislative tactic for these staffers, but the staffers believe as well that these polls are time-bound, potentially biased, and generally unreliable as political information.

Studies of public opinion about polls have established that citizens share, to some degree, the above perceptions of polling (for discussion, see Hollander et al. 1971). They are becoming somewhat more inclined to believe poll results presented to them by the media, but this may be because they have no vested interest in these results; they do not have an instrumental or strategic need for any particular polling outcome, and they have no need to persuade anyone with public opinion data. An instrumental need for public opinion data decreases the informational value of that data; persuasion and information cannot coexist easily.

To what resources, then, do candidates turn in order to acquire information about public preferences? Herbst (1998, 52–72) argues that legislative staffers use more informal means of calculating public opinion, such as interest groups and the media, which serve as a stand-in for the public. Policymakers, she notes, develop sophisticated means of accounting for bias among these groups; their communications are discounted according to their ideological bias. One problem with using these groups as stand-ins for the public, however, is that in doing so one presumes that these groups are conveying information from the public to policymakers; it is just as likely that they are conveying information to the public as well, and that they represent public opinion only to the degree that they persuade the public. This is a classic paradigm in literature on interest groups (see Wright 2003, 71–72). These information sources are thus not solely informational, either; they can be "spun" or used by legislators (or candidates) to persuade the public.

Eisinger (2003, 188–90) notes that legislators (and, one might again presume, candidates) use crowd size, mail, and other citizen contacts to evaluate public opinion. Unscientific techniques such as these are certainly vulnerable to rationalization; crowd size in particular is a famously bad tool for estimating one's popularity, as Miller et al. (1976) argue about the McGovern presidential campaign. A candidate's skill at interpreting these pieces of information correctly, at accounting for bias, is, again, indicative of the candidate's political savvy. Both Herbst (1998, 155) and Eisinger (2003, 188–90) caution that their questioning was about polling as part of the legislative process, not the campaign process, yet such processes certainly still affect the behavior of legislators on the campaign trail, and they certainly provide clues as to what candidates who do not or cannot poll do to gauge public opinion.

Eisinger (2003) notes that perceptions about the value of polls and other information sources guide policymaking more than does the actual accuracy of the information conveyed to the candidate or legislator. Herbst (1998, 87) concludes her study by noting that in the world of state legislative politics, "Democracy runs quite smoothly without attention to surveys, direct constituent contact, and other forms of conventional public opinion measurement." Is this the case in congressional campaigns? For an answer to this question, let us turn to the comments of the candidates.

Congressional Candidates' Measurements of Public Opinion

In the following pages, I turn back to my 1996 interviews to assess information gathering across different types of campaigns. For each candidate, there is a set of nested questions: Does the candidate actually have accurate information about voter preferences and his own chances? If so, how did the candidate acquire this information? And if not, why not? Did the candidate have no desire to acquire this information, was his political judgment flawed, or was the cost of information too high? These candidate interviews demonstrate that even while candidates were disdainful of opinion data, viewing it as a persuasive, not an informational, tool, they did have a sophisticated informational calculus. More competitive candidates (such as John Shimkus and Jay Hoffman) do indeed excel at gauging and articulating public preferences, but their ability to do this is not based upon the availability of allegedly objective information sources such as polls. The policy stances of less competitive candidates—of those similar to Betty Hull or Ken Blair—may not always resemble those of the most competitive candidates, but this is not a result of lack of information or misinformation.

The candidates' interview responses are arranged below into three sections. First, I discuss how they acquired information on voter preferences. Second, I analyze their attitudes toward the most frequently discussed form of such information, opinion polling, and their reflections on whether polling served an informational function or a persuasive function. Finally, I attempt to draw conclusions about the accuracy of the information they did acquire.

Techniques of Information Acquisition

In few areas of campaigning are the differences between the haves and have-nots greater than in the area of polling. As table 4.1 shows, all of the very competitive candidates with whom I spoke commissioned polls during their campaign. These candidates also tended to commission not just one poll, but several polls; only three of these candidates, or 21 percent, purchased only one poll. Forty-three percent purchased three or more polls, and 64 percent also were provided poll results by sources outside the campaign—generally the national or state party organizations, sympathetic interest groups, or the media. An almost equally high percentage, 81 percent, of somewhat competitive candidates commissioned polls, but over half of those who did commission polls only purchased a benchmark poll. Two of these candidates purchased only a tracking poll late in the campaign. Only 14 percent of the somewhat competitive candidates were able to purchase three or more polls. Meanwhile, all but one of the long-shot candidates were unable to conduct polls of any sort; the one long-shot candidate who did poll used a local polling firm rather than a Washington, DC, company and found that his poll was not accorded very much credibility by his party committee. Two long-shot candidates gained access to outside polls, conducted by their state parties, but most long shots made it clear to me that polling was never a feasible option for them.

Cost of polling was an issue for all of these candidates, yet costs were addressed in a different manner by the different types of candidates. Many long shots had little idea how much a poll would even cost; estimates ran from $3,000 to as high as $25,000. Whatever the cost, they believed they had little to gain from polling. One long-shot candidate remarked: "We didn't spend any money on polls because it made no sense. We had to put our money into the campaign, and the poll was just going to show we were behind. We knew we were not a targeted race no matter what our poll said" (Illinois). The reader will note that this candidates is referring to polling solely in the persuasive sense; she would have polled only if the poll would have shown she had a chance.

Somewhat competitive candidates were, as I mention above, generally able to afford some polling, yet if they did, these polls constituted a major part of their budget. Timing of the polls was important. Information from an early poll would be the most useful in guiding the campaign, yet money is scarce early in a campaign. A benchmark conducted late in the campaign risks describing a situation that is not changeable. As I note in chapter 6, the party committees encourage candidates to stock up money early, which can delay expenditures on polling until the campaign is already

Table 4.1. Candidate Polling by Competitiveness

	Long Shots	Somewhat Competitive	Very Competitive	Total
Poll	6%	81%	100%	62%
Benchmark Only	6	48	21	27
Benchmark and Track	0	10	36	13
Benchmark and 2+ Tracks	0	14	43	17
Track Only	0	10	0	4
Outside Polling	12	24	64	31
Outside Polling Only	12	4	0	6
No Polling	94	19	0	38
N	17	21	14	52

Competitiveness is measured such that long-shot candidates received less than 35 percent of the vote and spent less than $100,000; somewhat competitive candidates either received between 35 and 45 percent of the vote or, failing to do that, spent at least $100,000; and very competitive candidates received over 45 percent of the vote. The statistics for very competitive candidates include winning candidates.

underway. Despite the recommendation that candidates poll at the moment they are beginning their campaign, many must wait until they have already proven themselves as fundraisers (an activity that in itself benefits from good polling numbers). One very competitive candidate remarked that "We didn't poll until July 1. Our goal was to get $100,000 in cash in the bank by the June 30 FEC report. So we couldn't poll until after that" (Minnesota).

Among the most competitive candidates, however, cost was somewhat less of an issue, as was persuasion. The less competitive candidates worried about the cost of polls because the opportunity costs were steeper. A $20,000 poll would take $20,000 out of a budget that might only be $150,000 or so to begin with; it might cut an advertising budget in half. More competitive candidates were able to buy more polling without worrying as much about those polls' effects upon their budget. They were, then, more likely to talk to me about the content of those polls apart from the polls' impact (either directly, in terms of what they said, or indirectly, in terms of the polls' opportunity costs) on their campaign. The most competitive candidates seldom raised the issue of the cost of polls. They spent more time discussing the mechanics of the polls they had conducted.

The structure of polling for a well-heeled candidate is fairly uniform. Thirty of the fifty-two candidates conducted a benchmark poll with an established Washington polling firm. The most frequently mentioned items on these polls were name identification questions, responses to description of both candidates, incumbent positives and negatives, and associations of issues with the incumbent. The benchmarks these candidates conducted also featured a number of issue questions which several candidates reported were useful in gauging public mood. Timing was still an issue here, but it was not an issue of cost; rather, it was an issue of interpretation. The standard benchmark poll asks a vote choice question early, before describing the candidates, then asks the "incumbent reelect" question or gives a generic description of the candidates and asks the vote choice question again. For example, one candidate gave me the following example of a "blind" question: "Who do you want your congressman to be? Thirty-seven-year-old West Point graduate who's never held paid office, who believes government is too big and spends too much, and is conservative on most political issues, or sixty-year-old professional politician who's spent his life on the public payroll, who's spent fourteen years in Congress, and who's successful in getting federal money for the district?" (Illinois).

Needless to say, there is tremendous potential for question-wording bias here, but such questions do provide issue or candidate framing information and can make the early poll more informative than simple vote choice questions. Several candidates pointed out that the early poll is more informative for the campaign than is the late poll because any challenger's name recognition is going to be low early in the campaign: "You do polling during elections and you see the numbers move and you see why they're moving, that offers encouragement, certainly. It not only offers encouragement, it offers understanding, because nobody knows who you are when you first do polls. Everybody thinks they're better known than they really are. That probably brings both feet back to the ground, and probably both of your knees, too" (Illinois).

For a candidate who has interpreted the benchmark poll well and has the resources to continue polling, the tracking poll can be a test of advertising strategy. That is, it can be used by a candidate to monitor the effects of resource use. As such, its effectiveness is limited to those candidates who have the resources to commit to moving public opinion. Because of the much more limited length and sample size of the tracking poll, a tracking poll may only be as good as the benchmark it follows, as one very competitive candidate explained:

> We made the major thrust of our benchmark poll the incumbent. We knew in our benchmark that the incumbent lost doing his best positives to my best positives. We wanted to make it as big as possible, because if

you don't you're not getting good information. Then the track is like getting a flat response, like taking a snapshot. We were able to see that I was getting enough information out that it was causing his standing to deteriorate. He had huge name ID in all the polls, but we were able to see that in spite of his high name ID he was really low to reelect. (Wisconsin)

Such results are not necessarily issue information, but they are campaign information. The poll is meant to guide campaigning rather than to persuade others outside the campaign through its results.

If the very competitive candidates admitted any misgivings about polling, it was that they polled too much. There were several very competitive candidates who did not refer to useful campaign information gained from their polls, but few regarded the polls as a worthless endeavor. Some of the most comfortable winners I interviewed, however, shared the belief of the long shots that polling would not actually matter to the campaign; they already knew what the outcome of the race would be. In the winners' case, however, there were ample resources to poll, so the expenditure was not a matter of concern.

The above comments establish that candidates can gain useful information from polls. The benchmark, in particular, contains numerous issue questions that could provide the candidate with a quite accurate picture of the district and of whether his or her own ideas reflect what voters want from their representative. There are, however, many other sources of information on voter preferences. As table 4.2 shows, when I asked candidates "What were your most important sources of information about what voters wanted?" very few candidates mentioned opinion polls. Opinion polls lagged fourth, behind political experience, district and incumbent data, and voter contact, and barely ahead of interest groups.

Strangely, all three long-shot candidates who had access to any sort of poll—whether their own or polls commissioned by their party—made reference to those polls as valuable information sources. Two other long shots pointed out that they did not have access to polls of the district, but that they would conduct polls if elected to determine their legislative actions. Many candidates, however, insisted that they did not need polls to ascertain what voters wanted: "I learned about the voters by going around talking to people and reading the newspaper. I don't think it's magical. It was a matter of how I could learn most efficiently. Do you want to do a couple of polls, or do you want to send literature out? So I figured I knew the issues and would be able to find out what people are concerned about without polls" (Illinois).

Political experience was by far the most frequently cited source of in-

Table 4.2. Candidate Information Sources by Competitiveness

"What were your most important sources of information about what voters' views and concerns were in your district?"

	Long Shots	Somewhat Competitive	Very Competitive	Total
Political Experience	0%	43%	79%	38%
District/Incumbent Data	18	38	29	29
Voter Contact	35	33	14	29
Polls	18	24	29	23
Interest Groups	35	14	14	21
Previous Campaigns	12	29	7	17
Media	18	5	7	10
Presidential Campaign Cues	12	5	14	10
Party	6	10	7	8
Consultants	6	5	0	4
N	17	21	14	52

Note: Respondents were permitted to choose more than one category; column totals should not equal 100 percent.

formation for those who had held political office. Large percentages of candidates of all types also reported that they had researched their district thoroughly, and that voter contact was a major information source: "I didn't have the resources during my campaign to do polls to figure out where the voters stood. But the way I would campaign was to stand at shopping centers, and I would meet three hundred or four hundred people a day. That's more people than you meet doing a poll" (Wisconsin). Several candidates, mostly Republicans, also reported making use of information supplied by interest groups. Republicans of all levels of competitiveness mentioned receiving information from the Heritage Foundation and GOPAC; a smaller number of Democratic long shots reported that the Sierra Club had sent information they used during the campaign.

Finally, a less frequently cited but important information source was cues from other campaigns. Although Bob Dole was not a frequent visitor to the states I study here, many Democrats were able to infer from Bill Clinton's strategy in their states what they should be doing: "One of the things that you have to remember is that when you're running a campaign in the same year as a presidential election, you can look at what they're doing. When Clinton's here talking about Medicare, you figure they're doing that out of a poll, not just because they figure it's right. They're doing it because they've done twenty-seven polls. So certain issues you figure if it's important for them, it's important for you, too. If you have good political sense, it's not like rocket science" (Illinois).

Especially among the crop of second-time Republican candidates, polls conducted in 1994 were still a major information source. Twelve candidates I interviewed had run in the general election for Congress previously; all but four of these were Republicans who had run in 1994. Several candidates referred to polling they had done in 1994: "I don't think two campaigns are ever completely the same. But the issues stayed pretty similar. Clinton was popular in 1994, he was more popular in 1996. All that really changed was that in 1996 [the incumbent] had more of a record" (Minnesota).

All of the candidates quoted above had done some polling in their campaign except the two who specifically state in their quotes that they did not. There are no variations among these candidates in the information sources mentioned that are likely to be attributable to having polled; variation by candidate groups seems more likely to be related to finances and to competitiveness. No long shots, for example, mentioned prior political experience as a source of information because not many of them had any. Few other differences stand out.

Candidate Attitudes toward Opinion Polls

One could easily conclude, then, that opinion polls are scarcely worth their cost in terms of information. If one reaches this conclusion, however, then it would be valid to ask why the candidates who do not view opinion polls as a significant information source still invest in them.

For most of the candidates who had conducted polls, there was an informational component to the data they gathered even if gaining campaign guidance from such information was not the actual reason the poll was conducted. Thus, candidates cannot clearly be separated into an "informational polling" camp and a "persuasive polling" camp. I do classify candidate remarks, however, into the two categories. Results are shown in table 4.3. I categorize candidate references to actually learning what voters' preferences were as "strict information." I also employ a rather loose definition of information, which includes candidate comments about ways to frame questions for maximum effect on the public; ways to prioritize the issue stances they had and focus on those issues most salient to the public;

Table 4.3. Candidate Attitudes toward Opinion Polling

Categorization of candidates' responses about the uses to which public opinion polls were put in their campaign.

	Long shots	Somewhat Competitive	Very Competitive	Total
Opinion Polls as Information				
"Strict" Information	12%	14%	0%	10%
Framing	0	19	29	15
Set Priorities	6	5	14	6
Tracking Opponent	0	10	21	10
Targeting	0	19	21	13
Total	18	67	85	56
Opinion Polls as Persuasion				
Push Polls	0	0	14	4
Strategic Disclosure	0	0	29	8
Morale	6	10	14	10
Party Support	18	52	0	27
Contributions/ Interest Groups	12	29	7	17
Total	36	91	64	65
N	17	21	14	52

Note: Respondents were permitted to choose more than one category; column totals should not equal 100 percent.

ways to target particular issue constituencies or geographic constituencies; and ways to track the effectiveness of one's own message and one's opponent's message. In the persuasion category I place comments about push-polling; about strategically releasing polls to the media; about lifting the morale of the candidate or the candidate's supporters; and about providing poll results to the party campaign committees, interest groups, or other potential supporters and contributors.

In table 4.3, the persuasive uses of opinion polls outweigh the informational uses for long shots and somewhat competitive candidates. Differences are particularly stark among somewhat competitive candidates, 52 percent of whom used polls to try to gain party support. Although the very competitive candidates did lean slightly more toward using polls as information, they did not use them as strict information; instead, they used opinion polls to fine-tune their campaign. None of the most competitive candidates actually used polls to discern what public preferences were.

To be sure, there are varying degrees of informational content in the different types of poll uses I categorize here as "information." Very few candidates actually said that they learned about new issues or gained information that caused them to seriously rethink their campaign strategies. It should be noticed that none of the most competitive candidates claimed that their polls were used as information in the strict sense—that is, that they actually learned information about the constituency's voting or policy preferences that they did not already know. Most candidates insisted that polls told them nothing that they did not know. While such a claim illustrates the prejudices I discussed above toward politicians who act based on polls, several candidates actually seemed irritated not to have learned very much that did not accord with their intended campaign focus. The majority of informational comments fell under the loose definition of information. The most competitive candidates spoke of their polls more in terms of information than did less competitive candidates, but they tended to stress that their polls caused no dramatic changes in their campaigning, as the following comments show:

> On our first poll, we were trying to decide what the issues were and trying to discern the right language to communicate with people. Trying to find my strengths and his strengths and my weaknesses and his negatives. That was all. And as it turned out, the issues that I thought were important were the issues they thought were important. We framed them a little differently, but basically those were the key ones. (Minnesota)

> Our polling information indicated that when people were told how he voted, a third of his core support moved. We never had a true solid lead during the campaign, but we did have that poll telling us that if we could tell people about his record, we could win. (Ohio)

Informational discussions of polling tended, however, to be brief and often to be limited to individual issues that were particularly malleable—that could be phrased in a number of different ways in order to obtain different responses. Framing questions in such a manner tended to be regarded as a positive, informational side of polling to some candidates—they could find out how best to cast their ideas—and more negatively, as a way of slanting poll results, by others. In their least savory form, these experiments in question framing could, several candidates across competitiveness categories worried, be used in an unscientific push-poll that would be intended to persuade the survey respondent to vote a particular way based on information provided in the poll.

The balance of informational remarks and persuasion remarks tips when one moves from the most competitive candidates to the less competitive ones. It is in the middle competitiveness category, however, that most of the more caustic remarks about polling occur. Over half of the somewhat competitive candidates reported that polls were for consumption by the party, or were to be used to solicit contributions:

> You do two things with a poll. One is you do a poll to figure out our own viability, and the other is you do a poll to test a few messages. If things go well, you can go to donors or the party and say, "Look, we used this message, we think we can win this race." (Minnesota)

> The reason we conducted a poll, and we should have done a focus group too, was to get some Republican money, because they go only by the numbers. Then we polled again, the week before the election, for the same reason, because there were some additional dollars out there to be had that week. (Wisconsin)

Intriguingly, the somewhat competitive candidates spoke solely of persuading their party and potential contributors, not the general public. Among the most competitive candidates, the media were also fair game, as I showed earlier in the Hoffman/Shimkus case. That is, a good poll can be strategically disclosed to the media; for somewhat competitive candidates, however, a "good poll" is not necessarily one that shows the challenger winning. It is one that shows that the incumbent is beatable, that the challenger might win if he can present particular issues or lines of attack to the public.

Among these candidates, then, for whom polling is a means of making money and of getting party support, polls take on a less scientific tone:

> It boggles my mind that everything is so slanted, in both directions. I don't see any objective polls. A good example of that is focus groups. You get about two dozen people, and they're supposed to tell the candidate what it's all about. Nobody appointed them the campaign arbitrage, you know? Really, that's what candidacies are all about. It's about listening. But on a philosophical level, you take that information and you use it to articulate your message. That's not what I'm seeing, though. Instead it's all about polls and focus groups. (Ohio)

We did one poll, and it wasn't very good. So I told the national party if they wanted more polls, find somebody to pay for it. I know that polling is made to say whatever you want it to say, to convince people. [My opponent's] poll shows him up by twenty points. We know that wasn't true. Everybody knew it. If they poll in Minneapolis, they get one result. If they poll out here, then I'm going to do better. (Minnesota)

I would guess that since the poll was conducted by a national pollster who conducted polls all across the country, they tried out all the hot button issues—Medicare, Medicaid, some of the egregious budget votes. The poll certainly showed that Gingrich wasn't very popular. They tried all this stuff that was working somewhere else, and I assume they had similar responses here. But they didn't tell us anything about our district. (Wisconsin)

The long-shot candidates tended to have less to say about polling because they had less familiarity with opinion polls. Those who mentioned the persuasive component of polling were candidates who were certain they would not receive party money, and who thus chose not to conduct opinion polls because they regarded opinion polls as a device for trying to get party support or other interest group contributions. Those long shots who mentioned information received from polls included the lone long shot who did conduct polls and one other long shot who did not conduct polls but promised to do so if elected to find out what voters wanted.

Are Opinion Polls an Accurate Source of Information?

Estimating the accuracy of the information candidates did have is largely a subjective endeavor. The most relevant question in this regard is how accurate candidates' information truly needs to be. For a long-shot candidate, merely knowing that one is extremely unlikely to win may be sufficient; detailed information about voters' preferences on myriad issues is not likely to be particularly useful to the campaign. For a candidate who estimates that he is likely to get approximately 50 percent of the vote, however, such information can provide the crucial distinction between victory and defeat. The most important variable in this regard, then, is candidates' beliefs about how well they will do. Most of the candidates with whom I spoke had determined the vote share they were likely to get; these estimates ranged from 20 percent to over 50 percent. Some candidates actually supplied me with percentage figures about what they believed their chances of winning were. The majority of candidates, however, told me they believed their chances were "fair," "good," "poor," or used other such general estimates.

Although these interviews were conducted after the election, the most interesting result of my questions to the candidates about their beliefs was that candidates spoke just as frequently of being deceived by opinion polls as they did of finding accurate information about how well they were doing. Only thirteen of the fifty-two candidates—three of the seventeen long shots and ten of the twenty-one somewhat competitive candidates—told me that they felt they had overestimated their chance of winning the election. Others claimed that the estimates they made at the beginning of the campaign about the likely outcome were in the range of the eventual result. Of the ten somewhat competitive candidates who fared worse than they had expected to, all had conducted polls. Seven of these ten were from Minnesota or Illinois, states where there were also competitive senatorial campaigns, and many of them felt that their polls had overestimated their support because these campaigns had not boosted turnout as much as they had expected: "People trusted the results of our poll. Then they saw the results on Election Day and said, 'How can the polls be there and Election Day you're here? The spread is that far?' The thing is, again, we didn't have control of the top of the ticket" (Minnesota).

Candidates also voiced similar concerns about the effects of the presidential race, which seemed to most of the candidates to have been predetermined in their states. Aside from those candidates who blamed low turnout for their worse-than-expected showing, there were also those who had been cynical about the information they received from opinion polls even during the campaign:

> We got our hands on a poll through the grapevine about a week before the election that put us almost dead even. I need to tell you that I was surprised at that. I thought we would lose. I'm a very positive person, but I just did not believe there was a way for us to win, because I knew in a presidential election year [the incumbent] would bring out close to 70,000 extra voters, while we bring out about 4,000 more. I didn't want to bring anyone down, but I just did not believe those numbers. (Wisconsin)

Those candidates who had relatively accurate estimates of their chance of winning tended to rely upon district voting trends, upon the incumbent's past success, and upon the advice of prior candidates. Above, I noted that campaign consultants will encourage a candidate to poll before or immediately after entering a race in order to test his or her viability, to avoid committing resources to a hopeless cause. Few candidates whom I interviewed were able to do so. Even many quite competitive candidates waited until July of the election year or later to conduct benchmark polls. Polls thus did not determine strategy, nor were they a motivating factor in the campaign. Polls seem, then, more a result of information about probability of winning than they do a source of such information. That is, candidates poll more extensively as their expected vote approaches 50 percent. Accurate information about voter preferences is derived from other sources.

Conclusions

In chapter 3 I noted the rarity of convergence in congressional campaigns, and I noted that this lack of convergence is far more likely to be due to the failure of challengers, not incumbents, to seek vote-maximizing positions. This lack of convergence must be for one of two broad reasons—by choice or by error. The comments above about the plethora of information sources available to candidates, as well as the low cost and easy access of several of these sources, indicate that choice seems a far more plausible explanation than error.

The remarks of these candidates certainly should not be taken to suggest that candidates who conduct opinion polls are no different from the candidates who do not poll. They are. These differences, however, have little to do with the actual information conveyed in opinion polls. They are differences in resources. Opinion polls were not cited as the most important source of information about voters' views or campaign issues by a majority in any of the competitiveness groups. The most competitive candidates were more likely than were other candidate types to cite polls as a source of information, but they defined "information" in this context quite narrowly—they wanted to know how an opponent's advertisements were affecting their campaign, they wanted to tinker with ways of framing questions, or they wanted to investigate which areas or groups of voters were most receptive to their campaign. In few cases did candidates claim that opinion polls actually persuaded them how voters as a group approached the campaign issues.

Careful consideration of polling data may make the differences between a very competitive losing candidate and a winning candidate, but it seems unlikely to make more than a few percentage points worth of difference. For many candidates, the simple information that they were extremely unlikely to win was the only information needed. This does not mean that losing candidates did not understand public preferences; they merely saw no reason to adapt to these preferences. In sum, different types of candidates need different types of information, but having a sense of what voters want is a basic part of political intuition. Candidate information about public opinion is not a product of opinion polls, because they are reluctant to believe they need a survey research firm to tell them what their potential constituents would like. Information is not about polls for them, yet they continue to conduct them because polls are not about information for them either. One might decry the instrumental need on the part of many of these candidates for polls as persuasive tools. Many of the candidates might agree. Yet in the meantime, it appears, only a lucky handful of candidates have the luxury of considering polls as a source of information. These are the candidates who generally have the least need to persuade supporters, and these are the candidates who do, in fact, already know enough about the voters that they have little need to use public opinion information to make significant changes in their campaigns.

If the median voter model's lack of correspondence to these election dynamics is not simply a function of error on the part of candidates, then, given that incumbents do tend to follow a median voter strategy, candidate divergence must be the result of conscious choices by challengers. This chapter has laid the groundwork for consideration of the applicability of a sequential positioning framework to congressional campaigns. Whereas in this chapter my argument has been primarily negative—that candidates are not misinformed or misguided—in the subsequent chapters I seek to provide positive evidence for the existence of sequential positioning and expressive campaigning in congressional elections.

CHAPTER 5

"Like Throwing Golf Balls against the Wall": The Candidates Talk about Campaign Issues and Ideology

Students of American political behavior frequently (and perhaps correctly) downplay the role of issue appeals in determining the outcomes of congressional campaigns. The candidates themselves, the very vehicles through whom citizens are supposed to turn their preferences into policy, often deny that issues are a major determinant of their electoral fortunes. Even the most cursory list of criteria for voting decisions must take into account candidates' experience, competence, ethics, party affiliation, finances, and personality. Throughout this study I have argued that issue differences and ideological distance between candidates are an important indicator of the nature of elections—that candidates adopt issue positions in response to environmental factors such as the above criteria. A candidate has little leeway in changing his personality or financial base, and no candidate can change his or her past record short of misleading the voters. A candidate also has little chance of single-handedly altering the popularity of his opponent. The issue positions a candidate takes and the ideological appeals a candidate makes to the voters are among the only mutable aspects of a political campaign.

In the previous chapter I showed that the candidates with whom I spoke employed a variety of different means of gaining information about their opponent's popularity, the voters' preferences on policy, and their own probability of winning. Despite the skepticism evinced by some candidates toward polling and other more refined techniques for measuring public opinion, candidates nevertheless showed that they did not campaign blindly. The responses I presented suggest that challengers to incumbents do make accurate assessments of their own probability of winning and of the issue positions and popularity of their opponent. In that chapter I sought to eliminate the premise of simultaneous positioning except in the case where neither of the candidates is an incumbent.

In this chapter I explore the real action of the campaign: the strategic decisions of each candidate about which issue positions to take, which positions to emphasize, and how much of the campaign should be built around issue appeals. Here, I present evidence that the specific sequential positioning scenarios I hypothesized are indeed occurring—that candidates adopt positions after, and in response to, the incumbent, and that where candidates' chances of winning are low, they consciously adopt noncentrist, expressive positions. It is not possible to arrive at a distinction between a party-based campaign and an expressive campaign at this point, however, unless party control over candidates is an either/or proposition (this is the subject of the next chapter).

This is the most straightforward of the propositions from chapter 3 to prove—it requires merely that one ask candidates what the rationale for their position taking was. More generally, though, there are three broad areas of inquiry; each should show variation according to candidates' *a priori* probability of winning. First, how much ideological distance is there between candidates? If the incumbent is behaving rationally, ideological distance should be a function of the challenger's beliefs about his probability of defeating that incumbent. Where this probability is high, the challenger has an incentive to narrow the distance between himself and the incumbent, and to shift the focus toward other criteria—toward finer issue distinctions between the candidates, or toward nonpolicy vulnerabilities of the incumbent. As this probability declines, so also should the challenger's motivation to ape the incumbent's policy positions. This decline does not necessarily mean that the challenger will take divergent issue positions, but it does increase the chance that the challenger will take positions that are less geared toward winning and more expressive. Where the incumbent is not behaving rationally, of course, challengers have an incentive to move toward the median position that the incumbent has failed to capture.

While the different alternatives I outline in chapter 2 assume there will be a static environment following the initial positioning of the candidates, the actual world of electoral campaigns does, of course, involve adjustments in candidates' positions. These alternatives contain an implicit movement of strategic candidates from their *ex ante* preferred positions toward positions that would increase their probability of winning. Because it is impossible to measure the *ex ante* positions here, I instead look at the willingness of candidates to alter their positions during the campaign. Campaign stances are frequently updated to account for new information either about the issues or about public opinion. Thus, the second implication of my argument is that candidates' motivations for position changes will be affected by their probability of winning. Candidates will change their positions in response to public opinion only where they deem their probability of winning to be high enough that the change is worthwhile, or where they believe such changes will increase their probability of winning. Candidates who do not believe their probability of winning will be affected by changing positions will, as I have shown in the previous chapter, decline to seek out public opinion data. When they do change positions, these candidates will not change them in order to capture votes. They will do so in order to make their positions more compatible with each other, or they will revise positions in accordance with actual changes in their individual beliefs about "good" public policy. These changes will be made independently of any concern for maximizing probability of winning.

In a similar fashion, the rhetoric of the candidates should reflect the strategic or expressive concerns that prompted them to run in the first place. The third implication of my argument is that if candidates do make correct assessments of their chances of winning, they will also mention strategic or expressive concerns, issue positions they are not willing to compromise, and the role of their ideological beliefs in their decision to run for office. While all candidates may be assumed to have a strong interest in political issues and to have strong opinions about many of the major election issues, expressive position taking should be most clearly shown in the case of controversial or unusual issue positions. Instrumentally strategic positioning should be shown by a lack of such positions. In other words, candidates are unlikely to acknowledge that they had little chance of winning and then discuss ways in which they had oriented their campaign toward winning. Candidates who did believe they had a good chance of winning are equally unlikely to discuss ways in which they consciously failed to take advantage of opportunities to increase their chances.

Motivations for position taking are a far more sensitive issue for the candidates than are public opinion data or party assistance, and I certainly did not expect candidates to acknowledge having taken positions they did not believe were justified on grounds other than winning votes. Nonetheless, the results presented below contain many responses which point to significant differences in campaign strategy according to candidates' chances of winning. Single-issue candidates, the ultimate expressive candidates, only emerge in relatively long-shot races. These and other long-shot candidates spoke rather frankly about the "educational" function of their campaigns, and of trying to develop an issue agenda that made sense to them, regardless of its relevance to voters. Intriguingly, candidates with an outside chance of winning were the most concerned with staking out popular positions; it may be that the lack of other weaknesses in their opponent prompted them to concentrate upon issues more than did the other candidates. The very competitive challengers often felt that their opponents represented the district poorly enough that they did not have to take unusual pains to represent the median voter. The existence of a very competitive challenger, in fact, is an important indicator that the incumbent is out of step with the district on policy (see McAdams and Johannes 1987). In these cases, as well as in the open-seat races, the candidates often deemphasized their own issue positions, except in cases where their opponent seemed clearly in the minority. For each type, then, there is a trade-off between expressive position taking and instrumental position taking; a curvilinear relationship develops where the least competitive and the most competitive candidates are afforded some opportunity for expression, while those in the middle must concentrate more on seeking winning or vote-maximizing positions. The implications of the sequential positioning alternatives, then, are not only supported, they are also given further depth than one can provide in a simple model.

Do Issue Positions Matter in Campaigns?

A common tool used by political scientists in evaluating congressional elections is the presence or absence of a "quality" challenger, defined as a challenger who has previously been elected to public office (see Jacobson 1997a; Bond, Covington, and Fleisher 1985; Born 1986). There have been many different efforts made to introduce subtleties into the quality challenger measurements, but for the most part, these measurements have had little to do with the issues raised in the campaign. For instance, Jacobson (1997a, 113–14) discusses ANES survey questions on the traits citizens like or dislike in candidates. The factors most frequently mentioned by respondents include several attributes beyond an individual challenger's control come election time—performance and experience, district service and attention, party, and personality—and only two characteristics, ideology and (perhaps) group associations, that are clearly within a challenger's immediate control. Performance and experience are a matter of past record, which cannot be changed by a challenger over the course of an election, and district service is truly only applicable to incumbents. Even a candidate's personality, one might argue, can undergo limited changes. Advertisements can tout a candidate as a nice person, but a candidate's actual personal demeanor would be difficult to change. In three of the four election years for which Jacobson presents data, personality is by far the dominant "liked" characteristic of incumbents, with district service, and experience or performance coming next. Ideology or policy ranks third or fourth in all years except 1994, when it was the second most mentioned "liked" trait. Ideology is, however, the most frequently mentioned "disliked" trait for incumbents in 1988 and 1994. For challengers, ideology was second only to personality, and it in fact was the most mentioned "like" and "dislike" for voters in the 1994 survey. Incumbents, it appears then, can (and perhaps should) downplay their policy positions and ideological stances with some success; challengers have little else to bring to their campaigns.

Campaign issues thus appear to matter more to challengers than to incumbents, yet among the previous analyses of congressional challengers, the consensus is that candidates have little faith that voters consider the issues. Huckshorn and Spencer's *The Politics of Defeat* (1971, 195) reports that few of the challengers whom the authors surveyed thought their issue positions were of great importance in the race. Over 90 percent of the losing candidates reported that their knowledge of the issues had little effect upon their fortunes in the campaign. Nonetheless, the authors sensibly conclude, candidates still need something to talk about: "Even though the electorate is not listening, the candidates talk as though it were. And even though the election is not decided necessarily on the basis of confrontation and discussion of policy questions, issues and discussion still make up the substance of what is thought of as political campaigning" (Huckshorn and Spencer 1971, 226).

Kingdon (1966, 127) hypothesized in his study of 1964 candidates that losing candidates would be more likely to pick issues for their "policy importance" than would winners—a prediction that sounds similar to my argument. In a more recent study, Herrnson (1995, 171) presents 1992 candidate survey data that do appear to bear out Kingdon's hypothesis. Forty-six percent of challengers claimed that their advertisements and campaign appeals concentrated primarily upon their issue positions; another 18 percent claimed they were concentrating upon their opponent's issue positions. Only 12 percent of challengers focused upon "image" or personality, while 40 percent of incumbents made personality a focus of their appeals. Despite these differences, however, a greater percentage of candidates in uncompetitive races focused upon issues than did candidates in competitive races (53 percent to 41 percent). The ambiguity prediction from the sequential positioning alternatives thus seems to be supported here.[1]

A final concern regarding literature on congressional elections and issues is the presence of alternative campaign strategies. Not every candidate will adhere to a median voter strategy. Several of the more ideological candidates with whom I spoke claimed that their campaigns were not about capturing the median voter; instead, these candidates argued, they sought to selectively mobilize the uninvolved, the "silent majority," perhaps, and win despite the odds. It is important to note that even the most hopeless candidates did have some slim hope of winning. Most of the candidates who thought they had a small chance of winning staked their hopes on a less orthodox scenario or on the sharp increase in turnout which is often associated with presidential election years (see Campbell 1993, 36–62). Likewise, a candidate can take advantage of district heterogeneity to be "all things to all people," to have targeted appeals that will help disparate groups to think of the candidate along different lines. While certainly some candidates can do this successfully, these candidates are usually incumbents, not challengers (see Fenno 1978, 91–99). Most of the challengers certainly thought so; while they often pointed out ways in which the incumbent could dodge issues, they themselves saw few opportunities to profit from ambiguity unless they were already very competitive.

Candidates' Reflections on Campaign Issues

The findings I present in this chapter are arranged to parallel the course of events in a campaign, and they are again separated by candidates' level of competitiveness. In the previous chapter the different levels of competitiveness mapped well onto different strategies for acquisition of public opinion information. Here, I propose a stylized path toward developing and publicizing the campaign's issue focus for each candidate type. I work through general comments from candidates of each type, and rather than beginning my analysis with case studies as I did in chapter 4, I leave the case studies to the end to show how the different aspects of the campaign fit together. I have excluded open-seat candidates from consideration in this chapter (with the exception of table 5.2), in part because there are so few of them that it is difficult to speak meaningfully of them as a group, but also because explaining the dynamics of the three competitive open-seat elections would require a substantial digression into the individuals running and into competition theories that run far afield from the incumbent-centered argument I present here.

The comments of the candidates show dramatically varying strategies in regards to the relationships between information and issues. The longshot candidate has little or no need for actual information on the preferences of the district's voters; all he truly must know is that the incumbent is very popular. This is not to say that he has no information; as I argued in the previous chapter, he has all of the information he needs and he could acquire more were it cost-effective to do so. In this case, the incumbent, who is not threatened by his challenger, does not campaign aggressively against him. The challenger, who either has no interaction with the incumbent or has a handful of rather positive encounters with him, has neither the ability nor the motivation to go after the incumbent on nonpolicy grounds, and he can find few issues where the incumbent is blatantly out of step with the district. As a result, he chooses to campaign primarily upon his own beliefs about policy issues, regardless of the impact of these issues upon the incumbent or upon his own chance of winning.

The somewhat competitive candidate does have access to some public opinion data, and he does have the resources to pose a limited threat to the incumbent. He concludes that the incumbent's popularity is not based upon his issue positions, as he has reason to believe that these positions are not necessarily winning positions in the district. He concludes that the incumbent's popularity is due to a false image of centrism; that is, if the challenger can tell the "truth" about the incumbent, can point out areas in which he deviates from the center on issues, this image will collapse. The somewhat competitive challenger, then, takes more instrumentally strategic issue positions than does the long shot. If these issue attacks constitute enough of a threat to the incumbent, the incumbent will respond, which may bring nonpolicy matters further into the campaign.

The very competitive challenger emerges in part because the incumbent has serious vulnerabilities; more often than not, these are issue vulnerabilities. The incumbent may have taken unpopular positions on a variety of policy issues, and the challenger will have information on what these issues are and where the voters stand on them. The campaign will, then, be built upon areas in which the incumbent is vulnerable. There will not necessarily be convergence, since the incumbent is not staking out a median position. The challenger will also, as long as he is not viewed as being away from the median on issues, seek to turn the election toward nonpolicy matters—to question the incumbent's competence, ethics, or ability to look out for the district's best interests. The challenger will seek not only to address issues on which the incumbent is at a disadvantage, but to turn the campaign toward other matters where the incumbent is weak.

These stylized depictions of three types of campaigns, then, all begin with the incumbent; the challenger's strategy is a result of his or her evaluation of the incumbent's vulnerability. Before moving to the issues themselves and the results of these different types of campaigns, let us look at challengers' assessments of their opponents.

The Incumbent

I did not begin my interviews with questions about the incumbent; I began my interviews by asking candidates what prompted them to run for Congress. By the time we had discussed motivations for running, however, most candidates had made some reference to their opponents. If they had not, at this point I would ask them for their views of their opponents and how these views affected their campaigns. Late in the interview, however, I asked candidates "Who are some members of Congress that you personally respect?" To my surprise, four candidates—three of whom were long shots—named their opponents. To quote two of these candidates:

> I respect [my opponent] a lot. I can respect him and disagree with his positions and views. I respect him for the way he presents himself, his demeanor. And running against him, I thanked him for being decent to me. (Wisconsin)

> I consider [my opponent] my friend, and I would not have a hard time voting for him because he is somewhat conservative. . . . We met a couple weeks ago and he asked if I was going to run again, and I said absolutely not. So we talked about doing something for him. Not supporting him, but he suggested we put together a task force to study some of the issues we brought up in the campaign and how they relate to the district. (Minnesota)

I did not necessarily expect candidates to feel this warmly toward the incumbent, but I did expect varying levels of hostility toward the incumbent across candidate types. I expected that long shots—who had so little chance of winning that the incumbent would not bother to attack them—would be less likely to dislike the incumbent than would candidates who gave the incumbent a scare. I also expected that the more competitive candidates, most of whom had prior political experience, would take attacks from the incumbent in stride and would not take offense at hardball campaign tactics. It would be the somewhat competitive candidates, as well as a handful of long shots who were motivated to run out of personal distaste for the incumbent, who would have the most negative feelings toward the incumbent.

Table 5.1 demonstrates that for the most part, this pattern held up. When I asked candidates "What sort of relationship did you have with your opponent?" a majority of candidates of all types stated that they had a good relationship, but among the somewhat competitive candidates, this

Table 5.1. Candidate Evaluations of Their Opponents

	Long shots	Somewhat Competitive	Very Competitive	Total
Is the incumbent the kind of politician who would change his votes if he discovered that they were not favored by the majority of voters in the district? (Challengers Only)				
Yes	81%	81%	29%	73%
	(13)	(17)	(2)	(32)
No	19	19	71	27
	(3)	(4)	(5)	(12)
Did the incumbent campaign against you directly? (Challengers Only)				
Yes	6	52	100	43
	(1)	(11)	(7)	(19)
No	94	48	0	57
	(15)	(10)	(0)	(25)
N	16	21	7	44
What sort of relationship did you have with the incumbent during the campaign? (All Candidates)				
Good	50	48	71	52
	(8)	(10)	(5)	(23)
Bad	13	42	14	27
	(2)	(9)	(1)	(12)
None	37	10	14	20
	(6)	(2)	(1)	(9)
N	17	21	14	52

majority was much smaller than among the other groups. Fifty-five percent of somewhat competitive candidates who answered the question in either direction—that is, who claimed any "relationship" at all with their opponent—said the relationship was a good one. The corresponding figures are 80 percent for long shots and 82 percent for the very competitive candidates. It was here that I received some of the most spirited attacks upon the incumbents, as this somewhat competitive candidate's comments show:

> He doesn't like me because I tell the truth. It's like the cockroaches are able to operate in the darkness, at night. The minute you turn the kitchen light off, the cockroaches are all over the place. But the minute you turn the light on, zip! They hide, and run for cover. That's very much the way he and his organization are. Doesn't like the spotlight on, likes to operate under the cover of darkness, and we were able to put the light on him, and therefore he didn't like me. There was no question that he was running against me, personally. (Illinois)

The decision for an incumbent to personally attack his opponent was also related to the expected degree of competition. For most of the less competitive candidates, it was the failure of the incumbent to address them at all—to participate in debates, to appear at forums, or to directly address the issues challengers had sought to bring up—that was most frustrating. Thirty-three percent of the long shots professed to never having met the incumbent, and even two of the somewhat competitive candidates and two of the very competitive candidates claimed to have had no contact whatsoever with their opponent during the campaign: "If I were [the incumbent], would I have run my campaign differently? No. He played it brilliantly. He ignored me, and that was the right thing to do. He just totally ignored me. It's not good for democracy, but it's great for him" (Ohio).

Such behavior is, of course, standard operating procedure for incumbents. Only an incumbent with a serious challenger is expected to directly address that challenger (see Herrnson 2000, 185). There is also a median voter application to this scenario: if voters do not know the challenger's policy positions, they will not be certain which of the two candidates is farther from their own views. They will either be risk-averse, opting for the known quantity over the unknown challenger, or they will shift their thinking toward the experience and competence dimension, again opting for the incumbent on the grounds that the incumbent has the experience of being in the job to begin with. Thus, it is easy to say that incumbents are campaigning strategically in the races I consider, though this tells us nothing about whether they have taken issue positions strategically.

When I asked each of the candidates "Is your opponent the kind of person who would change his votes if he discovered he was out of step with the voters in your district?" the answers varied in relatively predictable ways. Eighty-one percent of long shots conceded that their opponents were strategic politicians by this definition, as did 81 percent of somewhat competitive candidates and only 29 percent of very competitive challengers (who may have been competitive precisely because their opponents had not taken positions strategically). These responses may be adaptations to the election results. Yet the specific content of the candidates' answers indicates a sensitivity to the ways in which incumbents seek to represent the median voter and noticeable variations in candidates' normative assessments of this trait—that is, disagreement about whether it was morally good or politically wise to cater to public opinion.

Long shots almost invariably pointed out that their opponents' policy positions had prevented serious competition—that they were relatively popular positions. They often sought to question whether this type of adaptation was the result of a lack of integrity or firm beliefs, as if to argue that even if a challenger does not always agree with the voters, his desire to speak his mind might be appealing to voters:

> [My opponent] is probably the best Republican member of Congress that we have. I ain't got anything against him. I just think it's time for him to retire and go home. The main issue that I wanted to raise, and which the media never let me hammer, is that I find it really hypocritical that he votes for things he doesn't believe in. . . . I felt the cooling down to my campaign when he turned around and supported the striker replacement, for example. (Ohio)

> First of all, you've got to understand that [my opponent] doesn't take a firm position on anything. He can go in front of any group he wants and say, "I voted along the same lines you want." So he was so middle-of-the-road that it's hard to say that there's a black-and-white difference between me and him on anything. There just wasn't. He'll come out in favor of a woman's right to choose, yet he'll still vote with the government and try to restrict it. Now when I say I'm pro-choice, I'm pro-choice. He'll flip on something like that, he can say anything he wants and it will be true. But when I have a position, it's a solid position. (Illinois)

> He's a career politician, he's been that way his whole life. At the beginning of his career he was much more conservative because his [state legislative] district was much more conservative. He became more liberal as his constituency was spread out over a district that was much more liberal. So he does that. Some people think that's being a total fake. There's a fine line between listening to your constituents and doing what you believe in, and I think you should find some middle ground there to try to, if you're a good politician, to represent their views as well as your own. I think that's why he has done very well that way, because he always listens to his constituents and adjusts his positions to their political whims. He moves to the polls. (Wisconsin)

There is a difference, however, between actually "moving to the polls" and merely giving the appearance that one is choosing positions that reflect voters' preferences. In 1996 numerous Democratic challengers sought to attack their Republican opponents' image for centrism by linking them to Newt Gingrich (see Jacobson 1997b, 156). While this was a national strategy, and one that may have been more related to Gingrich's unpopularity than to specific issues, several somewhat competitive Democrats described this tactic as a means of exposing the incumbent's lack of concern for voters' preferences:

His image in the district is still as a local figure, a local officeholder. One of the things that we failed to do, that we were unable to do, because of his image as a local council member, was to tie him to Gingrich. In Washington and among elites he may have that superficially, but among voters he doesn't have that image. He's just a local city council member on the national stage. (Ohio)

His moderate image came from a few high-profile votes, where occasionally he would break with the Republican leadership and vote for an environmental bill, or vote pro-choice. He voted for gun control, but that came after all sorts of hand-wringing and gnashing of teeth. He didn't want to vote for that gun-control thing. The same thing with minimum wage, he only voted for that after the bill was loaded up with tax breaks for business. It was after a lot of posturing and undecided this and that. He ends up getting these kinds of high-profile votes to bolster his image. Our research shows that he has pretty much voted like a conservative Republican. (Wisconsin)

Somewhat competitive Republicans had similar sentiments, claiming that their opponents' images belied their "Clinton-esque" liberalism:

He's not very ideological. I don't think he's got a policy vision one way or another. That's why he's done this radical transformation. When he was first elected, he was one of the most liberal members of Congress. But he's fashioned himself, much as the president did, as a very conservative Democrat. He's pretty skillful at that, but it's all staged. You really sense that there's a lot of politics there, just the sense that it's so wildly inconsistent. He votes one way one week and another way the next week. (Minnesota)

The real problem with Washington is this. I call it the good twin/evil twin scenario. The good twin stays in the district and says, "I'm for you, I'm with you on the issues, no problem." The evil twin is in Washington, and when they vote on bills when they come to the floor and when they vote on the motion to recommit, they do what their party leaders tell them to. And the local media is so stuffed with other things that you never really know what your congressman is up to. That was the main problem we faced, that nobody knew and we couldn't tell them. (Illinois)

Some of the same sentiments were shared by the most competitive candidates. For the most part, their opponents really did seem to be somewhat too liberal or conservative to hold onto their districts easily. I asked one Republican candidate what the biggest surprise he encountered during the campaign was, and he responded that

> It was how many people thought [my opponent] was a conservative. It's amazing. When you don't have strong campaigns against the guy for ten years, and he's not challenged in the media, they can come back and put whatever spin they want on it. That was the real challenge. He comes across as a very meek guy, inoffensive. His voting record may be offensive, but he's not an offensive person. We knew this guy is far too liberal for this district, yet the perception is that he's conservative. So the challenge was to point out his liberal voting record without beating up on him, because that could backfire. That's a tough thing to do. (Illinois)

For the most part, however, the stronger candidates were often baffled at the unstrategic moves they felt their opponents made. Several expressed that their candidacies were in part helped by merely taking advantage of media criticism of the incumbent. When I asked one candidate about some missteps his opponent had made in the previous Congress, he remarked that "We didn't even need to talk about that. There was an overall continuation of the points we were making, frankly not so much by us as by the media. I'm sure you read some of the coverage of things he had done. That just sort of continued throughout the campaign. I'm just amazed by some of the things he did. I think he had some qualified people on his staff, but they ended up doing a lot of dumb things" (Ohio).

All but one of the very competitive challengers were facing first- or second-term Republican Congressmen. This characteristic may make evaluating the very competitive 1996 challengers problematic, but one implication of these interviews is that less strategic incumbents are often those who face serious opposition. The Democrats facing first-term Republicans frequently discussed occasions on which their opponents declined to vote strategically: "He works very, very hard to be seen as an independent, but most of the time when he breaks with his party, it's because he thinks the party is being too moderate. When he breaks with the leadership, it's because they're selling out, because they're not conservative enough. That's who he really is, but the way he portrays himself is as this totally independent guy" (Wisconsin).

While the somewhat competitive candidates often held that their opponents had established a false image of sharing the views of most constituents, the most competitive challengers were aided by national- and state-level campaigns, and by the media, in undermining such attempts. Even where junior Republicans had actually made attempts to distance themselves from the media's portrayal of the "extremist" class of first- and second-term Republicans, they did not always have great success in doing so. Their relatively brief tenure also limited their ability to tout benefits they had brought to the district. Even where they had tried to do things for the district, challengers were able to exploit the disparity between these Republicans' zeal for budget cutting and their attempts to procure pork for their district. As one Democrat commented, "[The incumbent] did talk about how he put out his neck for certain things—he didn't just vote for them, he lobbied for them. And that was commendable. But he was the one who ran as an antipork candidate. He has his ideas about what should be done for the district, but what this race was clearly about was who best represents the ideas of the people of this district" (Illinois).

In short, while the most competitive candidates certainly had to clear some hurdles merely to get their party's nomination, even the candidates themselves seem to realize that one of most important keys to a competitive or successful challenge is being in the right place at the right time, with the right opponent.

Issue Strategies

The choice of an issue focus for a campaign is a two-faceted process. Candidates must choose not only which issue positions to focus upon, but they must also choose how issue-oriented their campaigns will be. I began my questions on the campaign's issue focus by asking candidates to name three or four issues on which they focused in their campaign. After discussing these issues, I asked the candidates whether they had made targeted appeals (that is, whether they had consciously focused upon different issues in different areas of the district), whether there were particular issue stances that they took which were particularly unpopular in their district, whether they changed their views on any of these issues during the campaign, and whether they discussed matters other than policy issues—for instance, whether they focused upon their opponent's ethics or competence.

Table 5.2 presents the issues candidates of different levels of competitiveness focused upon. Although the point should not be overstated, the most competitive candidates for each party appear to be somewhat more consistent in the issues they discuss than are less competitive candidates. Very competitive Democrats and very competitive Republicans each have one issue that all discussed (education for Democrats, welfare for Republicans), while the less competitive candidates are lacking such a common issue. Very competitive candidates of each party have a larger number of

Table 5.2. Candidate Issue Focus by Competitiveness

	Long Shots		Somewhat Competitive		Very Competitive	
Democrats	Healthcare	60%	Healthcare	80%	Education	100%
	Environment	50	Education	40	Environment	60
	Labor	30	Environment	40	Budget	50
	Abortion	20	Jobs	40	Healthcare	50
	Campaign Finance	20	Budget	30	Crime	40
	Education	20	Labor	20	Taxes	30
	Jobs	20	Transportation	20	Labor	30
	Welfare	20	Guns	10	Agriculture	10
	Budget	10			Guns	10
	Guns	10			Welfare	10
	Taxes	10				
	Transportation	10				
N		10		10		10
Republicans	Abortion	56%	Taxes	81%	Welfare	100%
	Welfare	56	Budget	63	Budget	75
	Taxes	42	Crime	45	Education	50
	Budget	28	Education	45	Agriculture	25
	Crime	28	Abortion	27	Crime	25
	Jobs	28	Welfare	27	Environment	25
	Education	14	Healthcare	18	Guns	25
	Guns	14	Guns	9	Taxes	25
	Housing	14				
N		7		11		4

issues that at least half of the candidates focused upon than is the case for less competitive candidates.

District characteristics play a large role in several of the issues of importance—for instance, agriculture was discussed by both candidates in Wisconsin's rural Third District, and public housing was a concern in Illinois's urban Seventh District. Putting these issues aside, however, it appears from this table that the most competitive candidates spoke most frequently about education, healthcare, the budget, the environment, and crime—issues that were stressed in the Clinton/Dole campaign and which were among the most common points of Democratic attack in Congress against the Republican majority. There is far less focus to the long-shot campaigns; while each of these issues is mentioned by long-shot candidates, their campaigns seem somewhat more idiosyncratic. Abortion, perhaps the most polarizing of the issues brought up, was mentioned more by long shots than by more competitive candidates, and none of the very competitive candidates made it a focal point of their campaigns. Finally, the reader will note that only eight of the thirteen issues raised by the candidates I interviewed also appear in the *Time/Congressional Quarterly* survey I drew upon to construct the scales in chapter 3.[2] References to term limits, gays in the military, defense policy, and foreign policy were altogether absent from candidates' comments on the most important issues in their campaigns.[3]

Merely asking about the issue focus of the campaign misses, of course, many nuances. I found little correlation between candidate type and the depth in which candidates were prepared to discuss these issues; many of the less competitive candidates had assiduously researched the topics about which they spoke, yet the more politically experienced candidates also had extensive knowledge about the issues they presented. There may have been more single-issue candidates among the long shots, yet this is more a reflection of political background and motivation for running than it is an indicator of differences in itself. Most of the long shots also bristled at being considered "single-issue candidates" by the media: "The campaign wasn't all about NAFTA, like the newspapers said. There were lots of other things too. That was all I heard in the papers, that I was wrong on NAFTA. Oh, and they also called me an old-fashioned Democrat. The campaign was about everything. Social security, Medicare, pensions, all of that. But you can't control what the paper says about you" (Ohio).

After brief discussions of some of the campaigns' issues and the effectiveness of issue appeals, I asked candidates whether they targeted their issue appeals—that is, whether they made specialized advertisements or presentations for different groups of voters in the district. Table 5.3 shows candidates' responses to this question and other questions about the role issue appeals played in their campaigns. While the ability to do this is in part a matter of money and public opinion research, the differences between candidate types cannot be completely explained away by these two variables. Only 12 percent of the long shots claimed to have done any targeting, as compared to 67 percent of the somewhat competitive candidates and 79 percent of the very competitive candidates. Several of the long shots claimed that the "package" of views they were trying to present could not be broken down for different groups:

Table 5.3. Candidate Issue Strategies

	Long shots	Somewhat Competitive	Very Competitive	Total
Did you target your message differently to different groups within the district?				
Yes	12% (2)	67% (14)	79% (11)	52% (27)
No	88 (15)	33 (7)	21 (3)	48 (25)
Was your campaign entirely focused upon policy issues, or did you bring up characteristics of your opponent, such as leadership, competence, or ethics?				
Issues Only	29 (6)	71 (10)	62 (32)	
Issues + Other	6 (1)	71 (15)	29 (4)	38 (20)
Were any of the issues you focused upon in your campaign issues on which the majority of voters in the district disagree with you?				
Yes	65 (11)	24 (5)	43 (6)	42 (22)
No	35 (6)	76 (16)	57 (8)	58 (30)
Did you change your views on any of the major campaign issues during the campaign?				
No	41 (7)	62 (13)	71 (10)	58 (30)
Yes, toward center	12 (2)	29 (6)	29 (4)	23 (12)
Yes, away from center	47 (8)	10 (2)	0 (0)	19 (10)
Do you think you were able to set the agenda at all for which issues were discussed by your opponent during the campaign?				
Yes	24 (4)	57 (12)	86 (12)	54 (28)
No	76 (13)	43 (9)	14 (2)	46 (24)
N	17	21	14	52

I really found early on that I couldn't attack the issues that I wanted to at the level I wanted because the receptivity of the public to the issues I wanted to talk about wasn't there, so I found that I had to engage in some basic education. I tried to persuade people that these were all things that were tied together and were tied directly to the actions that the Congress takes. (Ohio)

The advice I got from everybody was to have your three issues, just stick to your three issues. In fact, I got advice from a town committee member; she said, "Stick to education, stick to what you know." And I became understandably infuriated by that. I said, "I know about a lot of things." ... I talked about everything, every chance I got. But you know, these things don't lend themselves to sound bites. These are complex problems that are all interconnected. (Illinois)

More competitive candidates made frequent reference to regional or group strategies in their campaigns, but there was still some appeal to the notion of presenting a unified package of views:

What's interesting is that this district has very different sections. So I had to say that I had some moderate Democrat, fiscal ideas, but I had some very progressive ideas as well. The message was pretty similar across the district, but sure, I had to get to the heart of what people were concerned about. (Illinois)

There were a lot of things I would have liked to have said, but I wouldn't go on about them in front of groups. I couldn't talk about women's issues unless I was in front of women. I mean, I already am a woman, that's bad enough in this district. So here I sat as a woman, a challenger, and a Democrat. I mean, I might as well have slit my wrists! (Illinois)

I think the hardest thing for me was helping people connect the general philosophy that was converging with the current issues. If people understood that, [the incumbent], as well as most Republicans, would be looking for work. But it was very difficult to give people that combined message. You're used to thirty-second sound bites, the media wants to handle each issue in isolation, doesn't try to pull the package together the way that you see the package converging. It's very hard to have that conversation with voters. You definitely can't get it across in thirty seconds. That's probably why a negative campaign resonates more than a positive one. (Wisconsin)

I certainly would have gotten few affirmative responses had I asked candidates whether they ran a negative campaign. There were, however, sharp differences between candidate types in regard to whether they discussed their opponent harshly or made reference to matters other than their own positions on policy issues. In an attempt to place nonissue matters in a more positive light, I asked candidates whether they had focused upon their opponent's competence, ethics, or leadership skills—three avenues of attack that do not necessarily lead to mudslinging. The differences between categories are quite startling: only one long-shot candidate made such references to his opponent, while 71 percent of somewhat competitive candidates and 29 percent of very competitive candidates sought to shift debate in this manner.

Numerous long-shot candidates voiced similar sentiments about this sort of campaigning—that they had the opportunity to do it, but chose not to; that they knew things about their opponent that they could have used, but chose not to:

> Most of his ads were "Hey, I've been your representative for years, and here's what I've gotten done." There was no attack on me. The opportunity was there for me to attack him, he has some shady things in his past, but being a firm believer in the Constitution, I believe that he's innocent until proven guilty. That's not the kind of race I would run. (Illinois)

> [My opponent] came up to me once and told me he really enjoyed the campaign and how civil it stayed. We carried on very gentlemanly, and I think that's the way it should be run. I think that's what people want. They seem to say that. But if I had a couple of hundred thousand dollars, maybe the race wouldn't have been as nice. When you have money like that you can afford to be a bit snootier and a bit sharper. But that's just not me. I've never been one to be nasty unless I have a good reason. (Ohio)

> The only thing that I ever mentioned about [my opponent] was his voting record. I tried to keep it very professional. So did he. We've all got skeletons in our closet. Hell, I'm bound to. Someone could find something about me they could blow out of proportion. I told his campaign staff the first time I met them, "If I run, it's just going to be on issues, on what he actually did. I'm not going to attack him or anything like that." (Ohio)

Bringing up ethical questions or allegations about one's opponent, despite the unpopular image of such campaigning, was for most of the competitive candidates a strategic maneuver. The only very competitive candidates who did not do so were those who felt they did not need to—the winners. In many cases, their work had already been done for them, by others. Most of the rest, who needed something in addition, or perhaps in place of, strategic issue positions, sought to bring another element into the campaign:

> People didn't always get my argument. I said once or twice that even if

you were on his side, if you wanted his agenda to become the law, you had to look at his record of effectiveness. His opponent in the primary said that if you put all the bills that he shepherded through the legislative process, if you put them end-to-end, there would only be one end. I thought that was funny, so I used that. (Illinois)

This race was not at all personal. There was no mudslinging. But I did say that I think this is an exciting district, and the current representative was lacking in that regard. He's a backbencher. (Illinois)

[My opponent] is not a civil man, and I should have made that more of an issue. He's just mean, mean, mean. (Wisconsin)

Finally, I asked the candidates whether they had any policy views that were unpopular in their district and whether they altered their positions in response to this discovery. I tried not to put the second half of this question in a negative light; instead of asking whether candidates changed their views in response to public opinion, I asked if they learned anything during the campaign that "changed their way of thinking" about these issues. The candidates' evaluations of whether their positions were unpopular may be somewhat tainted by the margin of victory, although even some of the long shots thought their views would still be shared by the majority of the voters if they had the opportunity to make their case:

I think we'd come out ahead on all five of the issues we talked about if we had free and open public forums and if we had say five events from wintertime through springtime and then could go back and revisit the issues in the summer, I think [the incumbent] would lose on all five. (Illinois)

I suppose there's all kinds of things where most people don't agree with me. But the reason I want to be in Congress is because I feel I would do a job that would represent the people of this district in a responsible or honest manner. I would listen to them. It may not always be what they agree with on every vote, but I feel that it would be pretty close most of the time. Besides, I don't want to be there forever, anyway, and I told them that too. (Ohio)

Aside from abortion, an issue that virtually no candidate said was negotiable, regardless of public sentiment, candidates volunteered many issues on which they had changed their views during the campaign (or, in the case of second-time candidates, between their first and second campaign). I asked about changes in positions with the belief that a willingness to compromise one's position indicated a willingness to take positions strategically, a concern with maximizing votes or chance of winning. While many of the very competitive candidates claimed to already have established positions that they could not change (and which were positions shared by most voters), there was a greater willingness among somewhat competitive and very competitive candidates to change their views. Twenty-nine percent of the somewhat competitive candidates and 29 percent of the very competitive candidates acknowledged that they had moderated some of their policy positions during their campaigns, as opposed to only 12 percent of the long shots. The reasons for these changes were clearly strategic:

> There were a lot of issues that I was kind of on the fence about. Like, for instance, gun control. I didn't have much of an opinion about it. I went away from the party line, because especially in the central cities gun control seemed appropriate. (Wisconsin)

> Let me put it this way. I had always been interested in politics and I felt that's why I was a far better candidate for the job of congressman, because I was attuned to the national issues in a way that [the incumbent] was not. . . . But what he has done is he knows what plays in this district, and that's what keeps him in his seat. What I learned was about the electorate, about what they want. I learned about local politics, the dynamics of this area, and I had to make up my mind on all sorts of things that affected this area that I never thought about before. (Illinois)

Most of the more competitive candidates who said they had not changed their views argued that they had not changed precisely because they already shared their constituents' views, or that the campaign itself had dictated the terms of debate:

> On these talk shows people would ask all kinds of questions, and very rarely did I get any that surprised me. I think that we always knew what the issues were all through the thing. I knew which issues were important. That's why I had a campaign staff. (Illinois)

> Voters tend to respond to the issues that political actors drive into the debate. If you're a politician and you're not stupid you're paying attention to what's on people's minds, so there aren't any mysterious issues that appear halfway through the campaign. I knocked on seven or eight thou-

sand doors over the course of the campaign, and the people I met would comment pretty much on what they'd seen on TV. (Ohio)

Among the long-shot candidates there were several interviewees who said they had not changed any of their views during the campaign because they had already thought the issues out carefully, or because there was little to gain from changing their message. One of the most illustrative quotes in this regard came from an Ohio Democrat, who told me that "Really it comes down to, it was a single-issue campaign, and that single issue was abortion. Like it or not that's the way people vote. I support early abortion, and most people around here don't. I'd say I would have gotten 10 percent more votes if I'd switched that position, but I still wouldn't have won. So I stayed on the other side on that one" (Ohio).

Surprisingly, however, 47 percent of the long shots, as well as 10 percent of the somewhat competitive candidates, took my invitation to talk about changing their positions to indicate that they moved further away from the political center during the campaign—that the Republicans became more conservative than they had been previously, or the Democrats became more liberal. This is clearly indicative of a campaign that was not so much about winning votes as it was about expressing ideological beliefs. Most of these responses included reference to long and careful thought about the issue, about the best solution to a problem, or to reconciling different issues under an ideological or philosophical rubric: "I still get letters from people criticizing my stances on things. It doesn't do any good, but I tried to write back to as many as possible, just for my own intellectual clarification. I think that I did make some modifications on things like abortion, but it had nothing to do with votes. It had to do with my own basic views, my own feelings" (Illinois).

The Results

The degree of satisfaction that candidates derive from their campaigns depends in large part on what their expectations of the campaign are. At the beginning of the interviews, I asked candidates why they ran for Congress in the first place. I then placed their responses in one of four categories: desire to win, desire to present a particular set of policy issues and views to the public, distaste for the incumbent, and desire to help their party or to further their own political or nonpolitical career objectives. Many candidates gave more than one of these answers, and there are certainly elements of more than one of these desires in every campaign. Every

Figure 5.1. Candidate Motivations for Running

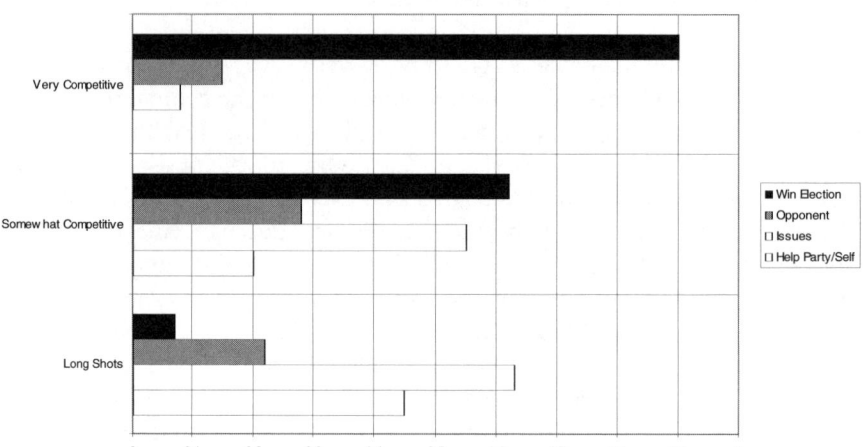

candidate, of course, would like to win, yet few of the long-shot candidates, for instance, mentioned this as a major reason for running. Likewise, although virtually all of the very competitive candidates stated that they ran to win, they certainly also were motivated to run in part because of their policy views. Thus, where candidates did give more than one of these reasons, I included each reason they gave.

The differences between categories here (as shown in figure 5.1) are again what one would expect. Long shots are more concerned with helping their party—they are more likely to be recruits, a matter I discuss in the next chapter—and they are more likely to have been inspired to run by particular issues than are the other candidate types. Somewhat competitive candidates are more likely to have been inspired in part out of distaste for the current incumbent, whether out of a desire to remove him from office or merely to make him more cautious in his voting, and the majority (67 percent) ran because they thought they could win. Among the most competitive candidates, winning was stated as the main objective by all but one of the candidates. Among the long shots and somewhat competitive candidates, many rationales for running that did not include winning were phrased as issue platforms: "I got involved for a variety of reasons. I think everything starts in your own universe, your own point of view. My own point of view was really looking at my own profession, looking at it from the perspective of increasing government interference, regulation, that sort of thing. I felt that things I had been feeling for years very likely would have a greater audience" (Ohio).

Other statements were phrased as direct attacks on the incumbent:

I got involved because of the issues and because of the what I would term "extreme" right-wing advocate that [the incumbent] was, and I thought it was extremely important to challenge him, make him pay attention to people, give them a choice. (Illinois)

I never thought that I would run, but then I started wondering "Why shouldn't I?" I'm exactly what the Constitution says. I'm a citizen, I've got every right in the world to do this. And I've got good ideas. Then [the incumbent] was the other inspiration, being the antienvironmentalist he is. His voting record is atrocious. I thought if the average person found out what he is really up to, he would not get their vote. (Ohio)

Among the more competitive candidates, statements about why they ran tended either to be phrased almost as stump speeches (which many of them probably were) or as simple "I would represent the district better" pronouncements. An example of each:

What prompted me to run is that my wife and I recently started a family. When you have children, you start thinking more about the future. I was concerned about the direction the country's going in, and I wanted to make a difference for my children's sake. (Illinois)

My reason for running was that I felt that the incumbent was not representing the people of the district. That has been a problem for the district for too long. (Ohio)

The manner in which candidates evaluated their campaigns afterward depended, then, upon what they expected from their campaign and why they ran. At the end of the interview, I asked each of them whether running for Congress had been worthwhile, whether they had benefited from it. This was intended more as a way to bring the interview to a close on a good note than as a question that would yield useful data. Nearly all of the candidates said that running had been a good experience, that they had met people, gained speaking skills, changed a few people's minds. Only three candidates said that they wished they had not run, and each of these three was a somewhat competitive candidate who had run exclusively to win. One candidate merely responded, "No. I gained nothing, and I lost a lot of money." Another candidate simply noted that he would not have run if he had known how poorly he would do. The third gave a more lengthy, and more colorful, answer:

> No, it really wasn't worthwhile. They used everything against me but the kitchen sink. I don't want to dredge it up emotionally and it doesn't matter to you, but I will tell you that it was like Abraham Lincoln said about being tarred and feathered and being driven out of town on a rail. If it hadn't been for the prestige of the whole thing, I would have just as soon walked before the campaign was even over. (Illinois)

Because most candidates had more modest or more varied motivations for running, however, many were eager to talk about ways in which they had benefited. I discuss candidates who ran because they wished to help their party in the next chapter. The remaining two categories of reasons for running, desire to address particular issues and dissatisfaction with the incumbent, both yielded statements at the close of the interview which square with the expressive campaigning paradigm. To see if expressively oriented candidates felt they had succeeded in presenting their views to a larger audience, I asked the candidates if they felt they had set the agenda for discussion at all in the campaign. To identify strategic responses by the incumbent—or at least, challengers' perceptions of incumbent strategy—I asked the candidates whether they believed the incumbent had responded to their campaigns by changing his behavior or his issue positions at all.

Agenda setting and influence on the incumbent are primarily a result of competitive campaigns—a well-financed campaign will be more successful in setting the terms of debate in an election, and a competitive challenge will certainly scare an incumbent more than will a long-shot, obscure challenger. Some of the less competitive candidates realized this:

> His strategy never changed. What did change was his voting in Congress, when he realized how unpopular Gingrich was becoming. So did I change his campaign strategy? No. Did I have an effect on his voting? Perhaps. But maybe he was just listening to public opinion, that's how these things get shifted. (Illinois)

> Every time we appeared together he would always stand there behind the podium and everything he said he came across as having set pieces to say and he was going to say them regardless of what I said or what other people said. And you know, that's pretty much how the whole campaign went. (Illinois)

Candidates' reflections on agenda setting again reflect the relative success of their campaigns in gaining attention; only 24 percent of the long shots felt they had set the agenda in any way, while 57 percent of somewhat competitive candidates shared that view, and 86 percent of the most competitive candidates felt that they had set the terms for debate. Reflections by the losing candidates about influence upon the incumbent were similar, although seven of the candidates (two long shots, four somewhat competitive candidates, and one very competitive challenger) felt that the incumbent was going to retire before the next election.[4] I was uncertain about whether candidates felt that the decision to retire would be a response to the challenger's campaign or an independent decision.

Several long shots did take pride in small contributions they had made to the campaign, however, as these two candidates demonstrate:

> It was mostly little things, like when we went to forums when we were speaking in front of crowds. He's got a bad back, he's old, so he just sits in his chair and talks to everybody from behind the table, but when I was there I was walking around, talking to people, so he had to start doing that a bit. (Illinois)

> He responded himself and his campaign responded more to the intellectual and debate-oriented points that I brought up because the press picked up on some of them. He didn't ever say they were my ideas, but the points I was making were relevant, and he felt that he had to respond to them. Actually, one of the things I hit him on early on was the fact that he never sponsored any legislation in Congress, so one of the first things he did after the election was he sponsored a bill to change rules in the Clean Air Act. He isn't even on any committees that would be dealing with that, so that's where I'm saying that it's a direct response to some of the things I did. He's just responding to some of the more substantive allegations I made. (Ohio)

Many of the more competitive candidates returned to the disjuncture between incumbents' image and their actual voting, arguing that they had had an effect on the incumbents in that they had forced them to spend more time in the district, or to downplay controversial positions, but that they had not actually changed their legislative behavior:

> He spends more time in the district now than he ever has. His office budget for travel is now the highest in the state. There's press releases all the time about him being back. So it has affected his behavior in the district, he's working harder than he ever has. But it hasn't changed his votes. Maybe on the margins, but not on anything that matters. (Wisconsin)

Philosophically, will he change? We'll see. He will use the word "bipartisan" more than he ever did before, but he's got one of the most partisan record in Congress, and that won't change. (Illinois)

Among the somewhat competitive candidates and the very competitive candidates, those who claimed not to have affected the incumbent said that the incumbent's failure to change was the reason for the closeness of the campaign and was indicative of a less strategic attitude on the part of the incumbent:

I don't think I did much to [the incumbent] because he's an ideologue, but I might have had some effect in making people think twice about the fact that I wasn't running because I needed to or for the money, I wasn't running for that, I was running because I believed in the issues. From that point of view, I feel it was worthwhile. I'd never urge people to go against their ideals, but I do have to disagree with [the incumbent] on policy grounds. These are issues that don't have anything to do with being a Democrat or a Republican. (Illinois)

I don't hold any animosity toward him, I don't think he's a bad guy, but he'll just do what he believes in. Is that right or wrong? I think it's wrong, and he thinks, obviously, that it's right. He'll always be voting with the ideological, conservative right. He won't change. (Illinois)

Finally, there were the incumbents who changed, who moved with the district or in order to preempt their opponents. These campaigns were perhaps the most frustrating to challengers, who could take some pride in influencing the incumbent but also realized that the incumbent's movement may have cost them their own chance of winning:

We had all these things we were prepared to use against him, but he took them away from us. Welfare reform was a big one, but then he took that away by voting for it. We expected him not to. It was like throwing golf balls against the wall. It's not going to stick to him, nothing sticks to him, there are no big issues down here that he's on the wrong side of. For certain people maybe there are, for maybe six thousand people, but you don't win an issue with six thousand votes. (Minnesota)

No question, we set the agenda. We moved him, we significantly affected his approach to being a congressman, with the paying attention to the suburbs. That was something he had never done before, and he did it very successfully. People were able to say that [the incumbent] isn't such a bad guy, he's not such a bad Democrat. While we set the agenda, he met virtually every issue head on. We set the high bar, and we were able to set it at a high level, and unfortunately he put his jumping shoes on and he was able to make the hurdle. (Illinois)

In sum, the goals of most of these candidates seem somewhat beyond their reach—those who seek to introduce issues into the campaign must settle primarily for introducing a small number of voters to those issues, expressing their views to only a few people, while those candidates who seek to win are the ones who actually introduce substantive issues to the campaign. More often than not, they do this only to see the incumbent appropriate those issues from them.

The above discussion shows that the circumstances of a candidate do play a major role in determining how that candidate will choose issues for his or her campaign and how he or she will present these issues. Long-shot candidates, as a group, have a more diffuse issue focus in comparison with other candidate types, and long-shot candidates are relatively free to tinker with their platform until it meets their own expressive or ideological standards. Somewhat competitive candidates demonstrate a narrower issue focus, as they seek to offset their opponent's popular issue stands, and a desire to search out their opponent's vulnerabilities on nonpolicy issues. The most competitive candidates have a much more uniform issue focus than do the other candidates, and the relatively more well-known vulnerabilities of the incumbent enable them to address the incumbent on policy grounds, while letting the media or other groups remind the voters of the incumbent's other flaws.

Issue Strategies in Three Campaigns

How does all of this information fit together in campaigns? The above discussion illustrates general attitudes and tendencies, but to show how all of these comments fit together, let us consider case studies of candidates who are, in many ways, representative of each type:

Expressive Politics in a Long-Shot Campaign

Wisconsin's Ninth District is easily the most conservative district in the state, stretching through solidly Republican northern suburbs of Milwaukee up through several rural communities to the small city of Sheboygan. Republican James Sensenbrenner has held the seat since 1978; since then, no challenger has garnered more than 30 percent of the vote and no Democratic presidential candidate has won more than 40 percent of the vote in the district.[5] Prior to 1996, Sensenbrenner had had an opponent in only one of the past three elections. Sensenbrenner is currently the senior member of the state's Republican House delegation and was at the time the chairman of the House Science Committee. His conservative politics have earned him a reputation as one of the more partisan members of Congress (see Duncan and Nutting 1999, 1507–1509), but his campaigning in his district has been less rancorous, limited to parades and fairly informal public gatherings. Although Sensenbrenner had an opponent in 1996, he still garnered 74 percent of the vote while spending only $140,000.

Sensenbrenner's opponent was retired school superintendent Floyd Brenholt. Brenholt mentioned to me that he ran in large part because he felt strongly that Sensenbrenner should not go unchallenged: "I've never run for office before, and I've never really participated in party activities before. I decided to get into the race for two reasons. There are many times when no one runs in the Ninth District as a Democrat, and I didn't want to see that happen again. The second reason was that I did have some feelings about these issues, and I thought at least to the extent that I could I should try to express those in the Ninth District and at least give people an option, somebody to vote for."

Brenholt ran an admittedly left-of-center campaign; his campaign literature included detailed summaries of his positions on a wide variety of issues; tables describing changes in national income distribution over the past two decades; and lengthy descriptions of his views on corporate welfare, campaign finance, and military spending. These are issues that few of the more competitive candidates gave high priority. Brenholt also addressed more popular issues such as healthcare, education, and the environment in his literature, unifying them all as responses to questions such as "Is it fair to all concerned?" and "Why is it always the poorest and most powerless among us who must sacrifice 'for the good of the country'?"

Brenholt raised only $14,000 in his campaign, far too little to do any polling. I asked him whether he was concerned during the campaign about how the issues he chose to speak about would resonate with the general public. He acknowledged that their appeal was limited: "I would guess probably that on a good number of those issues people split 30 to 70, maybe 25 to 75. In some ways, though, it was a good situation, because I knew my chances were virtually none. I didn't go around broadcasting that, but realistically, I knew what the chances were. But then the thing was, that freed me to do what I wanted to do to begin with, which was to say what I wanted to about the issues, whether the newspapers agreed or anyone else agreed."

Brenholt thus was not interested in assessing public opinion trends, and he said he did not change his views on any of the major issues of his campaign. He did note, however, that

> My wife and I spent a lot of time in libraries and bookstores trying to get materials for background on all of these things. When I got into this I really started looking into a lot of things. What I discovered in this campaign was that I would cite some of these statistics about wealth distribution, and people didn't believe it. They couldn't believe that those were correct. I think most people really want to do what's right for the vast majority of people, but I think they don't know. And one of the reasons they don't know is that they don't have time to search it out.

Thus, if Brenholt's views on any policy matters changed during the election, they shifted in response to his campaign research, not in regards to electoral concerns. Brenholt also ran his campaign with little reference to Sensenbrenner; he did point out in one of his leaflets that he and Sensenbrenner differed on issues such as the minimum wage and funding for the Department of Education, but for the most part he steered clear even of issue contrasts. Brenholt's literature instead focused upon campaign finance and the dominance of moneyed interests in Congress, as well as more basic questions such as "Who is Floyd Brenholt?" Brenholt said this was all done by design: "I intended right from when I announced my candidacy that it was going to be the kind of thing where I would push my own views, and not get on him for his views. I did try to list the things that the Republicans, including Sensenbrenner, are doing that I disagree with. The idea of the campaign was not to attack him. But I think it might have been more effective if I had been more forceful in explaining why I thought his votes were bad votes."

As a result, neither candidate antagonized the other: "I understand that when Sensenbrenner was on radio stations, he was complimentary to my campaign. He said that we disagreed on our views, but we weren't trying to get personal. I was not a big enough threat for him to get personal, and I did not want to. I'll be honest with you, I could not have survived a campaign like that. I'm not cut out for it."

Brenholt admitted that he did not run the campaign as well as he could have, but he did take pride in being able to talk over his views with some of the voters, and in being able to educate them to some extent. He was quite enthusiastic about benefiting from the campaign: "I think that one of the things that I was hoping for personally was that I would like to take two or three things after the campaign was over and I would like to stay involved in working on, for example, campaign finance reform or a better distribution of income. In this area, talking about sharing the wealth is not exactly something a lot of people are going to jump up and down about, but I think that having run I have a little more validity when I talk about that."

He did not, however, expect that his campaign will have any effect on Sensenbrenner or that Sensenbrenner's voting in Congress is likely to be influenced by whether he had an opponent or not:

> If he represents the views of 70 or 75 percent of the people, which I think he probably does, then it wouldn't be to his benefit to agree with something I said. He's got to vote the way that 70 percent of the people vote. I think the sad thing in this country is that people ought to be leaders, and I think too many of the people in Congress take their damn polls but they don't try to tell the people what the situation is. . . . But he might change in some areas [if he had a serious challenger]. I don't know that he would change that much. I suspect that he pretty much believes in what he's doing.

Brenholt's comments echo the views of many long-shot candidates about public opinion. His campaign, like many long-shot campaigns, was an attempt to change public opinion, rather than to respond to it. Like many other challengers in his shoes, he distributed campaign literature that was far more complex than the literature of many more competitive candidates. And like many other long shots, he did not stray from the issues he wanted to promote; he did not attack Sensenbrenner or try to create a hostile campaign. Brenholt was one of many challengers who noted that he ran the sort of campaign the public is perceived to want, a clean, issue-oriented campaign, but that these campaigns can only occur when the outcome is predetermined.

Choosing between Expression and Votes in a Somewhat Competitive Campaign

As of 1996, the Ninth District in Illinois had been held by the current incumbent even longer than had Wisconsin's Ninth District. Democrat Sidney Yates was first elected in 1948, and except for two years in the 1960s when he vacated the seat to run unsuccessfully for the Senate, Yates had not had a serious challenge for the seat since the 1950s. The Ninth District is solid Democratic turf; two-thirds of it is within Chicago's city limits, and the northern reaches of the district take in parts of Evanston, Skokie, and Niles, which are among the more liberal of Chicago's northern suburbs. Thomas Kazee's *Who Runs for Congress?* includes a case study of the district, and the authors of the study concluded that the Ninth would belong to Yates for as long as he wanted it. The study noted that while Yates had occasional challenges for the Democratic nomination, most ambitious Democrats in the area have seen fit to bide their time until Yates retires, rather than to seek to topple the powerful congressman (Layzell and Overby 1994, 163). *Politics in America* concurred, noting that "As Yates aged he could always tout his influential Appropriations Committee position to fend off the occasional younger challenger insisting it was time for the long-tenured incumbent to go" (Duncan and Lawrence 1997, 468–69).

In 1996 another of these younger challengers emerged. Joseph Walsh, a thirty-four-year-old analyst for a conservative think tank, raised more money ($117,000) than any of Yates's challengers had for decades. Walsh noted in his literature that he was "the first candidate for Congress in fourteen years—Republican or Democrat—to campaign actively for your vote." While most Chicago-area Democrats were coasting to victory, Walsh held Yates to 63 percent of the vote. Nineteen ninety-six was still a relatively comfortable victory for Yates, but his margin was the lowest it had been since 1966. Yates announced soon after the election that he would retire in 1998, setting off a frenzy of local politicians jockeying to succeed him.

Walsh crafted his issue strategy carefully, seeking to distance himself from Newt Gingrich and from Chicago's relatively conservative delegation of suburban Republicans. While many of his positions were standard Republican positions, Walsh touted his pro-choice credentials and his support for gay and lesbian rights; criticized "corporate welfare"; and concentrated upon school choice, government reform, and (naturally) term limits. Walsh's campaign literature made prominent mention of his former occupation as a social worker and of the *Chicago Tribune*'s description of him as a "moderate" (*Chicago Tribune* 1996).

The majority of attention Walsh received, however, was for his method of attack against Yates. Yates's opponents had been taking issue with his age for years, yet one of these challengers had noted in the Layzell and Overby study that such a strategy could easily backfire. Yates was a beloved figure in his district, and a campaign that was seen as being too negative could backfire. Walsh followed this advice, running what he described as a "playful" campaign. Walsh made issue of Yates's refusal to debate him and Yates's infrequent trips back to the district, going so far as to offer $1,000 to the first person to actually spot Yates in the district. During the campaign, he held an eighty-seventh birthday party for Yates; the incumbent did not attend. The campaign garnered a lot of attention for these stunts, perhaps so much that the issue message was obscured (see Neal 1996). I asked Walsh whether he thought that many of the voters had absorbed the issue message of the campaign. He responded:

> No, probably not the issue message. The voters absorbed our cute, playful anti-Sid campaign. They found out how old he was. We sent out a mailing to every Democrat in the district with a big picture of Sid on the front, that said "If only you knew . . ." And then you opened it up and boom, boom, boom, all these things about Yates. They found out things about Yates. And we tried to do it in a humorous, respectful way. And anything the voters got was based on that. That it's just not right that your congressman never comes home. And my thinking always was that if you get lucky enough to win, that then I'll engage these people in issue discussions.

Although the campaign materials Walsh distributed were not extremely detailed, he did try hard to tailor his issue appeals to the district. Realizing that the Ninth is a majority Democratic district, Walsh sought out Democrats and tried to win votes on the grounds that he would be back in the district frequently and he was more in touch with district concerns than Yates. He told me that he wished he had done more targeting of this nature: "I wish we could have started a year earlier and really built a grassroots network. There are a lot of people in this district who aren't registered, there are a lot of people who don't vote. There are a lot of ethnic groups that Sid Yates has never even heard of. It would be neat if we had done more to really build up a network from these groups."

Whereas Brenholt's campaign literature always noted his party affiliation, Walsh did not identify himself as the Republican candidate. With the numerous liberal positions he noted in his literature, a voter might have had trouble discerning Walsh's affiliation. Walsh emphasized many issues where he and Yates did not entirely part ways. I asked him where they did differ most sharply, and he responded that

> I'd say on most of the economic issues and on most of the role of government issues. I'd say—everybody tries to label you—I'd say I'm a socially liberal Republican. I'm liberal on things like abortion, guns, funding for the arts—all these issues, Sid and I did agree on, and he even admitted as

much in the paper. But even the issues on which we differed—and I'll raise my hand, we didn't run an issue-oriented campaign, we couldn't—we knew the only way that I was going to win was that the Democrat was going to say "I'm pissed off that Yates is running again, I'll give this guy a chance." But the issue that we did want to run on is that Sid Yates was a New Deal Democrat, and he was stuck in that frame of mind. Democrats and Republicans today know that you have to reform social security, they know that you have to reform welfare. And I'll throw myself into that mode.

Walsh was more forthcoming than any other candidate with whom I spoke about tinkering with his issue message:

I mean, accuse people of flip-flopping—I guess I changed my opinions on a few issues. When this campaign started, I was opposed to any government funding of the arts. A friend of mine kept feeding me material every week, and by May or June I realized there was some role for government. Or guns. A year ago I was a pretty big Second Amendment guy, but I became convinced that we need things like the Brady Bill or the ban on assault weapons. Three years ago, before I ever took a public stand on abortion, I thought of myself as pro-life. I've always been conservative, but I guess over the years I've become more libertarian.

Walsh noted that he may have even gone too far in this regard: "I really built up a defense mechanism during this campaign that I had to sound a bit more moderate. You have to nuance what you say, and I found myself doing that. I found myself sounding a lot more moderate at times than I wanted to be. Whenever I met somebody on the street, they would ask, 'What party are you?' and I'd say, 'I'm a Republican, but I'm a nice Republican.' All in one breath. I didn't like that, but that was the district."

Walsh ran a closer race than most observers expected, and he may have had a role in bringing about Yates's retirement, though he admits that it is impossible to know for sure. Walsh received the second-most votes of any Republican challenger in Illinois, and he actually received more votes than neighboring Republican incumbent Michael Flanagan. He remains convinced that he would have won had 1996 not been such a bad year for Republicans in Illinois. He shares with several other somewhat competitive challengers an attention to minimizing issue differences with the incumbent and with the district's voters. With no allies in his quest to inform the public of the incumbent's vulnerabilities, however, Walsh found it necessary to concentrate so much upon the incumbent and upon nonpolicy aspects of the campaign that he wound up dissatisfied with his ability to get his own ideas across.

Taking Positions to Win in a Very Competitive Campaign

Minnesota's rural First District has elected only one Democrat to Congress in the past century. In a state where Democrats held six of the eight House seats in 1996 (they are now down to four), it is one of the most conservative sections of the state. That lone Democrat, however, is former Representative Tim Penny, who represented the district from 1982 to 1994. Penny still is a commanding presence in the district, and both Democrats and Republicans seek to tie themselves to him. The First was also the home base of one of the Senate's most liberal members, Paul Wellstone. Upon Penny's retirement, his seat became one of the many Democratic losses in the 1994 election. Gil Gutknecht, a solidly conservative state legislator from Rochester, the hub of this southeastern district, won the open seat fairly easily and went on to become one of the more vocal Republican freshmen in the 104th Congress. Despite his district's conservative voting record, however, Gutknecht's seat was never regarded as completely safe.

Mary Rieder, a former staffer for Penny and an economics professor at Winona State University, had run unsuccessfully for the Democratic nomination in 1994, and she established herself soon after 1994 as the frontrunner for the nomination in 1996. Although Rieder has never held political office, she won the Democratic nomination by acclamation and tapped Penny to serve as her campaign chairman. She went on to run a campaign designed to portray her as a Blue Dog Democrat, a fiscal conservative in the mold of Penny and neighboring Democrats David Minge and Colin Peterson. Rieder also touted her endorsement by the Reform Party as evidence of her budgetary inclinations.[6] She raised $625,000 and was the beneficiary of an AFL-CIO advertising campaign that sought to call attention to Gutknecht's conservative voting record. She contends that she was actually ahead of Gutknecht in the polls a week before the election, and that she was the victim of a last-minute advertising blitz by Gutknecht and the Republican Party.

As was the case for many other competitive Democratic challengers, Rieder's campaign was focused upon fiscal issues that were also being used effectively in the Clinton campaign and by other high-profile Democrats. She stressed balancing the budget without cuts in education or healthcare, and she derided Gutknecht's call for a tax cut as irresponsible. Rieder took more liberal positions on the environment, gun control, and abortion, but she told me that her main intent in the campaign was to question Gutknecht's credentials on fiscal issues and to propose alternatives: "I think being an economist and a financial planner speaks to that. I don't know otherwise how to say 'Yes, she is a moderate, she's not a tax and spend liberal.' One of the things I'm going to do is write a piece about the Blue Dog budget, to say that's the kind of budget we should be looking at, not a Clinton budget."

She isn't quite sure how well she was able to establish her differences with Gutknecht. Despite the presence of Tim Penny in Rieder's campaign, Gutknecht had also tried to compare himself to Penny during the campaign. Rieder acknowledged that there were no real polar oppositions between herself and Gutknecht: "It was really kind of hard to draw out all the differences. I'm just not as right-wing as he is, but it was really difficult to nail him on right-wing stuff. We may not have done a real good job of that. The real problem was that people didn't know me well enough."

Rieder found that she did not have to go after Gutknecht on character issues, however; this is partly a function of Minnesota's strict standards for political advertising, but it is also a function of the extensive attention some of Gutknecht's missteps in the 104th Congress had received. AFL-CIO advertisements that aired before Rieder's campaign began softened Gutknecht up on several issues:

> The two ads that the AFL-CIO ran for me were the one on pensions, and I didn't do as much with pensions myself, and the one on education, that the Republicans wanted to cut all this money out of education. And then they did another one on where Gutknecht was getting his money. I didn't like that one very much, it was a radio ad and it was a little crass for me. But other people said they thought it was funny, so I just let it go, I thought that it might get us a couple more voters.

Rieder also left Gutknecht's most embarrassing gaffe alone. Gutknecht had been ridiculed in the Minneapolis newspapers for disputing the link between HIV and AIDS and for questioning whether AIDS is contagious (see, e.g., Hamburger 1996). Rieder felt that issue had already been exploited enough: "Maybe we made an error in not going after that more. People said 'Aren't you going to do a television ad on that?' And I thought no, I don't think so. That was getting old. But in retrospect, maybe we should have."

Rieder felt Gutknecht's major weakness was that he did not take her candidacy seriously until close to the election. He refused to debate her, and while Rieder was bringing in Wellstone, Hillary Clinton, Bruce Babbitt, Al Gore, and Donna Shalala, Gutknecht, she claims, was barely campaigning:

"He was just kind of there, he was telling people he didn't think he had any problems, that it wasn't going to be a close race. We were going to follow him around, but we couldn't even figure out where he was to follow him. I don't even know what he was running on. About three or four weeks out, he started going to the parades, but that's about it."

Although she eventually decided not to run again in 1998 (she did run in 2000), Rieder was entertaining the possibility at the time I spoke with her. She said she had not changed her views on many of the major issues during the 1996 campaign, but that she would think about changing the way she campaigns if she ran again. She noted that she was well informed about most of the major issues in the First District. As a resident of Eyota, a small farming community, she has a background on agricultural issues. She did admit that she did a lot of shifting on some of the minor issues in the campaign as the result of input from various interest groups or citizen's groups. In response to my series of questions on position changes during the campaign, she remarked that:

> Every group has their own questionnaire, and there are issues on the questionnaire that you hadn't thought about. But in general, the teachers wanted what I wanted, the nurses wanted what I wanted, labor wanting good wages and good jobs, these were all things I wanted too. In terms of my major positions, the things that I ran on, interest groups didn't influence my positions, but on some of the other issues that I had to discuss, I in general thought it was all right to go along with the positions of these groups.

Rieder may have gotten the attention of the media and received as many votes as she did in part because Gutknecht was not as active in the district as he could be, or because he was not as attuned to the politics of the district as he could have been. She believes that her campaign changed that: "He's already preparing for the next race. He's appearing on the radio a lot more. His staff is much more active in the district. He's not, but his staff is far more active. He's going to be a much better congressman between now and then. That may be enough to solidify his position in Congress."

Rieder also believes she had an impact upon Gutknecht's voting habits. She told the *Minnesota Star Tribune* (DeFiebre 1996) that she felt she lost in part because of her support for abortion rights and because she is a woman; on the major issues of her campaign, she senses that she may have thrown a scare into Gutknecht. She also told the *Star Tribune* that she expected Gutknecht to back off on measures to cut low-income heat-ing assistance programs and on cuts in education funding. In addition, she told me that "I don't expect that he's going to get a zero from the environmentalists again. He got zeroes from a large number of constituent groups. So I would suggest that he won't get zeroes again. He won't get 50–50s, but he'll probably score somewhere in the thirties with the things that aren't central to his beliefs. I don't think he'll vote against education as much."

The implication here, it seems, is that Gutknecht will moderate his positions on the things that he does not care about, but that he will maintain his current positions on the issues about which he does care. Because he is a member of the Budget Committee, this may still leave opportunities for challengers with Rieder's issue concerns to make headway against Gutknecht in the future. Yet even as Rieder mulled over whether she should run again, she was clearly skeptical about his vulnerability in the future. Like many serious challengers, she may have prompted Gutknecht to move toward the political center, to seek to ward off future opponents. As with many other strong challengers, Rieder's campaign relied upon the confluence of independent activity against her opponent, a voting record that seemed not to match the district, and an incumbent who had yet to establish a strong track record on the nonissue dimensions of competence or leadership.

Conclusions

Many of the points made by these candidates could certainly be applied as generalizations to political campaigns. The campaigns that citizens profess to like best—those where there are substantive differences on the issues, and where issue differences comprise the majority of campaign discussion, in place of attacks on the candidates' character or competence—tend only to occur in relatively unbalanced races. The races where both candidates seem very concerned with discovering and seconding the views of the median voter in the district are races in which policy issues recede into the background.

The choices of the candidates discussed here, however, were not made solely with reference to the voters. The positions and popularity of the incumbent were viewed by many of these candidates as the single most important factor in their campaign activities. Even those candidates who did not discuss the incumbent or take issue directly with the incumbent's positions only declined to do so because they felt that the incumbent was so powerful that they were not truly in competition with him for the voters' loyalties. These candidates frequently spoke of running to advance an agenda, to give voters a choice, to try to educate voters about political issues, to make sure that the incumbent's views were not the only views on the agenda—but they did not speak of winning the vote of the average citizen. As we move from the less competitive to the more competitive candidates, the calculus of negotiation goes up; that is, candidates are more willing to change their positions in order to account for voters' preferences. A cynic might say that they are more willing to follow, rather than to lead.

Long-shot candidacies, like that of Floyd Brenholt in Wisconsin's Ninth District, are frequently conducted with little media attention. They can be a learning experience for both the candidate and for any voters who care to pay attention. Brenholt himself was pessimistic about the effect of his campaign, yet it is apparent that he differed sharply with the incumbent, and with the average voter. Voters were, at the very least, given a choice by Brenholt and Sensenbrenner. More competitive candidates, like Joseph Walsh in Illinois's Ninth District, must balance calculated appeals to public opinion with criticisms of the incumbent, yet they must also worry about creating a backlash because of their criticism of a relatively popular incumbent. The most competitive challengers often find that a large part of the attacks on the opponent have been done for them, as was the case with Mary Rieder in Minnesota's First District. They frequently have the time and the resources to establish substantive issue differences with the incumbent, and they are aided in doing so by the perception that there are areas where the incumbent does not represent the median voter.

The only way to make sense of these campaigns is to employ an argument that begins with sequential positioning—with an acknowledgment that policy issues and pure political expression matter the most to challengers when the incumbent is either unbeatable or drastically out of step with the district on issues. The sequential positioning conception of political campaigning thus is clearly the most appropriate way of making stylized predictions about these campaigns. This is not to say that these candidates are all entirely emblematic of the predicament of candidates in their situation. There is certainly still room within the environmental limits of these campaigns for a challenger to run an exceptionally good campaign or an exceptionally poor campaign, to make accurate or inaccurate assessments of which issues will be effective or will appeal to the public, or to shrewdly exploit the incumbent's weaknesses or his own strengths. While resources are in many ways limited by the type of race being run and the type of incumbent being challenged, variations still occur, as in the case of the challenger who brings a vast personal fortune to the race. Despite these variables, however, the similarities are striking.

These similarities are rarely addressed by research that has been conducted in the past on congressional candidates. Surely the type of candidates that emerge is determined by the type of race that is expected. Both Floyd Brenholt and Joseph Walsh admitted that it was unlikely that they would have been their party's choice had their elections been expected to be close. The type of candidate who enters the race, however, is far less important for issue considerations than is the strategy adopted by that candidate. If a long-shot candidate lacks the desire to follow conventional campaign techniques, this is more a result of the campaign environment than it is of the candidate's skills or motivations. The question of whether one of the long-shot candidates would behave differently were the race to suddenly become much closer is somewhat moot, because such circumstances rarely happen.

The expressive campaign, or the degree of expressive behavior in a campaign, cannot be accounted for in any way other than in a theory which presupposes that campaign issues are an outcome, not a determinant, of a campaign's competitiveness. All candidates come to campaigns with a particular set of policy ideas and beliefs, but the nature of the candidates, and the nature of the beliefs, that are brought to any particular campaign are a result of the type of campaign which is expected. More often than not, these expectations are constructed based upon the behavior of the incumbent and the partisan inclinations of the district. One might easily argue that the majority of the candidates considered above were not behaving rationally if the premise was that they were seeking solely to win the election. Yet for most of these candidates, winning is not a realistic outcome. All candidates may hope to win, but candidate after candidate told me, "I wasn't about to give up my day job," or "I wasn't going to mortgage my farm for it." It is also evident, then, that some candidates were willing to adjust their political views to win; for others, such a change just didn't make sense.

Among the candidates who did not seem victory-oriented, then, the final question is how we can be sure that it is the candidates' own views that are being expressed. In the next chapter I seek to evaluate whether it is the views of the candidates, or of the candidates' parties, that are being expressed in the majority of House races.

CHAPTER 6

"You Don't Know Me, But Here I Am": Candidate Perceptions of Party Strength

In the previous two chapters, candidates made scant reference to partisanship or to their role as the standard bearer for a political party. Especially for candidates with as low a profile as many congressional challengers, however, it is inevitable that a substantial percentage of voters will know little about the candidates other than their party affiliation. Despite the fact that we live in an age of decreasing partisanship and increasing split-ticket voting, the candidates still argued that their party label was a major determinant of their success. The popularity of fellow partisans higher up on the ballot, such as presidential candidates Bill Clinton and Bob Dole, as well as gubernatorial and senatorial candidates in these states, was a frequent theme in the candidates' comments. The role that party organizations played, from the township level to the national level, was also a major source of both frustration and encouragement. Political parties, in short, are a much more important factor in the campaigns of nonincumbents than they are in the campaigns of sitting members of Congress.

All of the candidates' claims about voters' partisan cues, however, may say more about partisanship than about party. It is certainly possible that for many candidates, vote share is based more on candidates' party label than on anything they did in their campaigns. Given the evidence in chapter 3 that there is substantial polarization between competing candidates regardless of the competitiveness of the race (and given my allowance for party "sorting" in the alternatives in chapter 2), it is important to address whether candidate polarization is due to sorting by the candidates or due to pressure from the parties. In the previous chapters, I sought to build a case for viewing congressional campaigns as vehicles for candidate expression in cases where the challenger does not have a realistic chance of victory. It is equally valid, however, to view these campaigns as vehicles for political parties to express themselves. The possibility exists that parties can do so through a variety of means—through the primary process, through strongly worded advice to candidates, or through financial support. In this chapter I contend that while there may be theoretical reasons to wish this to be the case, it generally is not—and where it is, party expression and party pressure are not regarded favorably by the candidates themselves.

These claims open a can of worms regarding the manner in which parties can be identified. Because there is no monolithic, easily identified ideological entity called the Democratic Party or the Republican Party in the United States, the differences between candidate expression and party expression cannot be assessed without first gaining an understanding of what these candidates conceive their parties to be. While this may appear to be a straightforward proposition, different definitions of political parties abound. At times, we consider parties as aggregations of voters, while at other times we refer to parties as organizations of activists who slate candidates and recruit volunteers. At still other times, we refer to parties as teams of elected officeholders. It is tempting to begin and end a study of parties in congressional elections with a consideration of the national party campaign committees, but as Schwartz (1990) convincingly argues in her case study of the Illinois Republican Party, parties are perhaps best conceived of as *networks* that include organizations, officeholders, and activists. As I seek to show in this chapter, this is, at least, how candidates view parties.

Thus, the definition of a "strong" party—or a party able to help or hinder its candidates—is dependent upon the definition of party being used. In this chapter I shall distinguish between organizationally strong parties, which are successful in maximizing votes or election victories for their candidates across a number of elections, and ideologically strong parties, which are successful in presenting a clear, unambiguous set of policy proposals to the voters, regardless of the electoral consequences of espousing those views. Clearly, the view discussed above of party expression draws upon this second conception of party strength.

The states in which I conducted interviews provide a convenient contrast between these two party types. In Ohio and Illinois, states where the two major parties have traditionally been strong in the organizational sense, candidates reported little pressure from their party to adhere to any preordained set of issue positions; if anything, the parties pressured their more viable candidates to take moderate positions that were most likely to result in victory or to maximize vote share. In Minnesota and Wisconsin, states where the two parties have traditionally been more ideological and have a less effective organization, candidates indicated that the two parties often sought to pull candidates away from the political center, even where this may have cost the candidates votes. In the majority of cases, this ideological pressure came from local or state party activists and leaders who sought to influence the candidates' issue positions through recruitment and endorsements before the candidates were nominated. After candidates had been nominated, the two parties, at all levels, were seen by the candidates as a resource, either in terms of money or in terms of political capital. As one might predict, candidates in organizationally strong areas reported more frequently that, after they had been nominated, their party was helpful than did candidates in organizationally weak areas.

Candidates in organizationally strong areas also differed from their counterparts in organizationally weak, ideologically strong areas in their views on party membership and on the nature of their relationship with their party. The two candidate types shared similar views about the role of the national campaign organizations, the Democratic Congressional Campaign Committee (DCCC) and the National Republican Congressional Committee (NRCC) in their races, with the differences in the level of assistance from national organizations resulting from the candidates' competitiveness. Somewhat less intuitively, the candidates' level of party identification was stronger in organizationally strong areas than it was in organizationally weak (and ideologically strong) areas. This finding indicates that allegiance to one's party is a function not of ideology but of organizational strength—these candidates equated their fortunes with their party to the degree that their party could and had helped them.

As I have with the previous two interview chapters, I begin this chapter by briefly recapitulating the main points of the relevant theoretical and empirical literature. I then return to the *Time/Congressional Quarterly* survey data in order to provide a general assessment of the relationship between party organization and candidate convergence or divergence on policy. Finally, I present the major themes of the interviews, some illustrative case studies, and some concluding thoughts on the import of these discussions for the study of party behavior.

Party Strength: Organization or Ideology?

In bringing parties into this analysis, it is necessary to ask two questions. First, do parties have the capacity to influence any actions of their candidates? And second, if so, what sort of influence can they have on candidates' issues positions? That is, do they exert pressure upon candidates to adopt centrist positions, or do they seek to pull candidates away from their district's political center?

The contrast between viewing a "strong" party as an organization which gets its preferred candidates elected or as an organization with a clear ideological position is nearly as old as the study of political parties itself. In chapters 1 and 2, I sought to draw a distinction between positive and normative theories of candidate and party positioning. When we address party strength, however, it is the normative and positive theorists who are on the same side, with empirical analysts of American politics frequently on the other side. Frequently, in formal theories a strong party is one that can establish an agenda during campaigns and implement it while in office. The fact that the optimal spatial location of parties differs, as I noted, when one moves from the rather normative 1950 APSA Report to positive theories of party activities such as those of Downs, Riker, and others, is less important in this context than is the fact that both begin from the premise that parties can establish ideological positions.

There are few empirical studies of American politics that seek to use this measurement of party strength as a starting point (although I do discuss some of these studies later in this chapter), yet we should not entirely rule out the role of ideology in political parties. It may well be poor strategy for parties themselves to seek to establish distinct ideological positions, but we might still expect some efforts to do so within the parties. Even if parties do wish to establish positions, however, the question remains as to whether they have the capacity to do so.

Contemporary empirical literature in American politics often emphasizes what David Mayhew (1986, 20) defines as "material," rather than "purposive" benefits that parties provide to candidates. That is, empirical political scientists looking at American parties tend to see party strength as an organizational, not an ideological trait. When political scientists write about parties, it is almost obligatory to begin with V.O. Key's (1958, 180–82) tripartite division of parties: the party in government, the party in the electorate, and the party organization. In looking at congressional elections, it has traditionally been the party organization—and more specifically, the national party organization, in the form of the DCCC and the NRCC—that has been singled out as the lone influential actor (see Herrnson 2000, 88). In interviews with directors of the parties' national congressional campaign committees, Herrnson (2000, 92) found that the party's national organizational wing has little interest in an ideological "litmus test," and instead provides assistance to candidates based on their chances of winning. Assistance to candidates is apportioned according to fulfillment by the candidates of nonpolicy criteria, such as individual fundraising prowess and favorable polling numbers. The parties may provide research on the popularity among voters of different issue approaches, yet in doing so they are appealing to candidates' instrumental self-interest, not trying to secure commitments to their own ideological positions.

If we are to evaluate strength by using such measures, however, we must begin with the observation that both parties, at the national level, have very limited resources with which to assist and influence candidates. In any given election cycle, the two major national party organizations must decide which of the hundreds of House candidates to support. They can either concentrate their resources, choosing a handful of candidates to give full support, or they can diffuse their resources more broadly among a larger number of candidates. Overwhelmingly, the national party organizations have chosen the former option.[1] This tendency, however, ensures that while local and state level party organizations face similar considerations, one might ask whether these types of organizations have any role whatsoever to play in helping those candidates left out of the national organizations' decision making. Party organizations at all levels are more generous in their provision of volunteers, position papers, information, strategic assistance, and linkage with other candidates than they are with money. Such assistance is harder to track than is money, yet it comprised an important part of the candidates' evaluations of party assistance (see Kolodny 1998, 124–54; Herrnson 2000, 100–11). Certainly, financial support may be the best tool for national party organizations to use to try to influence candidates, and the fact that they provide such support to only a few candidates indicates that if parties at any level influence the positions of any but the most competitive candidates, it is not the national parties that do so. State and local parties, on the other hand, may be able to influence less competitive candidates, although they cannot do so through financial support (Schwartz 1990, 218–24).

The Maisel, Huckshorn and Spencer, Kingdon, Hershey, and Leuthold studies have all documented the opinions of congressional candidates regarding party assistance. Hershey concludes her analysis of financial support from party organizations by noting that "the candidates most likely to win are least likely to need the party's help in doing so. . . . Party help may be most keenly appreciated, and most influential, in campaigns with the slimmest chances of success" (Hershey 1974, 136). My findings corroborate this point. I also agree with Hershey that local party groups, individual party officeholders, and district-level organizations tend to be far more variable in their level of organization and in their interest in House candidates than are the official national party organizations.

This quest to look at the nonfinancial side of party assistance to candidates brings together Key's party divisions somewhat. While the national party organizations have traditionally been loath to become involved in backing candidates in primaries (although this was the case in some 2000 races, as the next chapter shows), they have at times assisted in candidate recruitment. Candidate recruitment, and various less formal means of encouraging candidates—for instance, soothing ruffled feathers from primary competition, providing technical assistance and advice, and providing issue information—have traditionally been the province of local party leaders, prominent members of the party rank-and-file in the electorate, and party leaders within government. Again, of particular concern here are the lower-profile House campaigns. Which party organizations take an interest in such campaigns? How (aside from the obvious financial differences) is party attention different in these campaigns from those of potential winners? Because there is no party organization that takes specific responsibility for the less fortunate congressional candidates, it is important to understand how the candidates view their parties, where they perceive any party pressure to be coming from, what they expect from their parties, and what types of interactions candidates have with their parties *as they conceive of them*. As the comments in this chapter suggest, most national party attention has little to do with coercion on issues, but state-level and local-level party actors do seek to exert ideological influence upon candidates, and they tend to follow predictable patterns in doing so.

A Brief Return to the Candidate Survey Data

To get a sense of what these patterns are, a brief detour back to the *Time/Congressional Quarterly* survey data is in order to put the candidates' comments in perspective. As I noted above, the states in which I conducted interviews provide a contrast between party organization types. The distinction between the more traditional, patronage-based party politics of Ohio and Illinois and the more ideological, issue-oriented politics of Minnesota is not my own; quantitative studies (Mayhew 1986, 66–77; Paddock 1998) and more impressionistic studies (Elazar 1972, 84–126; Fenton 1966, 117–54, 194–218) all agree on this distinction. Erikson and Wright (1989) show that these state distinctions matter in the positions of congressional candidates.

The task in this chapter, then, is to explore whether, if differences in party strength or party organization are reflected in candidates' positions,

Table 6.1. Candidate Ideology and Polarization by Party Organization and Party Culture

	Party Organization Level (TPO)					Elazar Party Culture Category			Total
	1	2	3	4	5	Moralistic	Individualistic	Traditionalistic	
All States									
Mean LQD	.636 (.178)	.608 (.170)	.390 (–)	.547 (.181)	.556 (.201)	.656 (.169)	.559 (.196)	.600 (.179)	.603 (.187)
Mean Vote Pct. Difference	27.7 (18.1)	28.3 (17.7)	16.8 (–)	26.9 (17.1)	31.6 (22.2)	26.8 (20.0)	30.5 (21.1)	27.7 (16.0)	28.8 (19.2)
Mean Democratic LQ	.816 (.143)	.746 (.156)	.580 (.244)	.734 (.169)	.847 (.139)	.833 (.121)	.830 (.152)	.743 (.165)	.805 (.153)
Mean Republican LQ	.183 (.149)	.150 (.111)	.131 (.080)	.210 (153)	.280 (.187)	.179 (.141)	.270 (.185)	.157 (.124)	.205 (.161)
N (Districts)	187	48	1*	31	98	121	139	105	365
Interview States									
State	MN, WI	--	--	OH	IL	MN, WI	IL, OH	--	
Mean LQD	.628 (.143)			.499 (.179)	.664 (.160)	.628 (.143)	.581 (.187)		.597 (.173)
Mean Vote Pct. Difference	24.2 (17.6)			29.7 (19.1)	26.4 (20.1)	24.2 (17.6)	28.1 (19.4)		26.8 (18.7)
Mean Democratic LQ	.849 (.123)			.726 (.173)	.868 (.128)	.849 (.123)	.799 (..166)		.815 (.154)
Mean Republican LQ	.224 (.163)			.259 (.169)	.180 (.144)	.224 (.163)	.219 (.160)		.221 (.159)
N (Districts)	17			17	17	17	34		51

Sources: 1996 Time/Congressional Quarterly Candidate Survey; Mayhew 1986, Elazar 1972. Standard Deviations in parentheses.
* The sole state with a TPO of 3 is Louisiana, which elects representatives through a jungle primary, followed by a runoff between the top two vote-getters. There is only one district where a Democrat faced a Republican in the runoff (therefore, only one LQD measure), although there are four Democrats and five Republicans with LQ scores.
Missing cases for LQD = 70 (16.1%).
F-test for H_0: No difference in LQD by TPO for all candidates: F = 3.82; p <.01.
F-test for H_0: No difference in LQ by TPO for all Republicans: F = 5.20; p <.01.
F-test for H_0: No difference in LQ by TPO for all Democrats: F = 1.02.
F-test for H_0: No difference in LQD by Elazar category for all candidates: F = 9.13; p <.01.
F-test for H_0: No difference in LQ by Elazar category for all Republicans: F = 21.3; p <.01.
F-test for H_0: No difference in LQ by Elazar category for all Democrats: F = 15.3; p <.01.

these differences are a consequence of party pressure or merely an accident of candidates' choices. To illustrate the connection between party organization and congressional candidates' positions, let us consider how two of the more comprehensive analyses of party organization by state map onto candidates' positions.

David Mayhew (1986) has developed a five-point measure of "total party organization" (TPO) by state, which sums individual binary measures of party autonomy, durability, hierarchy, ability to confer nomination on preferred candidates, and control of material incentives for party members. When we compare the LQD scores with TPO measures (see table 6.1), it is evident that Mayhew's party organization measures do tap differences in the degree of polarization between competing House candidates. Candidates are less polarized, and less consistently polarized (see the slight increase in the standard deviation as one moves across the table), where the states' parties are more organized. Organizationally stronger parties produce, on average, more centrist candidates, particularly in more competitive districts, but they neglect many candidates entirely.

It might be tempting to claim that these differences are a function of the behavior of only one party—that is, for instance, that the Republican Party in one part of the country (Mayhew's categories correlate somewhat with regions of the country) may differ sharply from the Republican Party in another region of the country. Or, in applied terms, we may merely be seeing the differences between Northern Democrats and Southern Democrats, or between New England Republicans and the remainder of the Republican Party. To test this, I have broken down the average liberalism quotients for candidates by level of party organization and party. The party LQ scores in table 6.1 show that although Republicans appear to be doing most of the moderating, these differences cannot solely be attributed to one party. Although the ideologies of candidates vary, the parties still move toward each other as party organization increases.

Elazar (1972) distinguishes states by the dominant political culture, arguing that there are three distinct types: individualistic (in which politics is aimed at efficiency, not ideology, and party regularity is prized), moralistic (in which ideology is more important than partisanship or party allegiance), and traditionalistic (in which deference and hierarchy are prized, and party competition is muted or absent altogether). Political culture, for Elazar (1972, 90), encompasses a set of perceptions about what is expected from government, differences in the types of people who become active in politics, and ways in which governing is conducted. The second set of columns in table 6.1 shows that candidate LQ scores also diverge in states where the political culture is more ideological. Although Elazar's categories are only weakly correlated with Mayhew's categories, they also demonstrate a potential party influence on candidates.

It is important to note, however, that it is more difficult to make causal arguments based on Elazar's descriptions than on Mayhew's. Because, for Elazar, different types of political culture breed different types of candidates, it is not the influence of parties that matters but simply the fact that different types of individuals are prompted to run for office. Thus, an exploration of the scaled data *may* suggest that parties wield influence, but we certainly have no proof that parties, under whatever definition we choose to employ, are applying ideological pressure to candidates.

We are, then, compelled to return to candidates' interview comments to assess the role of parties. The bottom half of table 6.1 compares the candidates from the four interview states to each other and to candidates nationwide. Differences by state in LQD scores here are not quite as pronounced as for the rest of the nation, primarily due to high levels of divergence in Illinois, the strongest party state in Mayhew's rankings. The high variation in the competitiveness of Illinois races may be one reason for this. Another reason may be Schwartz's (1990, xiii) contention that Illinois actually contains two party types—a more machine-oriented politics in the north and a more traditionalistic, Southern type of politics in the south. As I noted in chapter 3, other studies have agreed upon the distinctions between party organization and political culture types in these four states; this chapter serves in part to reinforce those distinctions.

The Candidates' Perspectives on Their Parties

In looking at candidates' comments about their parties, I seek here to draw out the state differences to see how they apply to candidates' interactions with their parties. There are three purposes here. First, in analyzing the candidates' interview comments I seek to provide evidence that (for the most part) it is the expressive voice of candidates, not parties, that comes through in the ideological positions and campaign strategies of those candidates who are unlikely to win election. This may be a function of an inability for (some) political parties to impose positions upon their candidates or of a lack of interest on the part of parties in doing so. Second, given what we know about the concentration of the national party organizations—here, the DCCC and the NRCC—on competitive races, I seek to show what the national parties do for candidates of different levels of competitiveness and how candidates can demonstrate their ability to compete to the national party organizations. And third, given the built-in contrast between state and local party organizations in Ohio and Illinois, on the one hand, and Wisconsin and Minnesota, on the other, I document the ways in which level of party organization can lead to, respectively, an emphasis by organizationally strong parties on encouraging potentially competitive candidates to take election-seeking positions and an emphasis by ideologically strong parties on encouraging candidates to take expressive positions that can at times be detrimental to candidates' competitiveness.

The reader will note, however, that (taking my cue from the evidence in table 6.1) I make few references here to differences between the Democratic and Republican parties. Some differences are to be expected—the main difference (aside from ideology) being that the Republican Party, defending its majority status for the first time in four decades, concentrated less upon aiding challengers than did the Democratic Party. Besides this difference, the converse of which has been documented by Sorauf (1992, 113–16) during the time the Democratic Party held the congressional majority, there are few differences between party activities that are relevant to questions regarding party strength, party assistance to candidates, or ideological pressure by the parties.

Party Identification

Contemporary arguments about the decline of parties have focused primarily upon voters. Fewer voters identify with the two major political parties than at any time since the advent of survey research—in the 2000 National Election Study, a full 40 percent of respondents classified themselves as independents (Sapiro, Rosenstone, and the National Election Studies 2001). Accordingly, we might expect that candidates share the voters' skepticism about party labels. This would also make sense from a rational choice perspective; a party label may be a relatively inexpensive means for candidates to convey information to those voters who do still exhibit strong partisanship, to send a signal about that candidates' policy positions. Such an instrumental use of the party label would, then, belie any sort of deeper faith or belief in the party's traditional goals for their own sake. On the other hand, one might argue that candidates, as individuals who are more deeply involved in politics than is the average citizen, should have a stronger sense of party identification than does the average voter. According to this line of reasoning, we might expect that candidates exhibit strong ties to their parties and assert strong opinions about what their party stands for.

The first section of table 6.2 shows clear patterns in party experience and party identification across candidate types. To begin with, Gary Jacobson's (1997a, 46–48) candidate quality work is supported by these interviews; of the long-shot candidates, none had previously held political

Table 6.2. Summary Statistics on Party Assistance

	Long Shots	Somewhat Competitive	Very Competitive	Total
Partisanship and Experience				
Previous Political Office	0% (0)	38% (8)	79% (11)	37% (19)
Other Political Experience	53 (9)	43 (9)	7 (1)	37 (19)
No Political Experience	47 (8)	19 (4)	14 (2)	27 (14)
Strong Party Identification	47 (8)	71 (15)	85 (12)	67 (35)
Recruited	41 (7)	24 (5)	7 (1)	25 (13)
Satisfied with Party Effort	29 (5)	19 (4)	64 (9)	35 (18)
DCCC/NRCC Assistance				
Money	6 (1)	33 (7)	85 (12)	38 (20)
Information	65 (11)	71 (15)	85 (12)	73 (38)
Training	47 (8)	24 (5)	43 (6)	37 (19)
Polling	12 (2)	19 (4)	79 (11)	33 (17)
Help With PACs	0 (0)	29 (6)	85 (12)	35 (18)
Set Expectations	12 (2)	47 (10)	64 (9)	40 (21)
No Help	29 (5)	10 (2)	7 (1)	15 (8)
Primary and Ideological Competition				
Primary	29 (5)	38 (8)	79 (11)	46 (24)
Competitive Primary	18 (3)	29 (6)	64 (9)	46 (18)
Ideological Pressure	24 (4)	19 (4)	21 (3)	21 (11)
N	17	21	14	52

office, although 53 percent had either held a position within their party, served on a congressional staff, or had run before. The balance shifts with the somewhat competitive candidates; 38 percent of them had previously held political office, generally as a state legislator, mayor, or county elected official. An additional 43 percent had previously held an appointed position in their party or had previously been the party's nominee, and only four had no political background. Seventy-nine percent of the very competitive candidates had political background, one had served on a congressional staff, and only two had no previous political experience. Both of these two had previously been television news personalities, so these two did have significant visibility in their districts which allowed them to overcome their lack of political experience.

Political background tells us little, however, about the relationship between candidates and their party. Surely candidates with prior political experience would be better known within their party, making them more viable candidates in a primary or for a party endorsement. But do these candidates make overtly partisan appeals? Do they identify strongly with their party? Although I did not ask the candidates directly how strongly they identified with their party, it is fairly easy to assess their relationship with their party from their comments. Candidates break down along roughly the same lines as they did on the political experience question: 47 percent of the long-shot candidates identified strongly with their party, 71 percent of the somewhat competitive candidates did, as did twelve, or 85 percent, of the very competitive candidates—the same twelve who had some political background. The candidates who did not indicate a strong relationship with their party, however, differ dramatically among themselves. Among the long-shot candidates, there is much talk of merely adopting the party label; for instance, I coded each of the three quotes below as evidence of weak party identification:

> I ran as a Democrat, but God knows, my policies are not Democratic policies. It was only because I ran as a Democrat that I achieved the kind of audience that we were able to achieve in a district that has been a Republican bastion for years. (Illinois)

> I told the party chairman I was going to talk about the issues I wanted to talk about in the election. My approach on issues was simply that a candidate is instructed by the informed, deliberative consensus of the voters. If you're in one of these districts that's designed to be Republican or Democrat and you're running as the candidate of the other party, the way around that is to say that my party is irrelevant. (Ohio)

> The way I look at things maybe is a bit broader because I have more of a people perception rather than the Democratic theory or the Republican theory. I would look at it more in terms of how it's going to affect people. Whether that's Democrat or Republican, I don't know. I think that's where we need to be. More so like the Democratic Party, I guess. (Ohio)

Among more competitive candidates, as well as some of the long-shot candidates, disaffection with the party was based more upon party factionalism; candidates often spoke of being "on the outs" with their party, of trying to encourage the party to move in a particular direction via their candidacy. For weak party identifiers, this was often a direction not favored by the party establishment:

> Even though I lost, I was able to address the issues that I wanted to, and I think I came out of it respected by the political insiders. I want to either force the Republican Party back to the center, or to help the Reform Party move either party back to the center.[2] (Minnesota)

> I was on the outs—I have been from day one—with the leadership in this district. These people didn't want me to run. We came to a shouting match when they put together a search committee. The search committee was put together for one reason, and that was to find someone other than me to run. (Minnesota)

> The thing I learned about politics is this: You've got two types of politicians. You've got the people who are in the political arena because they're idea people. They have great visions for America, they understand history, and that's what they want to go to Washington for. I fall into that category. The other candidates are business politicians. They're trying to figure out how to spend money to best influence their friends, their supporters. Unfortunately, in this state, a majority of Republicans and Democrats are business politicians. Idea politicians scare them. I was an idea guy, and I scared the Republicans. There's not a lot of crying in this state to think that I won't run again. (Illinois)

> Just because somebody has values, that they try to make an impact in society, that gives people something to get behind. Unfortunately, politicians are basing the things they do on public opinion. I think that the Republican Party is actually going to be the governing party. What philosophy is going to be guiding it, that's the question. I think most of the Republicans in office are closet liberals, and I wanted to break through that facade. (Wisconsin)

There may be an element of sour grapes to some of these comments, yet the last three of the above four quotes are from Republican candidates who fared quite well in their campaigns, garnering about 40 percent of the vote each in a fairly Democratic year. Their comments bespeak candidacies that were initiated not out of party loyalty, but out of a desire to move their party in a particular direction—in the final quote, to the right; in the others, to the center.

Among the most competitive candidates, there is little indication of dissatisfaction with the party. This may be in part because these candidates received resources that were denied to other candidates, but it also indicates that their candidacies were not aimed at changing the party's direction and that they expected and received full party support. The only candidates among these who did not have a strong background in the party still voiced views similar to those of candidates who did have some background. This indicates that personal coalitions were more valuable than party support, as shown by one strong candidate whom I coded as a weak party identifier: "The successful state reps have their own organization, and that's what happens at the congressional level. You need to work with the party, but you really need to build your own organization" (Illinois).

Among candidates with strong ties to their parties, the answers were somewhat more uniform. Many of the long-shot candidates ran out of a sense of duty to their party, out of a desire either to ensure that the party was represented or to help others on the ticket. Among candidates who spoke of being recruited by party leaders, this sentiment ran particularly strong. One of the most underfinanced candidates with whom I spoke simply stated: "We needed a candidate, and I said I would be the loyal opposition." Other strong party identifiers made similar, though more nuanced, points.

> The party has made it known that the fact that I ran helped the other candidates. That was the result. I kept [my opponent] busy, so he wasn't able to help the other candidates because he was worried about his race. (Ohio)

> I created a perceived concern on the part of a lot of Republicans throughout the district, and they demanded [the incumbent's] presence more than they ever had in the past. But also, the fact that he was here and not somewhere else campaigning for other people was one of the key goals of many of my national contributors. He's a renowned money earner for the party. (Ohio)

Several of these candidates claimed credit for turning out at least a handful of extra voters for their party in the presidential race, in local races, or in the Senate campaign in their state. All told, thirteen candidates claimed to have been recruited; seven of these thirteen were running in long-shot campaigns, while only one of these candidates ran a very competitive race. Perceptions of being recruited are somewhat subjective, since many candidates who said they had been recruited also admitted that they had made their interest in running known prior to being contacted by party leaders. Most of these candidates had been recruited merely to ensure that their party had a candidate; in three cases, however, candidates who reported being recruited said that they had been encouraged to run to save their party from embarrassment. In each of these cases, the party leadership was dissatisfied with the announced candidate or candidates on ideological grounds. To quote one candidate who went on to put together a rather last-minute, long-shot campaign, "There was a young man who was already running, he'd been running for two years and he started out with an extremely left-of-center position. That made some Democrats nervous, so behind closed doors I was asked to run. You gotta understand, these are very conservative Republican areas, so you got people who said, 'If he wins it, fine. But challenge him, and make him earn it'" (Ohio).

Views that I cast as strong party support among the more competitive candidates are somewhat harder to capture in interview quotes. Because many of these candidates had held previous office, they had a record of activity within their party, so their identification with their party often was reflected in references to their activities as state legislators, or in their close ties to national party leaders (an issue I will return to in my discussion of party assistance). Finally, six of the candidates reported having switched parties within the past decade. Four of these candidates were somewhat competitive, and three had held elected office in another party. With two exceptions, these candidates all came from areas in which their current parties have historically been relatively weak. Their switching may either be a sign of changes in party ideology, party strength, or, perhaps, opportunism.

Perceptions of Party Activities

Before dissecting the campaign activities of the candidates' parties at various levels, I first simply asked candidates, "Were you satisfied with your party's efforts on your behalf?" While some candidates diligently listed the activities of the national campaign organizations, the national coordinated campaign, the state parties, and the county-level or even township party organizations, most candidates gave a fairly inclusive, straightforward answer—no. This is surely to be expected, as the parties provide a convenient scapegoat for many candidates. Even many of those who said that they were satisfied quickly added that they had expected little help to begin with. To quote one second-time, somewhat competitive candidate: "You have to understand, I'm coming from a different place than everyone else. I didn't expect any money from anybody. So any help I got, I was happy about" (Ohio). In fact, this candidate was not coming from a different place than anybody else. Sixty-four percent of the very competitive candidates—including all but one of the victorious candidates—reported that they were satisfied with what their party had done for them, while only 19 percent of the somewhat competitive candidates and 29 percent of the long-shot candidates reported satisfaction with the party's efforts. Those who did not receive money, yet were satisfied, all noted that they were satisfied because they had low expectations.

Of the candidates who were dissatisfied with the party's efforts, most directed the brunt of their criticism at their national congressional campaign organizations. The second section of table 6.2 documents trends in national party assistance to candidates according to those candidates' competitiveness. Eighty-six percent of the very competitive candidates reported receiving financial assistance from the DCCC or NRCC, while only 33 percent of the somewhat competitive candidates and only one of the long-shot candidates reported receiving money. Those candidates who did receive money from the congressional campaign organizations often had little actual need for it—the median very competitive candidate raised $569,610. Despite the fundraising in these elections, though, the candidates still reported that money was the most important contribution of the party to their campaigns: "I'll say this: the money was the most helpful thing. We didn't want much more than that, because then they get into your campaign and they start running campaigns that are not geared toward the district. I wanted their money and I wanted to run, I didn't want a lot of advice that came with that that I would have to follow" (Wisconsin).

Many of those dissatisfied with lack of party support made general claims about how much more they could have done with even a small campaign contribution, but many of these candidates identified a less tangible sense of support which they found lacking:

> The DCCC is far too much numbers-driven, they don't have any awareness of districts. They don't even make an attempt to get to know the district. We kept saying this is a viable district, they kept saying no, it's not. . . . We kept them informed, though we didn't expect anything from them. The only time I ever asked them for anything was there is a moment in time when they cut off candidates. They announce to the world

that they're dead. I called six weeks before the election, and I said, "Do not cut us off. I never asked you for anything, you just can't do this to me. I haven't asked you for anything, all I'm asking you is not to do that." (Illinois)

The NRCC had the polling numbers, and they blurted out that they had the results and I was behind. There was fairly sensational news story where a representative of the national campaign team said, "Yeah, he's behind, we'll have to do something about that." It was not helpful. (Wisconsin)

Among the most bitter candidates were those who narrowly missed being targeted. These included many Republicans who did well in 1994 and were running for a second time in 1996. The three tiers I have set up here map fairly well onto national party services. All candidates reported receiving some amount of issue information and training from the national organizations—Democrats all referred to the DCCC's daily faxes and the opportunity to travel to Washington for a training session and meeting with President Clinton, while Republicans reported that they had also been offered campaign training and had received extensive information about their opponent's record and about the Republican Party's achievements in the 104th Congress from right-leaning, quasi-party interest groups such as GOPAC. Most of these candidates seconded the above quotes, claiming that it was not the lack of money that hurt them, but that the party's lack of concern for their race made it difficult for them to interest others in their campaign.

Most of the long-shot candidates were appreciative of the baseline assistance that the DCCC and NRCC provided—65 percent reported making use of the daily faxes and other strategy and issue information. Forty-seven percent attended candidate-training sessions in Washington; many of the attendees, not being party insiders, were quite thrilled with the opportunity to meet their party's political leaders. Twenty-nine percent of the candidates reported no assistance at all from their party, a response that may either be the result of not knowing what the national organizations had available or refusing assistance out of principle. Two of the long-shot candidates indicated that they had discussed the various "hurdles" the parties set up for candidates to receive further assistance—the ability to demonstrate fundraising prowess and to provide favorable poll results conducted by a pollster acceptable to the party.

This theme is much more prevalent among the somewhat competitive candidates. Forty-seven percent of these candidates made reference to expectations the party had of them. These candidates spoke of the need to poll early in order to gain party support and the need to raise $100,000 before the end of June of election year. In the words of one somewhat competitive candidate, "We went out there at the end of July, and they said, 'You're great, [your opponent] stinks. But it's a bad district. Go home, young man, and get media attention, and then we'll talk.' So between July and the election, we talked every week, but they wanted to see polling results. Obviously, they thought it was a hopeless cause. They finally came forward at the end and maxed out for us, based on polls" (Illinois).

These candidates were in many cases the losers in the battle for the targeted support of the DCCC and the NRCC. Several of them spoke of competing with the targeted candidates for funds; the high-priority races for both parties were spread evenly among the four states, such that many candidates felt that proximity to a more hotly contested race affected their ability to gain national party resources. While DCCC and NRCC directors deny that they limit their efforts within each state, some candidates argued that party efforts were indirectly affected in this manner; the most heated races received the most media attention and were at times priorities for the state party and party leaders within the state, thus deflecting attention from their races. To quote two somewhat competitive Ohio candidates,

> I think what you really compete with is whatever the other forty or fifty competitive races are nationally. That's more the sense. I don't think I competed with other Ohio candidates. There were a few other Ohio races that were higher in the pecking order than mine, but they were always going to be higher than mine, based on the Democratic performance of the district as much as anything else. That was the biggest uphill battle that you had to fight, that this was a tough district. (Ohio)

> Frankly, the Democratic Party does not have the money that the Republican Party does. I think they put all of their eggs in one or two baskets here in Ohio. They were successful in those particular races, but I think with my record of performance on behalf of working people, they could have been kinder to me early on. We would have been able to use our own resources to develop our story. (Ohio)

Some candidates in other states were more pointed about competition with their neighbors, however:

> There is a whole continuum that we were on. Supposedly they were going

to eventually get behind two of us. Gephardt had said that he had to win two seats here in order to become Speaker, so there was all this speculation about who would get assistance. Ultimately, four seats would be more accurate than two of them, is what we thought. Initially we were real hopeful that we would be one of them, but it became more and more apparent that open seats were a high priority for them. In some ways we should have figured that out earlier on. Unless we had a poll that showed us even or closer to even, then the open seats and the races against the first-term Republicans would be a higher priority for them. (Wisconsin)

Many of those who did receive financial support received it late in the campaign and found that they were unable to spend it. The somewhat competitive candidates also, however, made use of the party's baseline resources—24 percent attended training sessions in Washington, 71 percent made use of the daily campaign updates, 29 percent reported assistance from the national party in soliciting PAC contributions, and 19 percent reported receiving polling data from the DCCC or NRCC.

The most competitive candidates received all of the above, though their discussions often centered on money. Both of the two very competitive candidates who did not receive financial contributions from their national party believed they were deemed to be comfortably ahead of their opponents and not in need of money. One victorious candidate was quoted in district newspapers disputing this perception and expressing some bitterness about not receiving more support from the party, but after the election a spokesperson sought to mend fences: "I think his feeling was that this was one of the most targeted races. There were still issues where he needed help, and he felt he should have been able to reach out publicly and get help from the party. Obviously they were right, and we didn't need the help, but you never know" (Illinois).

The most high-profile candidates reported a whole array of national party efforts—training, money, PAC assistance, consultants, field directors, strategic advice, independent advertisements, and get-out-the-vote efforts. Most of these candidates had a fairly clear understanding of their privileged status: "The central function of the national party is the channeling of money to the most effective challengers and candidates and the most vulnerable incumbents. That was their primary importance. They also did a significant amount of opposition research, which we collated with some research other previous candidates had given us. Those were the two most significant tangible things the party did for us" (Ohio).

Few of the candidates reported assistance from their state parties; exceptions to this rule were Illinois Republicans and Wisconsin Democrats.

Wisconsin candidates reported that the Wisconsin Democratic Party worked fairly closely with the Clinton campaign and sought to coordinate the House races with state races and the presidential race as much as possible. Illinois Republicans were the only group that reported financial assistance from their party. Most candidates recognized that the state parties were more concerned with state legislative races.

One might suppose, then, that those candidates who were not targeted by the national party were wards of their local parties. In many cases, this is true. Canon (1990, 10) has argued that local parties play a large role in long-shot races, and long-shot races only, and Fowler and McClure (1989, 227) have downplayed the role of local parties in heated elections. Schwartz (1990, 218) argues in her study of the Illinois Republican Party that local parties do devote resources to long-shot candidates out of fear that their own organizations will wither if they do not actively support the full slate of candidates in their areas. In my interviews, I found few patterns in the degree of local party support. Urban Democrats often reported strong support from their local parties, yet so did many rural Republican candidates. In many cases, the reasons for strong local parties are quite specific to their areas, and these parties are often dependent on one or two individuals. One rural Republican remarked that

> I think what happened was that first of all we got very different responses from different levels of party organization. This, particularly as a rural district, has very strong local Republican organizations. The geography is that this district is larger than some states, so local parties, particularly because they tend to be rural and older communities, have more of a stable leadership. The same people have led some of those party operations for many years. We had strong support from them and a lot of help from them. At the congressional district level the Republican party was also quite helpful. They gave us the maximum amount, and we shared an office with them. (Minnesota)

Another rural candidate made a similar, but qualified argument: "With seventeen counties [in the district], you've got varying degrees of strength in the local parties. I would say they were all very committed to us, although you don't win a district like this with party strength. You win it with volunteers" (Wisconsin).

Local parties seem to play a prominent role early in the campaign; they often recruit candidates where no challenger at all, or no strong challenger, emerges. All but one of the candidates who reported being recruited said that they were recruited by local party officials. Divisive primaries can also be minimized with intervention from local party leaders, as the case studies below demonstrate.

By far the most frequently mentioned sources of assistance for candidates at all levels were incumbent members of their state's delegation. Even the longest of long shots reported some contact with one or two prominent members of their state's delegation. In Ohio, where the Democratic Party held only five seats in the 104th Congress, down from eleven four years previous, virtually every Democratic candidate reported extensive help from two members of the state's delegation, Marcy Kaptur and Sherrod Brown. Illinois Republicans reported similar assistance from Reps. Tom Ewing and Dennis Hastert, and most Wisconsin and Minnesota Democrats and Republicans reported help from the more secure members of their states' delegations. I asked one Ohio candidate who had been particularly frank about his long-shot status why he felt any of the sitting House members would help his campaign. His response was that

> Sometimes they will do this because they aspire to run for another office. They want to make contacts. You help these little guys working down here, and they'll be out there working for you. If Marcy wants to run for state office, or Sherrod Brown wants to run for governor, I'm going to remember that these people were with me. They knew my chances of winning were pretty slim, but they contacted me, and I'm willing to go to work for them. You want to keep members of the party happy because they can help you one day. (Ohio)

This type of assistance is not as spontaneous as it appears in the above quote; other candidates mentioned that the members whose names were frequently brought up had taken or been appointed to the position of leader of the state delegation, or as liaison between the DCCC or NRCC and their state's nonincumbent candidates. Even so, one candidate remarked that these members played a greater role in generating enthusiasm and providing moral support than did any of the official party organizations:

> [Brown] has done a great job of consolidating his seat, and now he wants to move up in the party hierarchy. As a challenger, my sense was the old barons, the old established people, were much less willing to do anything to get the majority back than were they younger guys. When we went to the Democratic Caucus for a big meeting and to the DCCC for a meeting, you didn't see the John Dingells of the world show up, which was odd when you think about it, because who benefits the most from getting the majority back? I didn't get the sense that Dingell was out there shaking the tree

trying to get money for challengers, but here's a young comer like Sherrod who really appreciates what it's like to have the majority. Also, Sherrod had been a statewide candidate, he might have statewide ambitions somewhere down the road. He was helpful. If he needs my help, I'll be there. If it came down to Sherrod versus other statewide figures, well, Sherrod did more for me in my race than anybody else, so who would I be inclined to endorse? I'd help Sherrod. So it's smart politics all the way around. (Ohio)

Several candidates running against representatives who had traditionally taken on the role of delegation leader saw their role as being enough of a threat to keep their opponent from playing a role in other races, as providing enough competition to ensure that their opponent stayed home and campaigned in his own race. The two earlier quotes from Ohio candidates about "keeping the incumbent busy" are examples of this. While neighboring political figures are often held by the candidates to be pivotal influences in their campaigns, however, they seldom leave behind strengthened party organizations in their own districts when they leave office. Nine of the districts in which I conducted interviews were districts which had traditionally been held by Democrats but had gone Republican in 1994. Another four seats were open. Few of the candidates in these districts found a local organization in place that had been nurtured by the previous incumbent. One Democrat running in one of these districts answered my question about local party organization by saying, "It's been pretty loose, again because [the Democratic incumbent prior to 1994] was so popular for so long that we didn't have to do anything. He always won, and the Democrats would just try to get their local people elected. They weren't real successful, and so we don't have a real strong party organization in this district" (Minnesota).

Another candidate shared a similar, though less complimentary story about the district's former representative: "He is in many ways a brilliant politician, but he has never been a party politician. He formed his own organization. He didn't share things. He always did his own thing" (Wisconsin).

And another put matters even more bluntly: "Politics is a very selfish game. You learn that everybody's with you as long as there's something to be gained. The local people, [the previous representative], they didn't think it was very likely to happen" (Ohio).

Ideology, Primaries, and Party Strength

The above discussion sheds some light on what makes for a successful campaign. Attention from the national congressional campaign organizations is crucial, yet this is often predicated on the past performance of the district. A Democrat running in an overwhelmingly Republican district is unlikely to raise the funds or generate the polling numbers to gain support of the national campaign organizations; the large gap between the haves and the have-nots in this regard appears to leave little room for the strength of parties at the local level. State parties play a relatively small role in House campaigns. The effect of state parties varies according to the parties' priorities and finances. In Ohio and Wisconsin, where there were no statewide races occurring, the state parties appear to have taken a greater interest in House races. Many Ohio candidates also pointed to the large role their state parties were playing in the presidential campaign, in light of Ohio's bellwether status in presidential races.

The candidates' perspectives on the relative strength of the parties in their districts, however, highlight several important points. First, party strength is not based on an ideological agenda; instead, for these candidates it encapsulates success at limiting ideological conflict, regardless of the disparity in issue preferences of party members or the party's would-be Congress members. Second, party strength paradoxically has little to do with the party's performance in any of the national-level races; districts that had been represented for years by Democrats prior to 1994 often had disorganized local parties, as did many Republican districts. Many districts that have reliably voted for one party at the presidential level likewise could not translate voting habits into organizational strength for other races. Third, party strength translates, according to many of these candidates, into ensuring that there is a deep talent pool of candidates and that the talent poll is winnowed and a nomination is made with a minimum of divisiveness, friction, or hard feelings.

A relatively small number of candidates reported any direct pressure on issues from their party at any level. Among those that did, however, the differences are striking. Virtually all of the candidates who did report some pressure reported that it was a result of the primary, that they were forced to run in one direction in the primary, and then another in the general election. This occurrence has become a staple of literature on presidential primaries—that the Democratic nominee, for instance, must run to the left in the primary, and then run to the center in the general election (see Bartels 1988, 7–9).[3] Candidates who reported fairly strong district or local party organizations insisted that this was not necessary: "I ran against [the incumbent] in the primary. The other candidates saw me as the front-runner, so they campaigned against me. But I stayed against [the incumbent] all of the time. I just presented myself as the one who had the best chance of beating him, and that's what the party leadership did, too" (Illinois).

Another candidate, who ran as an underdog in the primary, told a similar story:

> All three of us were concentrating on [the incumbent]. I was not fearful of making that my focus, because we were all three focusing on that. So I figured that whoever would win the primary would come out with a boost. I think that's what happened. The primary helped us a great deal, because attention was focused on the primary throughout the summer. Where the primary hurt us was with money raising. We were only able to raise $30,000, and that was like pulling teeth. But after the primary ended, we did it in style, all coming together. We had a unity dinner three days after the election, well attended throughout the district. People came together, and we raised almost $190,000 in the next month. (Wisconsin)

The effect of primaries should not be overstated—while primaries may at times exert an ideological pull of their own, the majority of House primaries are simply too low-profile and too dependent simply on name recognition and resources to make ideology a dominant factor. In addition, the candidates we might expect to place the highest premium on divergence—the least competitive candidates—are less likely either to have primary opposition or (when they do have opposition) to run in primaries that make enough of an impression on voters that these candidates are "tied" to primary positions.

The final section of table 6.2 compares the experiences of the different types of candidates in primary elections. Twenty-four candidates—79 percent of the competitive candidates, 38 percent of the somewhat competitive candidates, and 29 percent of the long-shot candidates—faced primary opponents. Some of these primaries were not considered to be particularly competitive by the candidates; six of the twenty-four candidates reported that their primary competitors did not cause them to spend money or had any effect on their campaigns, with all but two of these uncompetitive primaries occurring in the less competitive races. Eleven candidates reported some attempt by their party or members of their party to exert some ideological pressure upon the nominee—either by determining who the nominee would be, or by attempting to sway the candidate on issues. These candidates are not concentrated in any particular category of competitiveness—three were very competitive, four were somewhat competitive, and four were long shots. All of the candidates who reported such pressure, however, were either recruited by the party or faced a primary opponent. The sole such candidate who did not face what he or she termed a "divisive" primary or a contentious party endorsement claimed to be being pulled toward the center:

> A couple times we were told, "Look, if you don't start doing things in a fairly conventional manner it's going to be hard for you to raise money." Their advisors come in here and by the time they leave your head's kind of spinning, because there's a certain element of overwhelming you with "This is how you have to do it." . . . These guys would come in from Washington and say, "We've done all this national polling, we're talking to the DNC, Clinton's done a lot of polling, Clinton's going to win big in this district" and these were not the issues we were all that enthralled with. (Wisconsin)

Aside from this candidate, however, discussions of local party intervention on issues break down quite neatly—candidates who reported strong local parties felt that any issue pressure that was applied to them was applied in order to ensure a centrist candidacy, while candidates who reported weak local parties felt that issue pressure was exerted in order to pull the eventual nominee away from the political center. These latter types corresponded well with the areas that Fenton and Mayhew contend are weak party states. Several Minnesota candidates, Wisconsin candidates, and Chicago-area Republican candidates of all different levels of competitiveness talked about how they were pulled off-message by a divisive primary and were never able to unite the party behind them. One somewhat competitive candidate felt his chances were destroyed by his primary: "What [the other primary candidates] started to do was attack me as the frontrunner with all sorts of allegations, none of which were true. I think that might have diminished my candidacy in the eyes of at least some of the public. Republican voters still voted for me overwhelmingly, but that was really the beginning of the end. The primary was the beginning of the end of this campaign" (Illinois).

Another very competitive candidate had a similar story:

> I had been actively involved in the Republican Party for eighteen years, so I had a track record. At district caucuses, I was the one who was called on throughout the whole district to get up and talk on legislative activity. I am a politically moderate Republican. That doesn't mean I don't have a strong conservative record on many, many issues, including a number of social issues, but what happened here is a candidate came out of nowhere. He spent far more money in the primary than any candidate had ever spent up here. When he spent that amount of money, in attack

mode, I had to respond. I didn't have the opportunity to really develop a positive aura and talk about my record, talk about my plans. I was on the defensive very much in the primary campaign. . . . My opponent inflamed the passions of a number of groups in the party. He also distorted certain things. If you don't have the money to clarify these issues, if you don't have the money to tell your story, that stuff sticks. (Wisconsin)

Because the two parties in Minnesota endorse candidates prior to the primary date, some candidates can win the endorsement but lose the primary, or vice versa. In many cases, ideologically committed party activists can deny centrist candidates the endorsement, even though these candidates may be more electable. This difference is reflected in the statements of these somewhat competitive Minnesota candidates:

The candidate that will most likely emerge next time is a former military man. The first words out of his mouth at the district convention, that question was, "What are the most important issues to you?" His answer was "Life." There was nothing else. As he was saying this, someone was filming this event. Is he willing to take that conservative slant, to sell his soul as I did to get the endorsement? He probably will if he really wants it. I just think the Republican Party, unless we start coming together as an entity, will lose. Legislators do well in some areas, but they won't do well in the district as a whole. There's no coordination of efforts whatsoever. Legislators worked with me because I was one of them. They won't work with other people. I talked to somebody from [a county in the district] the other day. He's the old Republican guard, and the new Republican guard has just pushed him out. There's a lot of anger that has to be overcome, and that's going to lead to more defeats. (Minnesota)

The party activists in my district are very conservative. They didn't like my candidacy, and they will work against me if I run again in 1998. What I would like to do is get more moderates involved in the process. That's my biggest complaint, that I don't criticize the conservatives for doing what they do, they're simply using the process the way it's supposed to be used. My biggest concern is that moderates, you know, we like to bitch and complain, but we don't organize, so we have only ourselves to blame. (Minnesota)

Compare these responses with those of candidates from "strong party" areas of Ohio and Illinois. One somewhat competitive Democrat said that

> I guess I made the decision to run as soon as I won the party's endorsement, of the executive committee. You know how these things go. It begins with speculation, people start talking, you start talking to people about whether you should go, people started encouraging me to run, there started to develop a consensus among party leaders that I would be the strongest candidate among those who were thinking of running. There were some other party establishment folks who had been longtime members of the party who had been talking about it, but clearly wouldn't be the strongest candidate. The party chairman and leadership sort of dissuaded those folks that this just wasn't the right time. (Ohio)

A second-time Republican candidate took a more nuts-and-bolts approach to the local party organization: "I'd say that there are organizations there. There are organizations that you can mold and get to take a more active role. You don't have to go in and tell them what to do. They'll call you and say they're walking precincts, they want literature. . . . Our effort last time enabled us not only to endear ourselves to the local Republican organizations, but also to begin building a base outside those organizations" (Illinois).

Another second-time candidate had faced a primary, yet it proved not to be a divisive one. A campaign staffer remarked on the primary that

> The key thing was that he didn't stop campaigning after his last race, so when he declared and filed as a candidate he already had a base of support in all of these different counties. He knew the party structure, the party structure knew him. They knew that he was going to be someone who would be there to help. So he was not in a situation of saying, "You don't know me, but here I am, God's gift to the Republican Party in this district. I've never done anything for you here in this county, but now I want you guys to go out and campaign for me." It's the personal relationships in this district, particularly in the rural areas, that make a huge difference in terms of getting people in the party excited and involved in the campaign. (Illinois)

Sixty-eight percent of the Illinois candidates—six of the seven Republicans and seven of the twelve Democrats—claimed that the local parties in their districts were "strong," although their categorization of local party organizations included district, township, and county organizations. The same sentiment was shared by 56 percent (seven of twelve Democrats and two of four Republicans) of Ohio candidates, 50 percent (three of five Democrats, two of five Republicans) of candidates in Wisconsin, and 29 percent (two of the six Republicans, no Democrats) of Minnesotans. It is difficult to generalize these stories beyond the personalities of the individuals considered, but it is clear from the interviews that party strife rarely hurt Ohio or Illinois candidates, while it did damage several candidates in Minnesota and Wisconsin. This may also be an artifact of 1996—the same Ohio candidate quoted at length above about how his party's executive committee arrived at its endorsement also noted that the Democrats had lost the seat in 1994 because the party had failed to arrive at a consensus and a fairly contentious primary resulted.

The Role of Parties in Three Congressional Campaigns

To further illustrate some of the dynamics of party involvement in House races, let us consider three different candidates with whom I spoke. Ideally, case studies selected here should demonstrate the difference between strong and weak parties—that is, between organizationally strong parties and ideologically unified parties—as well as the difference between party participation in different types of campaigns. Unfortunately, however, the negative responses about party pressure I received from several of the candidates in Minnesota and Wisconsin must remain unattributed because these candidates were reluctant to be singled out as critics of their local party leaders. Thus, I limit the scope of this chapter's case studies to three campaigns, as I have in the previous chapter, and I note areas in which these candidates—and especially the long-shot and somewhat competitive candidates considered here—accord with or differ from the candidates in states or districts with more ideological parties.

A Long-Shot Campaign in a Strong Party State

The Twelfth District in Illinois is described by *Politics in America* as the state's most Democratic district outside Chicago (see Duncan and Lawrence 1997, 426). Schwartz (1990, 217), in fact, singles out the district's largest county, St. Clair County, as one of only two counties outside of Chicago where Republicans are reluctant to allocate money at any level. The Democrats here are conservative Democrats, however. The Twelfth stretches from East St. Louis and Belleville along the Mississippi River down to Cairo, including some of the poorest parts of Illinois. Several decaying industrial towns share the district with oil refineries and poor rural communities. The Twelfth has more in common with neighboring districts in Missouri and Kentucky than it does with the majority of Illinois congressional districts. Much of the Twelfth was represented prior to the 1992 redistricting by Democrat Glenn Poshard. After redistricting, Poshard's district moved east and Democrat Jerry Costello, a socially conservative Democrat with roots in the Democratic machine of the East St. Louis area, took over the district. As a neighboring Democratic candidate described the Twelfth, "The way my district is drawn, they cut off all the Democratic strongholds, they're all in Jerry Costello's district. The strength of the party there, as far as it being a party, there's a lot of strong county organizations out there in the smaller counties. The party organization in my area, because of the way the district is cut, is hard to put together."

Other candidates agreed that the Twelfth had been drawn to be the lone clearly Democratic district in southern Illinois. Bill Clinton and Al Gore won the district overwhelmingly in 1992, 1996, and 2000, although both Costello and Poshard's districts had voted narrowly for Ronald Reagan in the 1980s. Even in the 1980s, however, the Republican Party never mounted much of a threat to Costello. He has not had a well-financed opponent since the 1992 redistricting, and as of 1996 he had won each of his last three races with 66 percent or more of the vote. In 1996 the Republican candidate was draftsman and gun activist Shapley Hunter, from the small prison town of Tamms, near the district's southern border. Hunter raised only $4,800, and he had only minimal support from the national or state party in a campaign that yielded 27 percent of the vote.

Of the three candidates considered here, Hunter was clearly the most interested in party-building in his campaign, yet it is difficult to find evidence that his party influenced the views he expressed. As he put it, there is clearly much more party-building necessary in his district than in more competitive districts:

> The Republican Party here in Alexander County has been a pretty minimal force over the years, so immediately when they saw they had new blood in there they immediately made me county chairman, put my neck on the chopping block. It was through my connections as the county chairman that I met a number of people and became known as a solid conservative. When this year's congressional race came up, we had committed ourselves to have a conservative candidate to run in this district, and unfortunately the ones we had hoped would run, all of them more or less backed out. They thought this was not a winnable year for them, whatever their reasons were. I don't know what their reasons were for backing out. So the state central committeeman for this district was call-

ing around trying to find a good conservative, and he finally approached me. I told him up front I was an unknown with no money. He just said, "Give it the best you can, that's all we can ask." That's what I did. . . . I don't know how far down the list I was. We were working with [the other potential candidates] and we thought we would get a commitment from at least one of them all the way through to the primary, but when we got down to the filing deadline, they said they didn't believe Costello was beatable. At least, I believe that. I don't know their true reasons for not running. The consensus was that he just wasn't beatable. I actually think that he is beatable, given the press coverage of [Costello's recent ethics problems]. It would have been winnable for somebody who wanted to run that kind of race. But that's not the type of race I run, so I may have been my own worst enemy in that regard.

Hunter's campaign received very little press coverage; what campaign coverage there was was of Costello's ties to an alleged racketeer in the St. Louis area. As Hunter noted, he might have been able to use those ties to his advantage, but with a $4,800 treasury he probably would have had little success even had he tried. Hunter was aware that he would receive little assistance from the national party, and he did not appear to be upset about that: "I went into this race realizing that I had no money at all, and I knew that I was not to count on money from the national or state parties. I didn't want to try to burden them because I know there were a lot of races that were crucial, and I wanted to make sure that they had an adequate level of funding. I didn't want to be guilty of depriving someone else of that money. I wanted to run on whatever I could muster up here, with the time and money I was able to raise."

Hunter did not go out of his way to raise money, and he made a decision to take no PAC money. He did make use of information provided by the state party and of the national party's basic support for candidates: "I tried to keep as much track of Costello's record as possible. Part of that was due to the support we got from the national party. The RNC is very good about sending out packets on what they call the key votes of interest to the Republican Party."

Despite Hunter's current role as Alexander County Republican Party Chairman, his ties to the state and national party are tenuous. His chairmanship may provide evidence of Schwartz's (1990, 114) contention that Republican leaders in Illinois neglect the southern counties because their political culture is so different from that of the rest of Illinois. Hunter said that he had only recently become involved in the Republican Party. He was raised in a Democratic family in rural New Madrid County, Missouri, but argues that if the New Madridians of his youth "saw what the Democratic Party was like today, they would be Republicans."

Hunter also identifies little with the Illinois Republican "establishment"—he had not backed Illinois's Republican governor, Jim Edgar, in his previous reelection effort—and considered himself fortunate to be running in a year when the sole statewide Republican candidate, Senatorial nominee Al Salvi, was also seen as a political outsider. Hunter hoped that his campaign would help Salvi, and he also found that Salvi was helpful to him:

> Salvi was here several times, and his wife was here more than he was. Whenever he was down here he invited me to appear with him, and I was glad to go. I think the Salvi campaign and mine had a lot in common in that both of us were somewhat at odds with the party regulars. Al ran against [Illinois Lieutenant Governor] Bob Kustra [in the Republican Senatorial primary], who was the party's choice to run that race. He had the conservatives' support, but it took a lot of work after the primary to get the rest of the party behind him. In some areas he probably still didn't manage to get that support as well as he needed it. And I'm running down here as a virtual unknown and not a party regular, I just ran as a loose cannon pretty much down here in the Twelfth District. I think Al Salvi and I had a lot in common in that regard. He was supportive of Republican candidates everywhere, but I particularly noticed it when he was down here.

Hunter emphasized that he had few problems with his opponent, a sentiment that he shared with several of the long-shot challengers to politically moderate incumbents. He admitted that the next serious Republican effort would be when Jerry Costello leaves Congress, and that he was unlikely to be involved in that effort. Looking back on his campaign, he mentioned that "If it had been another 1994, they wouldn't have had to come down and find me. They would have had some candidates that would have stepped up. I think this district is winnable for the Republicans if you can get out and get the message out. But the timing is a big part of it."

Hunter thus seems somewhat ambivalent; on the one hand, he ran in order to help the Republican Party out in the district and hopefully in the state, but on the other hand, he is skeptical about the direction the party will take in the Twelfth District in the future. In response to my question about whether he expected to help out the 1998 Republican candidate in the district, he remarked that

It's hard to say. It depends who the candidate is and what their positions are. If they're a party regular, I would say no, I'm probably not going to have a lot of influence. If it's someone like myself who's an outsider, who's not a party regular, who's interested in working with a lot of the far right-wing groups that I'm more familiar with, then I may have some influence just through contacts. But I would say that the odds are that it's probably going to be a party regular next time and they're probably going to try to work through the traditional party structure.[4]

A Somewhat Competitive Campaign in a Strong Party State

In Ohio's Twelfth District, which is comprised of the eastern half of Columbus and several blue-collar suburbs, Democrats have had less success than in the Illinois Twelfth. Bill Clinton carried the district by a narrow 47 to 45 percent margin in 1996 but lost it by an equally narrow 42 to 40 percent margin in 1992. George Bush, Ronald Reagan, and Gerald Ford had carried the district by much more comfortable margins in the previous four elections, winning by at least 20 percent of the vote each time. Democrat Bob Shamansky had won the district's House seat in 1980, despite Reagan's popularity, but he was unseated in 1982 by a thirty-year-old Republican state senator, John Kasich. Kasich, chairman of the House Budget Committee from 1994 to 2000, carried the district comfortably until his 2000 retirement. Democrat Cynthia Ruccia, a Democratic Party activist with no previous political office, ran against him in 1994 and 1996, seeking to put together a coalition of black voters, blue-collar workers, and affluent liberals in her own suburb of Bexley. Although she raised over $250,000 in both of her bids, she received only 33 percent of the vote each time. Ruccia received some financial assistance from the DCCC in 1994 but reported less attention from the national party in 1996.

Cynthia Ruccia's campaign received far more media attention than did Hunter's, in part because it was a particularly nasty campaign and it featured several widely criticized campaign advertisements (see Eaton 1996). Whereas many competitive candidates rarely need to spend time convincing party leaders of their viability, such appeals were a major activity for Ruccia in her 1994 campaign:

> I had understood in looking at the way this district was redistricted in 1990 that a Democrat could win in this district because we had the same Democratic performance in this district as in [victorious 1996 candidate] Ted Strickland's district, maybe four-tenths of a percent less. It was not

going to be an easy race, but on paper it was doable. It took me time to sell the DCCC on that, but I got a fair amount of assistance after I had opened their eyes to it. Now when the 1996 election came around, it was a whole different story, because Kasich had been on his own meteoric rise at the time, so he became sort of a target. People became involved in my race for philosophical reasons. When it came down to party help, I got more than a lot of people got, but it's a horse race for them, they add up the numbers and see how people are going to do before they allocate the resources. They put me in kind of special category, but I didn't get to experience, for example, what [victorious Ohio Democratic challengers] Ted Strickland or Dennis Kucinich got. I wasn't in quite that category.

Ruccia received small financial contributions from the party in 1994, as well as a few in-kind contributions. The Democratic Party also directed several interest groups hostile to Kasich her way. Ruccia recognized, however, that beating Kasich would have been quite an upset. This is one reason why ties with the state and local party organizations were important to her; she argued that she hoped her campaigns would make her a more viable candidate for Congress or for another local elected office at some future point. She had hoped for a good relationship with local party officers, and she was partly successful in this regard. State party leaders were able to arrange for her to have President Clinton, Jesse Jackson, and John Conyers campaign in her district. The state party was not able to offer more than this, however:

> I was received very well by the state Democratic Party. What I really appreciated was that I always had access to [state party chair] David Leland if I needed some help, and he was always straight with me, told me what they couldn't do. I knew that in working with him, if I had specific requests, that if he could do it, he would do it. I didn't get any double talk. I caught on really quickly, though, that any help I was going to get was going to come from the DCCC. The state party supports state candidates, and the local party supports local candidates.

Ruccia reported friction within the local party, however, which stemmed from feuds over the Columbus mayoral race. She stressed that the local party itself was supportive, but that previous opponents of Kasich actively sought to undermine her campaign. Once Ruccia had emerged as the nominee, local party leaders sought to mend fences, but they were not entirely successful. Ruccia reported little help from any previous opponents of Kasich, with the exception of Bob Shamansky, the incumbent whom Kasich beat in 1982. Even though there was not a contested primary for the Democratic nomination, there were candidates who had aspired to run in the primary, and their ties to the Democratic Party may have harmed Ruccia's efforts in the general election. The closest thing there was to an attempt to affect the issues of the campaign, according to Ruccia, was criticism by the district's 1992 Democratic nominee of Ruccia's campaign.

Could she have won? Probably not. Kasich ignored her during the campaign, but she claims that she did manage to make him campaign and spend money within the district. As the other Ohio candidates quoted earlier noted, this is a major function, at least in the eyes of challengers, of running against an incumbent as powerful as Kasich. Like many of the candidates who sought the backing of the DCCC and NRCC yet fell short, Ruccia learned well the importance of money in a congressional campaign:

> I was as thrifty as I could be. I'm a businesswoman, so I do understand about the bottom line, where you can skimp and where you have to spend money. But what they expect in Washington, especially in the 1996 election, they were so obsessed about money. That's all anyone talked about. It was so amazing, they never wanted to hear anything at all except how much money I had, or if you had your own money to put into the race, and how you were going to raise it and where you were going to get it. Beyond that, no one was interested at all. You couldn't call them and ask them for anything without being grilled for ten minutes about money. Nothing else mattered.

The solution? Ruccia lowered her sights in 1998 to run for the Ohio House (also, unfortunately for her, unsuccessfully). In my interview, she told me that she hoped to build more of a base in the party by running for a lower-level office, and that perhaps this would help her run again for the U.S. House in the future.

A Very Competitive Campaign in a Weak Party State

It is difficult to distinguish between the two sequential positioning alternatives when considering very competitive candidates. This is so because in both, parties or candidates are willing to move away from their *ex ante* preferred positions where they can increase their probability of winning by doing so, and this is the case by definition for very competitive candidates. Thus, the fact that Lydia Spottswood, the Democratic challenger from the

First District of Wisconsin, ran in a state where parties have traditionally been more ideological and less well-organized does not have as much of an effect on her campaign as did the benign neglect of the Republicans in Shapley Hunter's campaign or the financial debates to which Cynthia Ruccia referred. Spottswood's campaign was a priority for her party's national organization, the DCCC, and it was thus not markedly different from the campaigns of very competitive candidates in Ohio or Illinois in terms of the attention it received from her party.

Wisconsin's First District, an industrial district in the southeastern part of the state which includes the cities of Racine, Kenosha, Janesville, and Beloit, is one of several districts that were targeted by both the DCCC and by organized labor. The First District had been represented by Democrat Les Aspin from 1970 until 1992, and then was represented for one term by Democrat Peter Barca from 1992 to 1994. Although the district has consistently leaned Democratic in presidential voting—Michael Dukakis carried it by a 51 to 49 percent margin in 1988, Bill Clinton defeated George Bush 41 to 36 percent in 1992 and defeated Bob Dole 50 to 38 percent in 1996, and Al Gore carried it by a 49 to 47 percent margin in 2000—Barca was a casualty of the Republican sweep in 1994, losing by slightly over one thousand votes to third-time Republican candidate Mark Neumann. When Barca decided not to run again in 1996, Lydia Spottswood, the Kenosha city council president, emerged from a four-candidate primary and went on to receive 49 percent of the vote in a losing campaign against Neumann. This race featured a blizzard of issue advertisements and independent expenditures by the parties, by the AFL-CIO, and by other interest groups.

Spottswood, although she was not well known outside of Kenosha prior to her election bid, did well in large part because of the high level of party support. She reported high levels of involvement from all levels of the party. She is one of the only very competitive candidates who reported any type of recruitment effort by the local party:

> In April, after I was reelected [to city council], I was approached by the county Democratic leadership to run for the state legislature. In May, however, we realized that we didn't have a challenger from the Democratic Party for the seat in Congress, and I had been a supporter of Les Aspin's and a supporter of Peter Barca's, and a moderate to conservative Democrat. I had not seen the incumbent closely—I do not know him personally, but I had a very bad feeling about how he approaches his job. I met with some key people in the district in the middle of May, basically to ask the question "Should I be changing races?" The decision was yes, I

probably should change races, because I had one opponent [in the state legislature primary] who I thought could do a good job. We then tried to figure out who else was out there with district-wide name recognition, it was necessary for someone to have that to run a good race, and that wasn't happening. The second question was who's out there with the ability to raise money very, very quickly. The consensus was that I was in the best position to do that.

Wisconsin's early September primary is one of the latest in the country, which can be a recipe for a long and draining primary. Spottswood ran in the primary against three other candidates, one of whom, Doug LaFollette, a relative of former Senator Robert LaFollette, had a significant advantage in terms of name recognition at the beginning. Spottswood said that several prominent Wisconsin representatives sought to influence the outcome of the primary:

> It was a strange primary. I was the first to announce, and in the beginning I took a lot of personal attacks from my opponents. What happened that changed the primary radically was that labor came to my support, and the Wisconsin delegation, Barrett, Kleczka, and Obey, announced their support as well. My primary opponents immediately became very hostile and defensive, and stepped up the personal, negative attacks on me. I suppose they just were doing what they thought they had to do to win. So from that standpoint you could describe it as somewhat divisive. I was the most conservative of the Democrats in the primary, and interestingly, that was the key to labor's support for me. Certainly, I understand their issues, but I think they also thought I had the best chance to win the general.

Hard feelings do not appear to have lingered after the primary, however. If there were any ill feelings after Spottswood won, they seem to have had little effect on the race. Peter Barca became involved in the race after the primary, but like the DCCC, he had remained neutral until that point:

> He didn't want to be involved until the general. Toward the end of the campaign he started to call us with suggestions, although he's apparently out of town a lot for his job. Later on he started making an effort to get in touch with us, more to answer questions than anything else. It was a little frustrating, because we thought he would have all kinds of help to offer us, but the good news is that labor made up for it, and the county and state Democratic Parties came forward and volunteered themselves.

Although the DCCC chose not to become active in Spottswood's campaign or any other Democrat's campaign until after the primary, it did provide research for all of the candidates in the primary. Once the primary was over, however, the DCCC became heavily involved. Spottswood summed up its activity: "They did help get some financial resources, contributions from the Democratic leadership in Washington. They also helped in terms of technical support and research that we needed. We had a consultant who would help us out, who would tweak us if we were not emphasizing something as much as we should. They did some independent expenditure; we were aware of it but didn't have control over it."

In response to a question about what the "tweaking" that the consultant did entailed, she responded that

> It was mostly technical. They were trying to track where we were with our budget, how we were using resources, what resources we hadn't tapped into that we needed to consider, how we were doing our media work and our buys, they were more decisions in that regard than "You're not talking about the same things as the president, you should be doing that." They weren't trying to make me a clone of the president. It was how well we were doing in the district and what they had in the way of resources that we might not be aware of information-wise, trying to gauge how we were relative to other field operations, GOTV efforts, all those kinds of things.

The state party served as a coordinator of efforts in the campaign, ensuring that the vice president, Tipper Gore, Dick Gephardt, and others were able to schedule time in the district, and identifying potential contributors within the state. Although resources also were being sought for the two open-seat races in Wisconsin, Spottswood's race is one of the few races I consider here where the Democratic Party, at all levels, was extremely involved in the campaign. In the end, the party's effort turned out to be insufficient to ensure victory. Several reasons were advanced by local journalists. One obvious reason might be that Spottswood was still outspent almost two-to-one by Neumann ($1.2 million to $700,000). News commentators also opined that the attack ads aired in the campaign may have turned off voters on both sides (Schultze 1996). Still others claimed that even though Spottswood got a boost from the primary, she did wind up spending money there that would have been more effectively spent in the general (Scolaro 1996). Spottswood was quoted in the *Milwaukee Journal-Sentinel* claiming that had she had two more weeks to campaign, she would have won (Schultze 1996). In my interview, she did place some of the blame for her loss on the late primary, but she also added that she thought her campaign had been beneficial for the Democratic Party in her district: "Our campaign kept the party energized in our district, despite the late start. I think most Democrats were stunned to see a woman virtually unknown outside my own city be able to close the gap so profoundly."

Each of these candidates illustrates several features of the relationship between candidate competitiveness and party assistance. Lydia Spottswood's race is one where the combination of a vulnerable incumbent and a strong local and state party effort brought about an extremely close race, a race that was a top priority for both the national Democratic and Republican Parties. At no point in the campaign was Spottswood's issue focus affected by the party. She had the resources and the desire to hire consultants to help shape the message of her campaign, but her party appears to have had enough confidence in her to let her run her own campaign. Meanwhile, the race in Ohio's Twelfth District featured a challenger who was aware of the resources that were available to a candidate like Spottswood, but who was also aware that these resources would not be available to her and that she would have to do much more to prove herself to both political elites and to voters. For the most part, her campaign does not appear to have been important enough to the national or state parties for them to try to affect her issue positions; disagreements on issues within the local party had enough of an effect that Ruccia seemed hesitant to claim that her campaign would have a long-term effect on Democratic fortunes in her district.

Shapley Hunter is somewhat more self-effacing than other long-shot candidates were, yet his campaign also demonstrates that long-shot candidates share several traits. These candidates tend to be individuals who recognize the futility of trying to raise large sums of money, of trying to bend the ear of the national party, and of investing a large amount of personal time or effort in an uphill campaign. Hunter, however, did have clear personal goals in his campaign, as did his party. Local Republicans sought to build a local party base among disaffected voters such as Hunter; Hunter sought to reach out to fellow conservatives and to build a base for candidates with similar views, as well as for himself. Hunter showed no signs of interest in the technicalities of receiving national party support, in part because he knew he had little chance of getting that support and that it was not worth his time to concern himself with the fundraising, polling, and consulting details of which Spottswood and Ruccia spoke. In a way, Hunter had more freedom than either of those two did—he had the freedom to do and say whatever he wanted, to let his conscience be his guide. Both Spottswood and Ruccia spoke of the difficult ethical decisions they had to make in their campaign, and about the effects of the political process upon beliefs and personal ideals. It is no surprise that many candidates of Hunter's ilk spoke more enthusiastically and freely about their campaigns than did a number of the veteran politicians I interviewed.

Conclusions

Political parties, in the words of the candidates with whom I spoke, are not merely tools to be used in elections, nor are they solely vehicles for ideological expression. The national party campaign committees function as service providers for those candidates who can garner attention from them, but other aspects of the party network are not as easy to categorize. It is not possible to completely discard the notion of party-based campaigning, to dismiss the notion that even (or, in some cases, especially) long-shot candidates are influenced in their position taking by the instrumental or ideological preferences of their party. It is also not possible, however, to attribute candidate position taking solely, or even primarily, to the preferences of political parties. In many cases here, the parties did not care what positions their candidates espoused. In others, the parties trusted their candidates' judgment to take positions that would best help them run competitive campaigns. And in still others, (the Hunter case in particular) political culture may have preceded any influence of parties themselves.

Research has established the central role of the national campaign organizations in contemporary congressional campaigns, and these interviews do nothing to diminish this role. This role, however, is not what Mayhew, Fenton, and Elazar are discussing when they analyze party strength and political culture. These interviews demonstrate that state and local parties—including not only official party leaders but elected politicians and other concerned partisans—do have an important role to play in national elections, particularly in the races of those candidates whom the DCCC and NRCC do not help. It is in these subnational organizations and networks that we can make distinctions in party strength and in which we can identify motives within political parties that go beyond short-term maximization of votes or probability of winning. A state or local party organization that mediates between national political figures and local candidates, coordinating their efforts, can help maximize a candidate's potential. Yet these parties may also be concerned with testing ideological appeals or reinforcing the priorities of the party at the state level or of the party activists, even at the expense of fielding competitive candidates in a particular district. A local party may help recruit candidates that are appropriate to a district, and it can provide some help for candidates who are not receiving help from national or state party organizations. Local parties, however, may also have their particular ideological agendas, and these may not accord with the views of the party's candidates or with majority preferences in a district or even among party members in a district.

These interviews demonstrate that party strength can vary dramatically across small geographic and political distances. It may have been difficult to unseat any House Democrats in Minnesota in 1996, yet the divisions reported by most of Minnesota's Republican candidates may have discouraged some of these candidates from running in the future. Minnesota's Republican Party was at the time of this study the weakest of the parties considered here in terms of its representation in Congress, and despite recent gains, internal strife may limit its ability to improve its fortunes in the near future. It is difficult to generalize about Minnesota's Democratic Party based on the lone interview here, but it seems to share with its Republican counterpart a more ideological focus and a lower level of organizational strength. According to Democratic candidates in Ohio, Ohio's Democratic Party, also in somewhat bad shape following the 1994 elections, gained back two seats in 1996 in part because of the efforts of younger Democrats to foster an organized, statewide effort. The parties in other states illustrate patterns described by Mayhew and Fenton; Illinois and Ohio did have stronger state and local party efforts and organization. In these states, financial and organizational effectiveness, rather than ideology, was a frequent topic of discussion, except in the case of Chicago Republicans. Wisconsin's state and local parties showed some sign of organizational strength, yet it is difficult to gauge whether or not this was because of high stakes—two open seats, one very competitive race, and three incumbents who had only narrowly been reelected in 1994—and extensive involvement by the national party organizations in Wisconsin in 1996. Despite the expected competitiveness of many Wisconsin districts, Wisconsinites were still more likely than were candidates from Ohio or Illinois to talk about ideological pressure from their state or local parties.

Why do parties matter in these elections? Earlier, I noted that 1996 was an atypical year because of the low number of uncontested seats. This is one indicator that both parties were particularly involved in the 1996 House candidacies of many candidates who had little realistic chance of winning. Clearly, the parties had some stake in each of these elections. In some cases, the parties exerted ideological pressure, while in others, they may have seen benefits in letting candidates express their own views, in letting enthusiastic political amateurs "swing away" at the incumbent.

As I pointed out in chapter 3, however, party organization and party culture is one of the major ways in which the candidates I have chosen are unrepresentative of all candidates. In the next chapter I explore differences in expressive campaigning across election years and across regions of the country.

CHAPTER 7

Expressive Campaigning in 2000 and Beyond

In a study such as this, in which the views of some candidates are presented as a representative sample of all candidates' views, two potential objections to making general claims seem evident. First, insofar as these candidates do *not* represent a random sample, and are drawn from four contiguous states, one might ask whether these candidates do in fact share important characteristics with candidates from other regions of the country. That is, have I thus far merely been describing trends in electoral competition that are peculiar to the four Midwestern states of Illinois, Minnesota, Ohio, and Wisconsin? What similarities or differences might we expect these candidates to have with candidates from states such as Alabama, California, Maine, or Wyoming? And second, why should we be confident that the 1996 election was "typical," that these candidates represent a fact of life in American politics or a trend in congressional elections, rather than an aberration due to factors peculiar to the 1996 elections?

By way of conclusion, in this chapter I seek to address both of these concerns, reiterating my argument as it applies to candidates outside of my original study. Many of the variables I have considered would seem somewhat impervious to change over time or across states—that is, there seems to be little reason to expect congressional candidates in some states to be superior information gatherers to those in other states. It also seems that while the issues that matter should vary substantially across states or across election years, the basic structure of ideological competition—that is, candidates facing vulnerable incumbents should seek to take popular positions, while candidates facing safe incumbents should not necessarily seek to do so—should not vary. And while the incumbency advantage may fluctuate somewhat over time, these fluctuations appear, at least in the past few decades, to take place within a narrow range—incumbency seems always to carry some advantage in House elections, no matter what the year is or which states we are considering.

It is worth investigating, however, the fluctuations that we may have theoretically informed reasons for expecting and the differences that may exist across years and across regions of the country. Therefore, I conducted a second set of interviews in the months following the 2000 elections in four different states—in Delaware, Maryland, New Jersey, and Pennsylvania. While these states are not as sharply different from the four Midwestern states I considered in 1996 as, for instance, states of the Deep South or the West may be, the application of the theory to these states does demonstrate that the expressive politics scenario does hold in other regions of the country. And while, for obvious reasons, it is impossible to project the theory backward in time to consider bygone elections, my conclusions regarding the 2000 elections demonstrate that the patterns of competition I found in 1996 were not atypical, and, if anything, elections in 2000 were characterized more by expressive campaigning than were the 1996 races. This second set of interviews does, however, reveal two notable wrinkles to the expressive politics argument. First, in terms of the timing of the elections, the proximity of the 2000 races to the impending 2002 redistricting resulted in a greater degree of forward-looking behavior on the part of candidates; that is, many 2000 candidates thought about the likely future shape of their district, and the feasibility of future campaigns for Congress, in considering the positions they would take in their campaigns. Second, peculiarities in the location (proximity to Washington, DC) and the electoral laws of this second set of states (namely, that in two of them state legislators were not up for election in 2000) may produce a higher-than-expected number of strategic and politically experienced challengers than we might otherwise expect.

Before summarizing the findings of this second round of interviews, however, three discussions of context are in order: a discussion of differences between the 2000 and 1996 congressional elections, a discussion of the differences in politics and political culture between the four Midwestern states I considered in 1996 and the four Mid-Atlantic states I considered in 2000, and a discussion of the import of these differences for our theoretical expectations.

Developments in Congressional Elections, 1996–2000

The 1998 elections were quite different from those of 1996 in some ways. The Democratic Party gained five seats in the House of Representatives, defying the predictions of virtually all election forecasters and defying the historical tendency of the party holding the presidency to lose seats in the midterm elections. The 1998 elections were also a reversion to the normal pattern of uncontested seats. Ninety-five incumbents, or 23.8 percent, ran without major-party opposition.[1] The 1998 elections garnered less media attention than did those of 1996, in part because it was believed that control of Congress was not at stake (see Brady, Cogan, and Fiorina 2000, 239–40).

In other ways, however, the 1998 elections were very similar to those of 1996, and the fortunes of incumbents and nonincumbents were also similar: 98.5 percent of incumbents seeking reelection won; only six incumbents were defeated. All six of the victorious 1996 candidates whom I interviewed ran for reelection, as did nine of my interviewees who had lost in 1996. Five of the six incumbents were reelected, and none of the nine nonincumbents were victorious.

All but one of the victorious 1996 candidates I spoke with won reelection, and most of them won without substantial difficulty. For instance, chapter 4's John Shimkus, despite the fact that his district was judged to be one of the most competitive in the nation in 1996, was not targeted by the Democratic Party. Shimkus received 61 percent of the vote. Of the losing 1996 candidates, several were expected to be potential winners in 1998. Foremost among these was Lydia Spottswood, profiled in chapter 6. Her 1996 opponent, Republican Mark Neumann, gave up his seat to run (unsuccessfully) for the Senate against Democrat Russ Feingold. Spottswood's district was deemed by both parties to be a potential pickup for Democrats, but Spottswood fell farther short in 1998 than she had in 1996, receiving only 43 percent of the vote (Duncan and Nutting 1999, 1490). Other candidates from my sample encountered similar results—of the nine candidates who ran again in 1998, only three improved upon their 1996 showing, and these three still lost.

More noteworthy were the candidates profiled in the previous chapters who declined to run. Although the Democratic incumbent Sidney Yates finally retired from Congress in Illinois, his 1996 challenger, Joseph Walsh (profiled in chapter 5), declined to run again, perhaps believing that 1996 had been his best chance. The Republican candidate for this seat, a man who had been the Republican nominee in two previous elections, ran a relatively low-profile campaign. The seat easily remained in Democratic hands. Several other 1996 incumbents whose districts were in the states I considered retired in 1998, but only one of these districts—Wisconsin's second district—changed party hands. While only three incumbents in the states I considered in 1996 ran unopposed, six incumbents from these states ran unopposed in 1998. One of these was Wisconsin's James Sensenbrenner, whose 1996 opponent, Floyd Brenholt, I profiled in chapter 5.

By 2000, competition in these states had grown even more lopsided than had been the case in 1996 and 1998. In contrast to my 1996 breakdown, in which I deemed twenty districts to be uncompetitive, twenty-two to be somewhat competitive, and eleven (three of which were open seats) to be very competitive, in 2000 there were again three uncontested seats (including Jerry Costello, whose 1996 race I discussed in chapter 6), but there were thirty-four uncompetitive districts, eleven somewhat competitive districts, and only eight very competitive districts. Of these eight very competitive districts, four were open seats. Of the unsuccessful candidates I interviewed in 1996, two ran again in 2000. Chapter 5's Mary Rieder made her second attempt to defeat Gil Gutknecht, but, as she had predicted in 1996, Gutknecht was more difficult to beat in 2000 and finished with 56 percent of the vote. The remaining first-time winners from 1996 all had solidified their districts by 2000, and none were seriously challenged. As in 1998, one notable feature of 2000 is the candidates I interviewed in 1996 who chose not to run in races that their party eventually won or in open-seat races. In Minnesota's Second District, Democrat David Minge was unseated by political neophyte Mark Kennedy; Minge's somewhat competitive 1994 and 1996 challenger did not run. In Ohio's Twelfth District, John Kasich retired and Cynthia Ruccia (profiled in chapter 6) chose not to run again; a far more politically experienced Democratic candidate emerged and this race became the most closely contested Ohio race, yet the Republicans held the seat. Other open seats in suburban Chicago, the Champaign-Urbana area of Illinois, and in Minneapolis were hotly contested but the 1996 and 1998 challengers either did not run or did not win their party's nomination.

In general, House elections in 2000 were both more competitive and less competitive than those of 1996, depending on one's measuring device. As the partisan balance in the House drew closer in the wake of the 1996 and 1998 elections, spending and campaigning in selected districts became more intense. Yet the number of districts that were highly competitive shrank. Excluding three candidates defeated in their party's primaries in 2000, the incumbent reelection rate in 2000 had grown to 98.5 percent—only six of four hundred incumbents were defeated. While several prominent Republicans retired as a result of the party's term limits on committee and subcommittee chairs, the majority of these retirements were by members who held safe seats. Only seventeen seats changed party hands, the third-lowest total since the 1940s (Jacobson 2001, 191).

According to *Congressional Quarterly*'s preelection handicapping, only nine of the four hundred incumbent-held seats were toss-ups or leaned toward the challenger, with an additional twenty-five that leaned toward the incumbent. Nineteen of the thirty-five open seats were judged to be competitive, for a net total of fifty-three competitive seats, the lowest total since 1990. According to Hernnson (2001, 169), a total of forty-three races were targeted by the AFL-CIO, one measurement of donors' expectations about competitiveness, and forty-three Republican candidates received assistance from a Medicare reform organization. These seats received a tremendous influx of money, interest group attention, and party attention, yet they represent a small number of House seats.

Campaign spending illustrates some of the inequalities at play in 2000. Average spending appears even more lopsided than in 1996 when we compare challengers and incumbents—the median challenger spent $51,408, the median incumbent spent $618,718, and the median open-seat candidate spent $900,795. Another means of addressing competition is in looking at the average disparity. According to Jacobson's index of average inequality, 2000 represents the most lopsided election year in recent history, approached only by the 1990 elections (Jacobson 2001, 193). The party campaign committees spent more money than ever in 2000, with the DCCC and the NRCC each spending over $50 million, but the focus of these spending efforts was on a small number of races (Herrnson 2001, 167).

It is somewhat more difficult to measure changes in the political environment of House races between 1996 and 2000. The 1998 elections had, of course, taken place in the shadow of President Clinton's impending impeachment trial, to which many observers attributed the Republican Party's unusual failure to gain seats at the midterm of a Democratic presidency (Herrnson 2000, 87–88). The 2000 elections shared several aspects of the 1996 elections—they took place at a time of economic growth, of tenuous partisan balance in the House, and the presence of a presidential election. The 2000 elections differed in that there were relatively few retirements, overall; the presidential election did not feature an incumbent and was far closer than the 1996 race; and, in contrast to 1996, congressional approval ratings were climbing (Herrnson 2001, 156). The lack of any presidential coat-tails is evident in the results of the 2000 races, where the minority Democrats gained one seat. Herrnson argues that impeachment had, for the most part, faded as an issue in all but two or three House elections (Herrnson 2001, 158), and congressional (as opposed to committee) term limits appear also not to have been a major issue (Jacobson 2001, 197). Although the 106th Congress continued a trend of polarization between parties, it would seem that the few districts which did change hands changed in such a way as to "sort out" instances of district-legislator partisan mismatch. All told, the issue context of 2000 does not seem remarkably different from 1996.

As Jacobson notes, however, the 2000 elections were not necessarily a harbinger for future House races; they are typical of the elections that precede a redistricting. In terms of spending and in terms of the number of competitive races, they followed a trend of the 1970s and 1980s in which seats are gradually sorted out after a redistricting and competition declines over the ten-year period (Jacobson 2001, 191). In terms of the number of contested seats, they followed the trend of having fewer uncontested seats in presidential election years, although the percentage of uncontested seats—15.8 percent (again, excluding Louisiana)—was substantially higher in 2000 than it was in 1996.

As a final note on the political context of 2000, there was unfortunately no issue survey of the breadth of the 1996 *Time/Congressional Quarterly* candidate survey that I used in chapter 3. Project Vote Smart again surveyed all candidates in 2000, with potentially scalable results, but the response rate was not nearly as high as the 1996 *Time/Congressional Quarterly* survey or Project Vote Smart's 1996 survey. Fortuitously, however, a candidate positioning study was conducted by Harvard political scientist Barry Burden which has findings somewhat comparable to my 1996 results (Burden 2001b). Burden's Candidate Ideology Survey simply asked all major-party House candidates to place themselves on a 0–100 scale of liberalism or conservatism. Burden was able to proxy incumbents' positions using first-dimension W-NOMINATE scores to obtain a total of 153 candidate dyads and 147 challenger positions. Scatterplots of differences between all Democrats and Republicans indicate substantial divergence between parties, but marked responsiveness to district voting (here, 1996 Dole vote) on the part of incumbents. As is the case in my analysis, challengers exhibit no significant responsiveness; the correlation between challengers' positions and district voting preferences is actually negative.[2] What little convergence there is occurs primarily in the most competitive districts, again supporting the notion of expressive campaigning for particularly disadvantaged challengers.

Political Differences across the States

A second potential obstacle to generalizing from my 1996 interviews is in the geographically unrepresentative choice of interviews. As I note in chapter 3, the need for familiarity with a state or region's political issues provides a compelling reason not to employ a random sample. Yet such a choice does cause problems in seeking to generalize. Accordingly, I also present the interviews here as a means of countering such objections.

Hence, a few brief words are in order on the level of political competition, the level of party strength, and the political culture of the Mid-Atlantic states of Delaware, Maryland, New Jersey, and Pennsylvania as compared with the Midwestern states in which I conducted my 1996 interviews.

New Jersey resembles the strong party states of Ohio and Illinois that I considered in 1996 in several ways. It is the nation's ninth-largest state, and it has historically had a strong yet evenly balanced party system that has lost influence over state-level or congressional politics in recent decades. It has historically been a battleground state in presidential elections but has recently been trending Democratic—the result, some argue, of a lack of a socially conservative base in its Republican Party (Barone, Cohen, and Ujifusa 2001, 974, 979). According to Zukin (1986, 11–15) New Jersey is anomalous because it has a highly educated, affluent (New Jersey has the second-highest per capita income in the nation) population yet its citizens know little about state political affairs because New Jersey has no major urban centers and is dependent upon New York and Philadelphia media for political news. New Jersey is the most densely populated state in the nation—it is 89 percent urban—yet it does exhibit an urban/rural split that is reflected in partisan divisions between the northern, more liberal sections of the state and a more rural Republican base. As noted above, however, New Jersey Republicans have tended to be somewhat more moderate than Republicans elsewhere, and issues such as the environment, education, and labor have tended to provoke defections among New Jersey Republicans from the national party. Strong Democratic machines in declining industrial cities such as Trenton, Camden, and Newark have been in decline, as have rural machines in the southern part of the state as New Jersey industry has turned toward developing pharmaceutical, telecommunications, and high-tech companies in the Princeton area (Moakley 1986). Because of its media dependence upon the large New York and Philadelphia markets, New Jersey is the second most expensive state in the nation in which to campaign, a phenomenon exemplified by the costly Torricelli and Corzine Senate races in recent years and the Bush campaign's decision not to invest resources in New Jersey in 2000. At the House level, this has resulted in a smaller number of vigorously contested House races, a larger number of uncompetitive races, and a comparatively small number of somewhat competitive races. Finally, House races in New Jersey may also be anomalous because members of the New Jersey legislature are elected in odd-numbered years, ensuring the state legislators can run for the U.S. House without giving up their jobs. In New Jersey, redistricting is done by a ten-member, bipartisan commission; New Jersey did not gain or lose seats in 2002. Currently, the New Jersey delegation includes six Republicans and seven Democrats, a figure unchanged in 2000 or 2002.

Pennsylvania is similar to New Jersey in its level of party organization, but the partisan divisions have been strikingly different. Both Democratic and Republican organizations have flourished in both the larger and the smaller cities in Pennsylvania, and both parties have also been relatively competitive with each other at the state level. As the *Almanac of American Politics* notes, however, Pennsylvania has made for an odd bellwether (Barone, Cohen, and Ujifusa 2001, 1298). Democrats in Pennsylvania have tended to be more conservative than national Democrats on cultural issues, and Republicans have tended to be more liberal than Republicans elsewhere on cultural matters. Pennsylvania is anchored by two large cities at either end of the state, Pittsburgh and Philadelphia, with a large swath—dubbed the "T"—in between. Western Pennsylvania, historically a more Democratic area of mines and steel mills, has trended toward the Republican Party in recent years, while more cosmopolitan and suburban eastern Pennsylvania has trended toward the Democrats. This has made for anomalous switches in congressional voting—Democrats have captured seats in affluent Philadelphia suburbs, while Republicans have won seats in poorer, more blue-collar areas of the state. Pennsylvania has the fifth-largest population of any state in the nation, but has been steadily losing ground, and House seats, since the 1930s. The *Almanac* notes that Pennsylvania politics resembles the politics of the 1940s (Barone and Ujifusa 1997, 1196); Sorauf (1963, 7–15) noted in the 1960s that one aspect of this legacy has been the dominance of a nonideological, patronage-oriented politics. Prior to the 2000 election, Pennsylvanians held four committee chairs in the House, and many members used these chairs to provide substantial public-works benefits for their districts. In 2000 Pennsylvania had twenty-one House seats; with one seat change in 2000, Republicans had, for the first time in over a decade, a narrow majority of eleven seats to ten Democratic seats. Reapportionment cost Pennsylvania two seats, and the redistricting plan, written by a Republican legislature and a Republican governor, was expected well in advance to hurt Democrats (see Barone, Cohen, and Ujifusa 2001, 1298–99).

Delaware, according to Mayhew (1986, 66), exhibits strong party politics similar to the politics of New Jersey and Pennsylvania. Like New Jersey, it is dependent upon an out-of-state media market (Philadelphia) for political news, and like New Jersey it boasts a relatively affluent populace which is not concentrated in any major urban area. Delaware has also been politically competitive—it was the nation's longest-running bellwether prior to 2000—with a pragmatic politics centered around support for the state's pharmaceutical and banking industries. Political divisions in the state arise between the more Democratic area of Wilmington, the state's largest city, and more rural areas in the southern part of the state, with the affluent yet somewhat socially liberal area of New Castle County and the Wilmington suburbs holding the balance in statewide elections. Delaware is the lone state I consider with a single, at-large House seat; while Democrats now hold both Senate seats and the governorship, the House seat has been safely in Republican hands since 1992. While one might expect that state Democrats, given a lack of other House races to consider, would devote more attention to the state's House seat, races against incumbent Rep. Mike Castle have been surprisingly low-key.

Finally, Maryland, though adjacent to Delaware and Pennsylvania, has a somewhat different political climate than the aforementioned three states. Maryland has traditionally been considered more akin to the southern border states in its politics. Accounts by Fenton (1957, 171–202) and Mayhew (1986, 84) have called attention to factionalization in the Maryland Democratic Party, as the Democratic machine in Baltimore has competed with a Democratic faction in the western part of the state. By most measures, Maryland is now one of the most Democratic states in the country, with all statewide offices held by Democrats from 1986 until 2002, an impregnable Democratic majority in the state legislature, and substantial margins for recent Democratic presidential contenders. Yet as of 2000 the state's eight-member House delegation was evenly split between Democrats and Republicans. This was the result, some argue, of miscalculations on the part of the Democrats in the 1992 redistricting, in which a second majority-minority district was created but two Democrats were defeated running in their new districts (Barone and Ujifusa 1997, 661). Maryland has the largest black population outside of the Deep South, a large population of reliably Democratic federal and public employees, and the nation's sixth-largest metropolitan area in Baltimore, the Baltimore suburbs, and the Washington, DC, suburbs. Historically, however, the Washington suburbs have played a small role in state politics, with most successful politicians at the state level arising from the Baltimore area. Current bases of Republican support include the more rural Eastern Shore and the Baltimore suburbs, while the poorer western area of the state has been more akin to the South, producing socially conservative Democrats and tending often to cross party lines and support Republicans.

Each of these states is classified as a 5, a strong party state, by Mayhew (1986, 46–66, 84–89), with the exception of Delaware, which rates a 4. One would expect an absence of the types of ideological parties I noted in the previous chapter in Wisconsin and Minnesota, and thus one would

Table 7.1. 1996 and 2000 Candidates Compared

	All 1996 nonincumbents	1996 Interviewees	All 2000 nonincumbents	2000 nonincumbents in DE, MD, NJ, PA	2000 Interviewees
Democrats	54.4% (255)	57.7% (30)	49.9% (200)	47.6% (20)	57.1% (8)
Republicans	45.6 (214)	42.3 (22)	50.1 (201)	52.4 (22)	42.9 (6)
Winners	15.5 (72)	11.5 (6)	9.4 (41)	7.1 (3)	14.3 (2)
Long Shots	34.3 (161)	36.5 (17)	54.6 (219)	57.1 (24)	42.9 (6)
Somewhat Competitive	39.9 (187)	38.5 (21)	30.2 (121)	21.4 (9)	21.4 (3)
Very Competitive	25.8 (121)	26.9 (14)	15.2 (61)	21.4 (9)	35.7 (5)
Open Seats	11.3 (49)	8.3 (4)	8.0 (35)	7.0 (3)	14.3 (2)
Uncontested Seats (Third-party candidates not included)	3.2 (14)	–	15.8 (69)	9.3 (4)	–
N	469	52	401	42	14

expect that where party influence exists, it would be influence to adopt more pragmatic, centrist positions. These states contain a paucity of rural districts as compared with the four Midwestern states, and thus, perhaps, the nature of many of the issues should vary. In addition, one might expect that, on average, Republican candidates should be more moderate than Republicans in the Midwest. A primary difference between these states and the Midwestern states should be a lack of moderately competitive campaigns; in most of the districts in these states, media campaigns are extremely expensive, and apart from a small number of competitive districts centered around smaller cities in Pennsylvania, there should be few races where major media buys are not essential to victory for challengers.

The summary statistics in table 7.1 bear out this contention, and they also demonstrate areas of difference between the House races in these states and other races in 2000, as well as slight differences between the candidates I interviewed and all candidates in these states in 2000. As the table shows, my selection skews slightly toward Democrats, as compared with the aggregate numbers in these states, and it skews slightly toward more competitive races. Insofar as all groups are represented here, however, this skewing should not substantially alter the generalizability of my interviews to the states as a group.

What Might We Expect to Be Different? What Might We Expect to Stay the Same?

As the above comments indicate, there are important differences between the 2000 elections and the 1996 elections, and between the political context of Mid-Atlantic states as opposed to Midwestern states. These differences, however, should have minimal effect upon the variables of importance to this study—information, issue positions, and party involvement. They do provide some extensions to the theory, but they do nothing to refute it.

We should not necessarily expect any difference in candidates' information acquisition strategies across either time or place. In chapter 4 I argued that the only potential difference we might expect across candidates in information is that better-financed candidates might rely more heavily upon polling data. Insofar as polling data was rarely treated by candidates at any level of competitiveness as a source of information about voter preferences, however, and insofar as the degree of information about voter preferences necessary to candidates is different for candidates at different levels of competitiveness, difference in how well informed candidates are is not particularly relevant to the accuracy of their assessment of their chance of winning or of what positions, if any, will help them to win. Because the candidates I consider here are, on average, less competitive than my selection of 1996 candidates, we should see fewer candidates who were able to conduct extensive polls, but this change does little to affect my basic conclusions on information acquisition.

The nature of issue competition also should be little changed from 1996. As I note above, the only potential major issue that was not present to a roughly equal degree in 1996 is impeachment, and there is little evidence that the impeachment trial played a large role in more than a small number of 2000 races. While some candidates with whom I spoke mentioned that they had discussed their views on the president's impeachment, even these few candidates acknowledged that it was not a major focus of their campaigns. There are certainly some differences in the issues raised that can be attributed to region—energy and mining issues in Pennsylvania, tobacco farming in Maryland, and so forth—but the presence of these issues should have little effect on overall ideological strategies or candidates' reasons for running.

The involvement of the party campaign organizations in House elections did change noticeably between 1996 and 2000. Fewer seats were targeted by the parties, and there were only a small number of vigorously contested seats in the Mid-Atlantic states I consider here. Although one of the Maryland elections was close, none of the seats in Maryland or Delaware were a focus of attention for the DCCC or the NRCC. Three New Jersey seats and three Pennsylvania seats (of which one in each state was open) were targeted by the parties; I was able to interview candidates in three of these six races. If we consider the forty-five House seats in these states in comparison with the rest of the nation, the ratio of six of forty-five seats with substantial party involvement is not significantly different from Herrnson's estimates of party involvement nationally, nor is the percentage of these seats among my interviewees. As I seek to show in my comments on the interviews, candidates' reflections on the role of the national, state, and local parties also do not seem at odds with those of the 1996 candidates.

We are thus left with several more idiosyncratic factors which make these interviews a source of corroboration and of slight extension of my 1996 interviews. There are several factors unique to these states and to the 2000 elections that do go somewhat beyond my initial theory. First, in regards to the year, the impending redistricting and in particular the impending loss of two House seats in Pennsylvania ensured that many of the challengers were looking toward the 2002 elections in their campaigns. In Pennsylvania, some candidates could be expected to view their 2000 bids in part as a means of establishing their *bona fides* with their party in the event that redistricting rendered their district more sympathetic to their party. The same could also be expected to hold true in Maryland, where Democratic challengers took pains to point out to me that Maryland is now the most Democratic state in the nation in terms of state legislative partisanship, yet its U.S. House delegation was evenly split between the parties.

Other factors are state-specific. All four states had Senate races in 2000; three of these four (all but Maryland's) were at least moderately competitive. There is one at-large seat in this group; although one might expect that the presence of only one House race would increase the attention paid by the state parties to this seat, in fact this race was largely ignored. Two states considered here—Maryland and New Jersey—did not hold elections to state office in 2000. New Jersey holds elections in odd-numbered years and Maryland holds elections for both houses every four years—most recently, in 1998. This ensures that the strategic calculus for state legislators is not the same as it is in states where they would need to give up their seats in order to run—they have less to lose—and may result in a larger number of experienced candidates running in less competitive races that they would otherwise sit out. Finally, the proximity of these states—particularly Maryland—to Washington, DC, may ensure that even among challengers who have not held elected office there is a larger-than-expected number of challengers who have significant knowledge of congressional politics and congressional experience, as lobbyists or staff. These geographic peculiarities would seem to indicate that we may see more politically savvy candidates in the types of races where we would not necessarily expect them in other states. The fact that expressive campaigning still seems present in the majority of these campaigns indicates that this phenomenon will be with us for some time.

The 2000 Candidates

Let us first consider the variables discussed in the previous three chapters, with an eye toward identifying similarities or differences between the 1996 Midwestern candidates considered in the three previous chapters and this chapter's 2000 Mid-Atlantic candidates.

Information

In chapter 4 I noted two features among my 1996 interviewees. First, as one moves from less competitive to more competitive candidates, the use of sophisticated public opinion polling techniques increases. This is unsurprising; it is a function of resources. Second, however, in that chapter I also provide evidence that candidates with access to public opinion data cannot be said to be better informed, in any way relevant to their chance of winning, than are those without such data. This is so because candidates do not use public opinion data as a source of information about voter preferences. Among those candidates with public opinion information at hand, polls are viewed as a tool for acquiring party support, as a means of garnering attention in the media, and, hopefully, as a campaign tool to be used against their opponents. That is, a favorable showing in a poll can be presented to potential supporters, or it can be trumpeted in order to persuade the public that a candidate is indeed viable. Candidates of all levels of competitiveness draw upon their own background in the district, the views of voters or political elites in the district, or upon the incumbent's past record as a means of learning public sentiment. This type of information is easily available to all. Furthermore, the simple knowledge that one is highly unlikely to win no matter how well one represents public views is, in itself, a piece of information which may trump all of the other, more subtle, aspects of voter preferences.

Among the 2000 candidates with whom I spoke, I encountered views which paralleled those of the 1996 candidates quite closely. Among these candidates, as well as among 2000 candidates more generally, there was a much greater percentage of "have-nots" than was the case in 1996. As a result, an even smaller number had access to polling data than was the case in 1996. Half (seven of fourteen) of the candidates with whom I spoke conducted any polls, none of the long-shot candidates, two of the three somewhat competitive candidates, and all of the very competitive candidates. Among the long shots and the somewhat competitive candidates, there were some who had access to polls previous candidates had done in their district. As one remarked, "[The previous challenger] took a zillion polls, and he told me privately, 'Don't waste your money doing that.' It doesn't tell you a great deal. If you really don't know whether you're winning or losing, and you've got a lot of money to throw around, then maybe. But it costs a lot of dough. . . . I never had a choice anyway" (Pennsylvania).

Long-shot candidates drew instead upon means ranging from consideration of past voting trends to sentiments expressed in public gatherings to gain a sense of what voters wanted:

> If you do the analysis of the numbers, it might be possible to get 52 percent of the vote here. You go back to the 1992 presidential vote, and look at how the different counties vote and how they changed. . . . On issues, you can do the same thing. For example, on HMOs, 10,000 people were dumped from their HMO coverage, and there could be 30,000 to 40,000 people who know somebody who was cut, so you know at least that many people care about that issue. (Pennsylvania)

> One of my supporters was a professor of English at the community college in the area and asked me to come talk to his students. I asked them several questions from a Pew Foundation survey, and then we talked about a whole bunch of those issues. They were very talkative—I learned several lessons from that. (Pennsylvania)

Among the somewhat competitive candidates, as was the case in 1996, there was more of a struggle to acquire polling information, but the intent of this acquisition was more to influence the DCCC or the NRCC than it was to learn about voters' positions for campaigning purposes: "We did a standard poll with about 350 responses, and when the pollster had seen the preliminary results he upped it to 400 so there was no way people could criticize the poll. It showed [the incumbent] with 37 percent reelect numbers. I thought we could go out and raise money based on those numbers, but we couldn't get anybody interested" (Maryland).

Finally, the very competitive candidates included three who were recipients of extensive support from their parties and two who were not. The two who were not targets both did manage to raise enough money to do extensive polling—one was largely self-financed and the other received heavy labor support—but both also noted that their polls were primarily designed to be persuasive. The three targeted candidates spoke of polling as the very competitive 1996 candidates did; they were able to conduct several polls, they often disseminated their results strategically, and they often were able to keep a running tally of how the campaign was faring in response to major advertising buys of their own or of their opponent. The campaign manager for one victorious candidate actually had a poster of the trends in the campaign's tracking polls on display in his office to note the consistency in polling results throughout the campaign. Several of these candidates also noted that they had paid extremely close attention to presidential polls in the area and had set expectations about how well George W. Bush or Al Gore needed to do in their districts for their campaigns to be helped.

In sum, information acquisition and use strategies in 2000 were similar to those of the 1996 candidates with whom I spoke. Polling was actually more frequent among the highly competitive candidates I consider here than it was among the most competitive candidates in 1996; this may be a function of the large campaign budgets of several of the 2000 candidates. There is little evidence, however, that candidates with less public opinion information were at a disadvantage *because* they were unable to measure public opinion accurately. Likewise, few of the candidates admitted to doing anything more than tweaking their message slightly on account of any information they gathered through polling. The less competitive candidates had creative and often unorthodox means of gathering information about voter preferences, but they did not appear to have been led astray by this information; in most cases, they learned that their campaigns had little support among voters, and this piece of information rendered more precise measurements of public opinion relatively useless.

Issues

Although some of the issues of relevance changed between 1996 and 2000, the broader issues strategies of candidates did not. Among the 1996 candidates, as I noted in chapter 5, candidates of different competitiveness levels exhibited distinct patterns—uncompetitive candidates made little effort to discover the incumbent's strengths or weaknesses and generally ran their campaigns with little regard to the incumbent; somewhat competitive candidates exhibited the strongest attempts at convergence of any of the candidate types, although in many cases only because, in their opinion, the incumbent had co-opted their issues; and the most competitive challengers were able to point out issue differences with the incumbent in large part because the incumbent did have issue vulnerabilities. Among open-seat candidates it seems that candidates seek to converge on the most prominent issues. Similar patterns exist among the 2000 candidates.

Again, there is substantial divergence among the least competitive candidates, in part because the least competitive candidates have little intent or hope of engaging the incumbent in debate on the issues. For instance, the following three candidates are clearly running expressive campaigns:

> I think there are different philosophies between the parties. There are many issues that I disagreed with [the incumbent] on, particularly on taxes. Some of these affected a large part of the district, but others didn't. It was not a personal vendetta on my part against [the incumbent] or his party. I just feel that opposition whether you win or lose is healthy. (New Jersey)

> The Democrats right now don't talk much about religion. That was one of my reasons for getting into the race, because there's no real reason in my mind for separation of church and state. I believe God should be part of our decision making, and my campaign was about sticking to my guns about that, even if the voters or my party didn't like that philosophy. (Delaware)

> There were a lot of issues that I did not bring up because that would be attacking him. I tried to sell myself rather than attack the congressman because again, remember that you're working on the fundamental belief that you're not going to win, although you don't tell anybody that. (Pennsylvania)

The somewhat competitive candidates, as was the case in 1996, were more frustrated with their lack of success in raising issues. Many Democrats, for instance, reported that they had thought the Clinton impeachment would be a particularly divisive issue but that it did not resonate with voters. Others spoke of their uphill climb in trying to persuade voters that, in their opinion, the incumbent was not as much of a "moderate" as voters may have thought. The somewhat competitive races did feature more similar candidates than did several others. As one Republican-turned-Democrat remarked of his opponent, "He's about as progressive as a Republican can be on some issues. There are areas where our views coincide, but there are significant areas where we disagreed. I wanted to get through this campaign talking entirely about issues. The scenario was that while he expressed strong support for some issues, how he voted was different in Washington, more along the lines of traditional Republicans. We had some success on that, but clearly not enough" (Pennsylvania).

Finally, the most competitive candidates were often able to point out substantial disagreements and adopt strategies that diverged sharply from those of their opponents, in part because the incumbents did seem to be somewhat mismatched with their districts. As one Democratic challenger remarked,

> The only way to run against her, I felt—and this was borne out in our polling as well—was not to knock her. She's basically a moderate-voting individual who doesn't do anything, but she has tremendous name recognition and she's nice. But there were a lot of issues I could go after her on. She supports the death penalty, I don't. She supported some of the tax cuts, I don't. On a lot of issues, she waffles, but this is now the Democrats' seat to lose, so I could say exactly what I wanted and talk about the issues. (Maryland)

Another very competitive challenger had similar comments on his lack of a need to compromise: "I just spoke my mind. I can't do it any other way. To be very honest with you, I think that's what got me as far as I got. He said he was running on his record, and I said fine, so am I—I'm running on his record too. Because I think this is a Democratic district" (Pennsylvania).

For many analysts, campaigns at all levels in 2000 were somewhat devoid of issues (see, e.g., McWilliams 2001). As was the case in 1996, however, the starkest differences between the candidates on issues occurred in relatively uncompetitive races. It is only in these races that both candidates have the luxury of establishing strong issue positions. It is in these races that we see expressive campaigning on the part of the challengers, the raising of issues because of a belief in the importance of those issues for their own sake. In the more competitive challenges to incumbents, we again see the spectacle of challengers searching for issues to use against a rather ill-defined incumbent, or of challengers seeking to differentiate themselves on issues without adopting unpopular positions. Insofar as there were fewer candidates in 2000 in the two upper competitiveness categories, it would stand to reason that expressive campaigning was on the rise in 2000.

The Role of the Parties

In chapter 6 I noted disparities in the levels of party support for candidates of different levels of competitiveness. This, in itself, is unsurprising. What is more noteworthy, however, is that less competitive candidates do have the ability to draw upon the resources of their parties. They make greater use of "free" party information—they are likely to see their parties as a means of gathering issue information, and they are often counseled in their campaigns by local party officials and, at times, by members of their parties' congressional delegations. The type and level of this assistance varies across states, as does the amount of pressure exerted by the party to adopt any particular set of issue positions. In states with traditionally weaker parties, such as Wisconsin and Minnesota, parties can exert pressure upon candidates at all levels to adopt noncentrist positions; in states with traditionally stronger parties, such as Illinois and Ohio, parties exert no pressure upon less competitive candidates and can at times help steer more competitive candidates toward the political center. In this latter case, any steering does not represent ideological pressure as much as it entails the sharing of information on how to exploit an opponent's weak spots most effectively. Among the middling candidates, those on the bubble of receiving party support, the most tension emerges between the parties and their candidates; in such cases, candidates were most critical of their parties' choices about whom to back and felt the most pressure to "produce," to meet party fundraising targets or polling targets.

It is in the area of party support that one might expect the 2000 candidates to differ most from the candidates I interviewed in 1996. The states I selected in 2000 all have a history of strong, competitive political parties; the potential exceptions to the trends of 1996 in Ohio and Illinois would be Delaware, where the lone challenger had an absence of competition for state-level party resources, and Maryland, a state with a weak Republican Party and a Democratic Party that has seen conflict between party organizations in Baltimore and elsewhere in the state. What is notable in 2000 is the relative absence of a role for the party in the majority of races in the states with the strongest party systems, the fact that the Democratic Party intervened unsuccessfully in the primaries in two of these states' open-seat races, and the fact that some of the most competitive candidates were not running in races targeted by their party.

None of the long-shot candidates with whom I spoke in 2000 had a prior history of holding electoral office, although most had been party activists or held unelected public office. One of these candidates had previously run as the nominee of the Reform Party, while another subsequently capitalized upon his House campaign to win election as a county commissioner. In contrast, one of the three somewhat competitive candidates was a New Jersey state legislator while the other two were current or former House staff members. Three of the five very competitive candidates were elected officials; the other two included a prominent union official and a former Senate staff member turned Washington lobbyist. Of the five very competitive candidates, the three current or former elected officials were targeted by their party while the other two, although they raised substantial amount of money from organized interests, were not party targets.

The long-shot candidates reported some dissatisfaction with their party's level of assistance but were realistic about having no expectation of party support:

> They had information available for candidates. They have Web sites you can have access to. There's a lot of people running, so obviously you're not going to get 100 percent personalized attention, but I think to some degree they'll help a person develop what kind of issues they want to run on and what's important to that particular person. (New Jersey)

> In an area like this, which is 100 percent Republican, they just leave their candidates blowing in the wind. They don't say, well, let's give him a little, maybe we'll get some exposure. I would call the DCCC regularly and they would give me previews [of party events in the district], but that was all. (Pennsylvania)

These candidates reported receiving advice and reported being told frankly by national or state party officials early in their campaigns not to expect financial assistance; for the most part, the greatest assistance received by these candidates was invitations to either speak or at least hand out campaign literature at rallies for the presidential or senatorial candidates.

Somewhat competitive candidates, as was the case in 1996, exhibited the greatest frustration with their parties; many of these candidates reported early, positive discussions with their parties, only to fail to receive assistance that they had felt they might expect. It was in these races that candidates believed themselves to be losing out to neighboring, inferior candidates. In Pennsylvania, for instance, many Democratic candidates griped about the extent of DCCC support for the party's two targeted nonincumbents, challenger Patrick Casey and open-seat candidate Terry Van Horne, and many Republican candidates complained about NRCC support for challenger Stewart Greenleaf and open-seat candidate Melissa Hart. The Van Horne/Hart race, in fact, perhaps because it wound up not being particularly close (Hart won with 59 percent of the vote), inspired gripes from candidates of both parties that the DCCC and NRCC had paid too much attention to a race that was destined to be an easy Republican victory. Even candidates outside of Pennsylvania pointed to this race as an example of misguided targeting priorities for both parties, albeit particularly for Democrats. Resentment over this race was compounded by the fact that the preferred candidate of the DCCC failed to win the primary and Van Horne was judged by many to be a seriously flawed candidate.

Somewhat competitive candidates were the quickest to allege that their races could have been competitive had their parties fully understood the dynamics of the district: "Over time, because [the incumbent] has won, people have sort of taken on an exaggerated sense of how conservative the district is. So the local party is demoralized, and they don't put in the effort that they should. The state party is the same way. Maryland was a given for Al Gore and Paul Sarbanes, and they should have said we don't need to help those guys, let's see if there are any races this year where our efforts will pay off" (Maryland).

Many of these candidates reported that their party, for better or for worse, was best viewed as an assortment of individual politicians' organizations. This provided an opportunity for help where individuals were sympathetic, but it was an impediment to drawing upon an established group of individuals or source of campaign assistance and information:

> There isn't really a New Jersey Democratic Party. It's a bunch of individual fiefdoms. You've got the Torricelli fiefdom, the Lautenberg fiefdom, the Pallone fiefdom. . . . Torricelli and Pallone were helpful in fundraising and getting me to events. The official Democratic Party county chairs talk big, but they can't really do very much. (New Jersey)

The Democratic Party here isn't particularly strong. There's a perception that they were stronger when [a previous Democratic incumbent] held the district, but in reality there were three organizations—the Democratic Party, the Republican Party, and [the former incumbent's] own organization. That's just the way people are. They're attached to an individual candidate or campaign. (Pennsylvania)

Finally, the highly competitive candidates who did receive party support all reported complete satisfaction with the level of support they received, and all reported that this support had no issue-related strings attached to it. While in Pennsylvania and New Jersey there were three races apiece targeted by the parties, none of these candidates reported a sense of competition for attention with the other targeted campaigns:

The NRCC was very fair to us. One advantage we had was our consultant was doing both of the most important Republican races [in the state]. We knew everything that was going on in the other races. They were very different campaigns, but there was a lot of intermingling. I think the NRCC liked that too, because this campaign was very focused on what was going on in New Jersey. In 1998 they were all over the place, but this year the message was tailored to the individual local districts, which I think was what Denny Hastert was going for. (New Jersey)

We were complaining about how they shouldn't spend money . . . on whom, I don't recall. You can always find somebody else's campaign who's being supported who you think doesn't need the money either because they're safe or they don't have a chance. But I don't have a lot to complain about with the NRCC. My staff was pulling their chain, but that's really just part of their job. (New Jersey)

Both of the highly competitive candidates who were not running in targeted races noted a lack of constraints from their party on the issues they raised and both admitted to running campaigns that diverged sharply from the incumbent's on issues. In terms of their own satisfaction with the issue focus of their campaigns, these candidates exhibited a high level of satisfaction, but both also admitted a frustration with the party's role akin to the views of the somewhat competitive candidates:

The decision on this race was made before it even started. The Democratic Party believes its own press—that this is a race nobody can win—and it becomes self-fulfilling. There were some real issue differences here, but they didn't pay attention to the issue differences. That's a tremendous advantage for an incumbent. . . . [But] that allowed me to be free. What did I have to lose? I could say exactly what I wanted when I talked about the issues. People like that kind of straight talk. I'm lucky because I didn't have to pander. (Maryland)

Let's face it, you're sitting back in Washington and you hear there's another local union person running, you gotta prove yourself, and you've gotta raise money. I hit every target they set. I think at first they looked at this as a seat they could win, but in the final analysis, did I get the support from the DCCC I should have received? No. In a way I understand that, but in a way I don't understand. Where I got beat there wasn't a lot that was going to change those people. To be very honest with you, I just spoke my mind in the campaign, and that's what got me as far as I got. (Pennsylvania)

Both of these candidates, then, had the luxury of running expressive campaigns, and both demonstrate that, under certain circumstances (a vulnerable incumbent, a lack of attention from the party) such campaigns can result in upsets and propel to Washington candidates who differ dramatically from their predecessors. Although both lost, both outperformed many of the targeted candidates nationwide, and their campaigns attest both to the potential fallibility of parties' targeting decisions and to the potential for expressive campaigning to produce results felt within the Beltway. They indicate that expressive campaigning can potentially bring candidates to Washington, but in addition, their campaigns may, both candidates hope, result in useable information for them, their parties, or other party candidates in subsequent elections. Both candidates indicated that they were either thinking of running again in 2002 (one did, albeit unsuccessfully), were involved in attempting to recruit candidates for 2002, or, at a minimum, that they had evidence that their campaigns would prompt their parties to take a closer look at the district in the future.

Two factors are noticeably absent from the comments of all of the 2000 candidates. First, none made reference to any coat-tail effects for either Bush or Gore. Virtually uniformly, Republicans noted that, in fact, Bush had underperformed relative to the vote percentage they expected him to receive in their district, yet they hastened to point out that they did not believe this affected their campaigns. The two victorious Republican candidates both had set goals for how well they believed Bush would need to do for them to win their races, and in both cases they won despite Bush's failure to reach these targets. Among the three unsuccessful highly competitive candidates, as well as the less competitive candidates, all said that they had done better than they would have expected given their party's presidential candidate's showing in their districts. Second, no candidates reported pressure from their parties, at whatever level, to adopt particular issue positions. Some candidates noted that they believed their opponents may have been pressured by their parties to adopt positions they would not otherwise have taken. The closest any candidates came to noting any party pressure was the former Reform Party nominee, who stated that he felt Democrats had been particularly suspicious of him initially because his positions in the past had been at odds with traditional Democratic positions.

Overall, the comments on parties are substantially similar to those of the 1996 candidates. Candidates' thoughts on the information they acquired about the issue preferences of the voters, the strategy behind their own issue focus, and the role of the parties seem to indicate that the findings I have drawn out are relatively consistent across time and across regions of the country. While one might not necessarily expect the main themes of chapters 4, 5, and 6 to change dramatically across time or region of the country, these interviews provide evidence that expressive campaigning is certainly a general characteristic of most congressional campaigns. The interviews do not, of course, exhaust all potential variations in campaigns—one might, for instance, look at midterm elections, or at other distinct regions of the country—but they do indicate that the races I considered in the Midwest in 1996 are not atypical.

New Wrinkles

While politics and political culture in Pennsylvania, Maryland, Delaware, and New Jersey do not appear to exert any effects on the candidates here that put them in a substantially different light than the Midwestern candidates I considered in 1996, there are, as I note, a few smaller differences among these candidates that one might expect to alter the types of campaigns waged. The presence of an at-large district in this sample might have indicated that this is a district that state-level political actors would pay more attention to; the fact that this was not the case—the Delaware district has not been competitive for several elections—shows the limited interest state or local parties have in House elections.

The fact that state legislators in Maryland and New Jersey were not up for reelection in 2000—and thus had less to lose by running for Congress—may have led to more competitive races than one would expect in some districts. This may indeed have happened in some districts; at least three districts that I consider, as well as at least three that I did not consider from these states, featured candidates from one of these two categories. The fact that three relatively uncompetitive Maryland and New Jersey districts featured politically experienced challengers may attest to this; it may indicate that strategic politicians ran in some of these races despite steep odds against success, and it may therefore indicate that we should expect more policy convergence in these races. This phenomenon may have inflated challenger vote totals, pushing some races from the "long-shot" to the "somewhat competitive" category. The same holds true for the two suburban Maryland districts that drew current or former congressional staff members or lobbyists—here, political experience, albeit in nonelected office, is at less of a premium. If these peculiarities do betoken greater competition, though, this would in fact indicate that in other areas of the country the 2000 House races would actually have been prone to be more lopsided, and more prone to producing expressive candidates, than my interviews here show.

One factor of the 2000 races, however, is of particular importance if we are to assess the overall competitiveness of House races and the potential role of expressive campaigning in the future. One would expect that the fewer districts that are targeted by the parties and the more narrowly spread resources are for challengers, the greater the number of issue-oriented, noncentrist expressive campaigns. One might infer from Jacobson's (2001) argument that the relative paucity of competitive House races in 2000 was due to the confluence of three factors—the growing cost of waging a competitive House race and the secular trend toward a smaller number of races focused upon by the parties; the slender Republican majority in the House during the 106th Congress and the correspondingly small number of seats the Democrats would need to capture to gain the majority; and the decade-long trend of redistricting cycles, in which turnover tends to be lowest in years ending in zero, only to increase following the redrawing of House districts.

These three factors are, of course, relevant to the amounts of strategic and expressive campaigning in any election year. The secular trend argument would lead us to believe expressive campaigns should continue to increase in number. The balance of power in the House would indicate that expressive campaigning should remain with us, to its present degree, for at least the next election cycle or until one party establishes a substantial majority in the House. Yet if 2000 was a year in which many potential challengers, as well as their parties, sought to wait until districts were redrawn, we might infer that expressive campaigning is a phenomenon that wanes and waxes over the course of each decade.

Three of the four states I considered in 2000 were facing an impending redistricting, and in two of them, a dramatic reshuffling of districts was expected. In Delaware, of course, there would be no redistricting, and in New Jersey few candidates expected redistricting to dramatically alter the existing districts. Pennsylvania, however, was to lose two House seats by the 2002 election, and the clear intentions of the Republican state legislative majority and Republican governor to seek greater advantage for Republicans in the House led to much speculation on the part of the candidates with whom I spoke. In Maryland, the apparent discrepancy between the state's unbalanced partisanship and balanced House delegation also prompted speculation on the part of the candidates about what their fortunes might be in a subsequent run or what lessons state legislators might have learned from their campaigns that would affect redistricting. Some of the candidates with whom I spoke in 1996 alluded to a two-election strategy for gaining office. The fact that in 2002 many districts would be altered led to a different type of two-election strategy, in which some candidates viewed 2000 as their only chance, after which the incumbent might be drawn into a safer district if threatened, while others felt that a strong showing in 2000 might prompt sympathetic legislators to attempt to draw districts in which they would be more likely to oust the incumbent in 2002.

Apart from looking at the unique circumstances of the individual states, it is also important, for one final time, to isolate the competitiveness categories in order to look at what perspectives candidates should have on redistricting. Long-shot candidates should have little reason to have any personal stake in redistricting; their districts would have to become dramatically different for them to anticipate more favorable circumstances in a subsequent bid for office, and even if this is to be the case, they ought not to expect their party's nomination if the district does become competitive. Somewhat competitive candidates may well be mulling over a subsequent bid should their district be drawn to their party's advantage. The most competitive candidates might be anticipated to be ambivalent; for some, a better district could certainly put them over the top, but they might not find this necessary to believe they have a chance in the future. And, obviously, candidates who won would likely prefer the district to remain the same or to become slightly more favorable to them but not to have the district dramatically redrawn.

Matters do play out in this fashion among the candidates whom I interviewed. While several of the long-shot candidates speculated about what the future might bring in terms of redistricting, they did not indicate that redistricting would influence their own fortunes. These candidates were most likely to talk about fairness, about the overall composition of their state's delegation, or about improving their party's chances in the district or elsewhere without reference to future candidacies of their own:

> I would hope that this county would become one district. I know that they will try to strengthen the Republican control of Congress through redistricting, and I'm afraid that our county will be divided between three districts. That would be a disaster because we wouldn't have any representation. We'd just be being used for the northern part of the county for votes against [a neighboring incumbent]. (Pennsylvania Democrat)

> I don't think I'll have a chance to run again in that the governor's plan will prevail. He'll get his way and we'll have three Republican congressmen from up here. It's a political move, obviously, but anyone who opposes it and who's a Republican partisan is at the minimum on the horns of a dilemma. (Pennsylvania Republican)

Meanwhile, somewhat competitive candidates generally admitted to be toying with the idea of another run and hoping that their views on future redistricting decisions would be taken into account. In Democrat-controlled Maryland, for instance, one Democratic candidate who subsequently ran again in 2002 remarked: "I'm definitely considering running again. We're actually putting together a group, meeting with the county committee chairs and the senators' staffs. We're going to analyze where we did well, where we fell short, to build a plan. We've got a four-to-four delegation in a heavily Democratic state where the incumbents win 87, 86, 77, and 65 percent, so it doesn't take a genius to figure out what you need to do to win more districts" (Maryland).

In Pennsylvania, where Democrats expected to lose at least some of the few competitive districts they held, one somewhat competitive Democrat was more sanguine, mixing "fairness" motives and personal motives: "The uniqueness of this district is that since the redistricting of 1960, the district has been this county plus something. You don't find too many congressional districts that are identified with one county. There's always been an attempt to keep it that way, and there should be, but this time there probably will not be. It's a fast-growing area, so it has to change in some way. As a Democrat, it probably is not going to change to my benefit" (Pennsylvania).

Among the most competitive candidates, the prognosis of what was likely to happen in terms of partisan control was similar in each of these states, although candidates' own forecasts about their future seemed less dependent on redistricting. The campaign manager for a victorious Pennsylvania Republican noted that some lobbying to preserve the district or slightly improve it was already underway: "It's not going to get any worse. If there was a Democratic majority that controlled the legislature, they could carve up our district. But since one district in the Pittsburgh area has to be done away with, the rest have to be expanded. We would like to pick up a number of constituents she represented in the state senate. Being a former state senator, she clearly has ties to the state legislature. Given the makeup, I think it will be a slightly more favorable district" (Pennsylvania).

Finally, somewhat competitive and very competitive candidates in New Jersey concurred that there was little chance New Jersey's new districts would aid challengers of either party; again, they mixed normative views on how redistricting should work with glum assessments of any future benefits to them:

> I think districts should be as compact as is mathematically possible, that gerrymandering should be impossible. The more I study redistricting, the more I think people are going to abuse it. We have a bipartisan commission which does this, which usually means it will be a bipartisan gerrymander, which usually means an incumbent protection gerrymander. The most vulnerable Democrat and the two most vulnerable Republicans are adjacent to each other, so there are all kinds of mutually advantageous deals that can be made. I think it will be a go-along, get-along situation, so I'm not real optimistic with regards to the district being as competitive as it is now. I don't mind if I'm wrong, since I don't intend to be here next year, but I think it's important for the national party that we have more districts in New Jersey that can be won by Republicans. (New Jersey)

In previous chapters, I did note that some candidates were willing to engage in campaigns in order not necessarily to win, but to run against expectations in hopes of gaining more support in a subsequent bid. Such candidates would be likely to adopt vote-maximizing strategies even toward a losing end. To the extent that an impending redistricting might lure candidates into the 2000 race, we would again expect fewer expressive campaigns in affected states in 2000. Only one group of candidates in this study, however, could realistically expect such an outcome—Maryland Democrats. Of these four candidates, two (whom I did not interview) clearly had such a low chance of victory that they would have been unlikely to gain from redistricting; we are thus left with only two candidates who might have expected future benefits from redistricting. For the majority of

2000 challengers affected by redistricting among my interviewees, then, an impending redistricting seems likely to discourage intentions of building upon a coalition and, thus, more likely to encourage expressive campaigning.

Conclusions

The 2000 nonincumbent candidate interviews provide support for the argument advanced in the preceding chapters regarding the relative lack of candidate convergence in House elections. They indicate that the vast majority of House candidates, from the least competitive to the most competitive, design their campaigns in accordance with their beliefs about their probability of winning. In the majority of these races, candidates know that they have little or no chance of winning, and they adopt issue strategies accordingly. These candidates tend not to be motivated by the prospect of winning, and they adopt positions that can be rather extreme relative to the median voter in the district. Candidates do so because they wish to express ideas that would otherwise go unheard, to rally fellow partisans, or to educate voters. Although it is not possible to predict how frequent such campaigns will be in the future, a variety of trends noticeable when comparing the 2000 elections with those of 1996 indicate that as the number of competitive House races has declined, the frequency of expressive congressional campaigns would logically seem to have increased. Even apart from the unusually uncompetitive redistricting year of 2002, secular and less cyclical trends indicate that these types of races will remain a major part of the American political landscape for some time to come.

What is the impact of unbalanced competition in American House races? What might the impact be in the future? In the next chapter, I evaluate the normative consequences of these types of campaigns and of the prevalence of unbalanced, uncompetitive elections more generally.

CHAPTER 8

Conclusions: Expressive Politics and Invisible Politics

In the end, cynics might say, there is no getting around the fact that almost all of the candidates profiled here lost. However we might wish for a political system that provides a place for people like Floyd Brenholt, Betty Hull, or Shapley Hunter, it is hard to move beyond their opponents' gracious words in their victory speeches. One might assume that on election night, Reps. James Sensenbrenner, Phil Crane, and Jerry Costello thanked Brenholt, Hull, and Hunter for running spirited campaigns and for talking about the issues. This is standard campaign rhetoric. But does it mean anything? Could one say that congressional politics or voters are somehow better off because of campaigns such as these?

It is difficult to measure the effects of such campaigns, or to measure the more general effects of the prevalence of lopsided campaigns. Although this book is a study of congressional candidates, I first became interested in the effects of long-shot, losing campaigns through a study of presidential campaign politics. One might argue that presidential candidates in a similar long-shot position—for instance, a Barry Goldwater, a George McGovern, or a Walter Mondale—also adapted their strategies to their undeniable underdog status. There is ample evidence that at some point in their campaigns, these three candidates reconciled themselves to the inevitable and sought solace in exploring ways in which they might make a difference even in losing. It is also clear that these campaigns made a difference at some level. In the case of Goldwater, several books have been written about the effects of Goldwater's campaign on the Republican Party (Goldberg 1995; Perlstein 2001). Goldwater campaign insider Stephen Shadegg argues that Goldwater spent October of 1964 arguing that even if he lost, his campaign would serve as a wake-up call to Americans, as a "defen[se] of American society against its own indulgence, slothfulness, and apathy" (Shadegg 1965, 241). Karl Hess, another campaign staffer, noted the importance for the party of Goldwater's control of the Republican National Committee:

"this, for the future of the party, would be second in meaningfulness only to an election victory" (Klinkner 1994, 72). In the waning days of the McGovern campaign, McGovern himself told *Newsweek* that "if we don't [win], maybe some other, more effective political leader will come along and market these ideas better than I can" (*Newsweek* 1972). And Mondale defended his campaign in September of 1984 by saying, "I may lose this election, but at least I will say something in defeat" (Gillon 1992, 380).

These may all be rationalizations, but given the lessons the parties' subsequent candidates might be said to have learned from these campaigns, it would seem that each of these three, recognizing the long odds against victory, sought to reap other benefits from his campaign. Can the same be said for congressional candidates? Are there district-level stories to be told that parallel the Goldwater, McGovern, or Mondale stories?

I would not have undertaken this study if I believed these campaigns make no difference. At a minimum, these campaigns can teach both political theorists and empirical political scientists lessons about how to understand congressional campaigns, and perhaps campaign politics more generally. In this chapter I close the book by reiterating the main tenets of my argument, by exploring the lessons researchers can learn, and by exploring the normative consequences of these campaigns for American politics.

Invisible Politics and Invisible Politicians

In this book I have sought to demonstrate that a new theory is needed to explain the issue strategies of challengers to incumbents. In particular, it is necessary to explain the strategies of candidates who emerge to challenge extremely popular incumbents—incumbents who are highly unlikely to be unseated. In chapter 3 I demonstrate empirically that incumbents and challengers differ in the degree of "rationality" in their issue positions—if rationality is defined as seeking to adopt vote-maximizing positions, positions which cater to the preferences of the median voter. But it is too easy to dub the positions of losing candidates "irrational." Instead, I have argued here that we should see divergent issue positions as responses to unbalanced competition, as positions taken not in order to win but to express political views that would otherwise go unheard.

Giovanni Sartori (1976, 95–96) describes the intra-party decisions which precede establishment of issue positions as "invisible politics." We are unable to definitively get inside the heads of politicians in order to discern the reasons for the issue positions they take or the personal compromises they make. Stylized reductions of their incentives, such as Mayhew's "single-minded election-seeking" or Fenno's three-pronged categorization of congressional incumbents' motives, have been of great use in simplifying the strategic calculations of members of Congress and deriving testable hypotheses. But they are mere approximations of members' personal decision-making processes. And they definitely do not get us very far in understanding the decisions of nonincumbent candidates. The invisible politics of which Sartori speaks, however, is, he writes, "more simple, and more genuine" than is visible, or "rational" political behavior (Sartori 1976, 96). In the case of the candidates I describe here, it is a politics of actual preferences, actual beliefs, which are often put forward without reference to instrumental concerns.

The candidates studied here are invisible in another sense, however. They ran campaigns which garnered scant media interest, scant voter interest, and even scant interest on the part of the incumbent. Not all of the candidates studied here ran "invisible" campaigns, but the majority did. The invisibility of these campaigns has brought about much research by political scientists, but it is ultimately research which moves us toward explaining why incumbents are so safe, and away from the campaigns of those who challenge incumbents. This is our loss, as these campaigns are an important part of political discourse, and they are often happening right under our noses.

The explanation I have provided here for the strategies of these candidates does not diverge dramatically from established game-theoretic models of candidate competition. My explanation does not contain precise candidate equilibria, and hence it does not rise to, or aspire to rise to, the sophistication of many well-established models. This is because the intuition behind it is quite simple. Spatial models of candidate competition generally can be distilled down to three essential variables: information, both about voter preferences and about one's opponent's issue position; candidate positions themselves; and the outcome (or expected outcome) of the election given any set of candidate positions. If an incumbency advantage is established, I argue, it must inhere in part to the positions of the incumbent, and it must be a piece of information that is known to both candidates. Where an incumbency advantage exists, then, information is neither particularly costly nor scarce for either candidate—in the incumbent's case, because of the resources that come with incumbency; in the challenger's case, because the incumbent's performance and positions are observable.

Where voter preferences and the opposing candidate's positions can be known to a candidate, this must only be because that candidate does not adopt positions at the same time as her opponent. That is, candidates position themselves sequentially, not simultaneously. Where candidates are taking positions sequentially and the first mover has behaved rationally, the vote maximization assumption seems somewhat suspect for the candidate adopting positions second. After all, what is the purpose of a candidate in a plurality or majority rule, first-past-the-post election expending resources in order to get more votes than are necessary to win, or seeking as many votes as possible in what is doomed to be a losing effort? Here, I propose two different alternatives, which I dub the *expressive campaign* and the *party-based campaign*. The intuition behind these alternatives is that where an incumbent has an advantage and has adopted a median position, a challenger's probability of winning is virtually nonexistent. For a challenger in such circumstances, the goal is the campaign itself, not its outcome.

In chapters 3 through 6 I have sought to document the various tenets of this argument—that challengers do not tend to take positions in accordance with voter preferences; that they have information that is "good enough" for them to be aware that they are doing this; that they are eager to speak at length about their desire to express their policy views, even at the expense of votes, in their campaigns; and that parties can influence challenger positions but that well-organized parties choose not to do this. Thus, I conclude that both sequential positioning alternatives hold, that these constructs do serve to explain the strategic choices made by these candidates. In chapter 7 I provide evidence that the patterns noted in the previous three chapters are not atypical, that they are not patterns limited to one particular set of states or one particular election year. Furthermore, chapter 7 presents the possibility that the frequency of expressive campaigns may increase with documented trends in the safety of incumbents. Expressive campaigning, then, may wax and wane over time but remains a major component of American congressional elections.

There are three sets of implications for this argument—implications for theorists of candidate competition, implications for those who study American politics, and implications for those with a normative belief in the importance of competitive elections and substantive discourse about issues in those elections. In the remainder of this chapter, I thus entertain the implications of my argument for each of these fields of inquiry, and I note areas in which additional research would clarify and extend my argument.

Implications and Directions for Further Research: Theories of Candidate Competition

At the most basic level, the research I present here should encourage those who would construct theories of candidate competition to look more closely at the sequential nature of electoral competition. The work of

Groseclose (2001) and of Feld and Grofman (1991) that I discuss in chapter 2 presages a move in that direction, but the theory I elaborate here seems to square well enough with the self-reported strategic decisions of challengers to incumbents that I find it remarkable that sequential theories of candidate positioning have not gained wider currency. Similar theories of behavior in legislatures have been proposed (see Baron 1995), as have expectation-based models concerning candidate entry (see Cox 1997; Greenberg and Shepsle 1987). It may only be a matter of time before such theories are applied more extensively to campaigns and elections.

The theory I propose here contains several assumptions which represent breaks with established literature. I have sought in the qualitative chapters of this book to demonstrate their validity for the elections I cover. Each of these assumptions can, I argue, be extended and elaborated upon. I shall consider each of these in turn, in accordance with the sequence of empirical chapters I have provided here.

Information

The full information assumption has often been questioned when it has been employed to explain politicians' choices. I have weakened this assumption somewhat, by demonstrating that the candidates considered here had information thresholds—that they were able to acquire "full enough" information for the purposes of their campaigns. In addition, in a sequential model the second mover has the luxury of being able to base choices upon his or her beliefs about the level of information the first mover has. For instance, a challenger can observe the positions taken by an incumbent, and if that incumbent has had substantial electoral success at those positions, he or she may well assume that the incumbent has identified the median. If that challenger wishes to capture the median, then, all he or she has to do is to ape the strategy of the incumbent.

This begs the question, however, of how incumbents gain their information. Hall (1995) addresses the import of the full information assumption for studying legislators' behavior and concludes that its frequent use in establishing models of legislative behavior provides a test of the assumption, a test which it has frequently passed. The full information assumption seems less controversial, however, in the framework I use here. The unidimensional framework and the relatively simple constraints provided by voters' ability to process information about candidates—is a candidate, for instance, for or against gun control?—makes the full information criterion much easier to meet in electoral competition than it is in legislative activity. Nonetheless, an elaboration of where and when information thresholds exist in campaigns, or when a particular level of information is enough, would be welcome.

Issue Positions

Measuring candidates' issue positions is another substantial problem for testing spatial models of candidate behavior. The scale I employ in chapter 3 has no provisions for weighting according to intensity, and it is composed of a series of yes/no question responses—it does not measure whether candidates have more subtle preferences over each of these issues. This is a problem that plagues many spatial analyses. Political scientists have labored to measure the positions of incumbent legislators, yet nonincumbent candidates are far more difficult to measure. I have sought to overcome this problem through my reliance upon the open-ended interview questions I posed to a subset of these candidates, but even before more data are collected on these candidates, a clearer means by which to identify the ideal points of candidates—particularly those without a legislative record—must be constructed.

Candidates' Preferences

One area in which further work is possible using the framework I provide here, and without either conducting a tremendous amount of extra research or laboring to resolve theoretical quandaries such as those I outline above, is in gauging the trade-offs between candidates' *ex ante* ideal points and positions taken to maximize utility in terms of votes or probability of winning. In the theory I present here, I judged it to be somewhat of a detour to provide indifference curves or other mathematical mechanisms for assessing how a candidate moves from maximization of utility along one dimension toward utility maximization on the other. This all should depend upon the weight each candidate assigns to each incentive. For the sake of illustration, I proposed a simple stylized depiction of this movement with a tipping point—either the challenger believes himself or herself to be competitive (and hence maximizes proximity to the district median) or does not (and hence maximizes proximity to his or her noninstrumental ideal point). One could, of course, posit other, less clear trade-offs; for instance, a candidate's utility along one dimension could decline in a linear or curvilinear fashion across different positions. A candidate could weigh these two values differently, and thus find some winning positions inferior to certain losing positions (that is, some issue stances may be nonnegotiable) or the candidate may find probability of winning not to be the stark either/or proposition I have established here. Elaboration of these tradeoffs would not be difficult, although testing them would be. Continued movement among political scientists away from solely positing election-seeking goals or outcome-based goals toward study of more purely ideological or expressive motivations would certainly aid in the development of electoral models which feature candidates with varying prospects for success.

Political Parties

Finally, rational choice theories which posit a role for political parties must take fuller account of the differences between in-parties and out-parties, or in the case of my argument here, of parties which do have an opportunity to be competitive and those which do not. In the ongoing debate between Krehbiel and much of the rest of the positive theory community, Krehbiel (1998, 165–72) has argued that inserting parties into legislative models does not help us gain leverage upon legislative decision making. The most important criticism leveled by Krehbiel is that responsible party government or conditional party government theories cannot be tested because they have no provision for estimating legislators' "true" ideal points—they measure party strength using voting outcomes, which, in turn, are the phenomena they are seeking to explain.

Analysis of nonincumbent candidates provides a way around this problem in two ways. First, it provides a baseline for judging candidates' preferences prior to reaching office, although this baseline is still complicated by our inability to conclusively distinguish between expressive and strategic positions. Second, however, it also provides, as I posit in chapter 2 and demonstrate in chapter 6, a means of gauging party unity in elections. It may seem paradoxical to look for the voice of the party in the campaigns of candidates who lose their election bids, but this may be the greatest opportunity in American electoral politics to seek to identify party positions without such positions being contaminated by election-oriented behavior. At the very least, identifying party positions in this sense can provide a means of estimating how far election-seeking politicians or officeholders deviate from such party positions.

Implications and Directions for Further Research: The Study of Nonincumbent Candidates

At a minimum, the research I present here should also call to the reader's attention the paucity of research on congressional challengers. Although Congress may well be among the most studied of American institutions, we know precious little about individuals who run for Congress save those who win or come close to winning. The Maisel and Stone (1997; also Stone, Maisel, and Maestas 1998; Stone and Maisel 2003) candidate emergence study should be of great help in identifying the barriers to competition in many congressional districts, but the congressional candidates who do emerge are rarely studied on the scale I attempt here, let alone on a national scale. There are substantial costs to undertaking such a study; I have sought here to go beyond the scale of studies such as those of Kingdon, Huckshorn and Spencer, and Leuthold, but a truly random, qualitative study of congressional challengers remains prohibitively expensive for the average researcher. It is much easier to conduct qualitative, interview-based research in Washington, where all incumbents are gathered, than it is to venture out across the country to track down unsuccessful candidates.

Surveys such as the *Time/Congressional Quarterly* Candidate Survey discussed in chapters 3 and 6 are one means of remedying this problem. Because the *Time/Congressional Quarterly* study appears not to have been constructed with statistical research in mind, however, its utility for this project was somewhat limited. Many congressional candidates run such low-profile campaigns that they are eager for attention, whether the source is political scientists, journalists, or any other interested party. All but one of the 1996 candidates I was able to locate were eager to speak with me; their enthusiasm indicates that they would be a valuable source of information for any researcher.

More specific implications and research subjects coincide, as is the case with the theoretical implications, with the organization of this book:

Information

My argument about information acquisition is that candidates do, regardless of their financial resources, have the ability to gather relatively accurate information about voter preferences. I investigate such information acquisition through relatively open-ended questions to candidates about their information sources and about their rationale for position taking. My conclusions in this regard are admittedly a judgment of the veracity of candidates' claims and the plausibility of their claims about public opinion. Using district-level survey data on political issues would provide a valuable means of verifying candidates' claims. In addition, investigating the specific questions asked when candidates do poll, how voters respond, and how well-constructed these surveys are for objectively measuring public opinion would provide a better sense of the value of such polls in measuring voter preferences. Unfortunately, most of these polls are proprietary, and the candidates I interviewed who conducted polls often seemed quite removed from the administration of such polls and not well enough versed in survey research to understand the potential uses of such polls. More detailed studies of such polls thus await the cooperation of the firms who conduct them.

Issue Positions

In the theory I have presented here, I posit two different incentives for position-taking-strategic maximization of votes or probability of winning, and expression of one's actual political beliefs. There are, of course, many other motivations for position taking. As Maisel (1986, 24) argues, many congressional candidates adopt positions with an eye toward the future, toward another race for Congress or another office, or merely with an eye toward gaining customers for their businesses.

Any model which posits *ex ante* preferences begs the question of how these preferences arise. Such a question is, of course, so large that it goes far beyond the scope of this book and far beyond the issue of studying congressional candidates. Two more modest means by which the formation of issue positions could be studied are, however, to study congressional candidates before and after their campaigns or to track these candidates for a period of time after their campaigns end. I chose not to interview candidates during their campaigns because of concerns that I would not be able to interview them—they would, after all, be busy campaigning—and because I was concerned about the veracity of any information they would provide me. A pre-/post-interview format would, however, enable the researcher to measure how much candidates' views or statements change after the campaign. In addition, a study such as the Maisel and Stone study would be of use insofar as it gathers information about potential candidates before they actually enter the race.

Likewise, tracking candidates after their campaigns would allow the researcher to investigate whether candidates who take positions geared toward helping them in the future—in another race for Congress, for instance—do benefit from their campaigns in this manner. Surely some candidates profiled here had such goals in mind—of my case-study candidates, John Shimkus was a second-time candidate for Congress when he won, Lydia Spottswood and Mary Rieder would go on to run again in 1998 and 2000, respectively, and Cynthia Ruccia ran twice for Congress before deciding to use her knowledge and name-recognition to run for a lesser office. Evidence on whether candidates benefit in repeat bids for Congress from their first race is mixed (see Squire and Smith 1984; Levitt 1994; Mack 1998; Milyo 1998; Boatright and Taylor 2001). More qualitative research could, however, shed greater light on the realism of candidates' future-oriented goals.

Political Parties

The conclusions I reach about the role of political parties in these candidates' campaigns have been explored by numerous researchers. Such studies are hampered, however, by the difficulty of gaining access to all that goes on within political parties at their various levels. Especially with the increasing role of the national campaign committees in congressional campaigns and the corresponding decline of the local party machines which were the subject of so much party research in the past, it is difficult to identify the role of smaller party units—of the county-level or district-level party organizations. In many of the campaigns considered here, these organizations served as little more than clubs for a small group of the party faithful. Nonetheless, these organizations are important units of study if we wish to shed light upon the candidate recruitment process. Again, efforts such as the candidate emergence study and the Kazee edited volume may help in this regard. The party decline and party centralization arguments leave little room for these types of party organizations. Yet, as I show in a number of the campaigns considered here, party organizations at this level do play a vital role in campaigns. In states with more ideological parties, they may prevent viable candidates from emerging; in states with less ideological parties, they may serve a vital function because they do encourage viable candidates and they may keep a semblance of party organization—of organizational memory, perhaps—in place to be drawn upon in the future. Here, a comparison of competition over time, holding region (and therefore party organization) constant, may provide some answers.

Normative Implications

Throughout this book I have eschewed normative claims about the candidates I study here or about the implications of my theory for representative democracy. In chapters 1 and 2 I sought to distinguish normative theories of how candidates for office *should* behave from positive theories of how we might actually expect them to behave. As I argue in chapter 1, however, it is possible to understand the genesis of spatial models of candidate competition as a response to normative theories of responsible political parties. Thus, because my theory does posit a role for political parties, it does speak to the prescriptive elements of responsible party theory.

In addition, the candidates whom I consider here are of theoretical interest precisely because they could reasonably expect to lose. Because the vast majority of them did lose, it is difficult to draw normative lessons from their campaigns. These candidates present a paradox because we may well look at the positions they took in their campaigns and conclude that they deserved to lose—they took positions which did not represent the preferences of a majority of their would-be constituents, and most voters, accordingly, voted against them. To claim, based upon these candidates' commitment to running for office against overwhelming odds, and based upon their often principled adherence to unpopular positions, that they deserved to win would be somewhat unfounded; it would be a normative argument against the positive theory I have outlined here. In fact, it would be nothing more than an expressive statement on my part.

These two claims do lead, however, to several normative results of my theory. First, and most importantly, this theory does provide some grounding for investigating party responsibility. Following Riker's (1982a, 1982b, 1997) withering normative argument against the responsible party theory, it is evident from the actions of candidates in states which feature ideological, divergent parties that responsible party government is not possible, but that responsible parties are. In other words, a responsible party is a losing party. Conversely, a party which expects to lose has the luxury of taking "responsible" positions. We are able to identify party ideologies in the campaigns of losing candidates, while they are absent in the campaigns of more competitive candidates. This may well have a normative, expressive value—it gives extremists or holders of unpopular views a vehicle for expressing their views, albeit in a losing effort. Those who search for "a choice, not an echo" often need look no further than their own congressional district to find divergent policy views—but they only find them because the outcome of that election is virtually preordained.

Second, one might respond to this finding by seeking to reward such candidates—by, for instance, calling for campaign finance reforms which would remedy the inequalities which exist in congressional campaigns. While there are certainly sound arguments to be made for campaign finance reform, my argument is not necessarily one of them. Campbell (2003) has shown conclusively that the most recent campaign finance reform legislation, the Bipartisan Campaign Reform Act, will have little effect on competition. Even campaign finance reforms that do affect competition would not, according to the logic of the sequential positioning alternatives I propose, yield significantly different types of incumbents. Divergent pairs of positions occur because one candidate has little or no chance of victory. If that candidate's probability of winning is increased, there is no reason not to expect that candidate to abandon such positions and adopt a more centrist strategy. There is also no reason to expect that the types of ideologically motivated candidates who emerge as long shots would secure their party's nomination if the expectation was that the race would be competitive. I have argued here that the "quality candidate" measurement developed by Jacobson and others has little bearing upon spatial competition, but the type of candidate that emerges certainly is a major determinant of the type of competition which results. In remedying campaign funding inequalities, we might engender more visible congressional races, and we might well expect greater turnover in Congress. We would not, however, necessarily introduce dramatically new ideas into the policy process. In the end, I would argue, the more we seek to reward divergent, "responsible" party agendas, the more we seek to reward them, the more they will recede from our grasp.

Third, however, one does not need to be elected to office to "represent" voters. As I noted in chapter 1, a median voter scenario predicts that those who hold extreme views, or even views slightly away from the political center, can be left out of government entirely. Few would argue that in the current U.S. system there is not significant variation in the views of elected representatives. Yet the issue positions of congressional challengers, and the similarity or dissimilarity of those positions to those of other elected representatives, can tell us how much of legislative activity corresponds to the merely descriptive traits of ideological or partisan minorities within congressional districts. They can tell us much about the degree to which our legislature does represent ideological minorities within the public. That is, if there are ideas present in the campaigns of congressional challengers which are absent in the discourse of congressional incumbents, we might conclude that significant minorities of the public are not represented in governmental policy deliberation.

To bring this rather theoretical argument into the real world, one might point to the fact that congressional representatives are, on occasion, said to represent constituencies other than their geographical constituency. Mansbridge (2003) refers to this as "surrogate representation." An African American representative, for instance, might be said to represent the views of African Americans in general, even where those African Americans said to be represented do not reside within his or her congressional district. The same is often said to hold for other racial or ethnic groups, for women, for gays and lesbians, or for religious or ethnic minorities. The same is also said, albeit less frequently, to hold true for members of Congress who espouse particularly extreme ideological sentiments. A particularly liberal member of Congress—a Paul Wellstone or a Ted Kennedy—is often said to represent the views of other liberals nationwide. We cannot conclusively separate out the election-seeking motive of candidates such as these from these candidates' actual *ex ante* ideal points, but we can do so in the case of many congressional challengers. Matching the positions and issue emphases of particularly liberal congressional challengers to those of incumbents, in this case, can tell us to what degree the policy preferences of the left actually do find representation within Congress. Not only can we identify pure partisan views, but we can also identify particular issues that may or may not find representation within Congress.

To take this argument a step further, one might also hypothesize a particular drawing of legislative districts such that particular ideological views find no representation within government. One might suppose, for instance, that holders of a particular view are divided such that they are a majority in no congressional district, but that they represent a large minority of the constituents of a larger geographic entity. Rural areas of a state, for instance, might be allocated to congressional districts such that they are a minority within each of several congressional districts even though the sum total of rural residents within the state might be equivalent to one or more congressional districts. Such views may not find representation within government, but given the often low costs of mounting a congressional challenge (especially a long-shot challenge that few election-oriented politicians would undertake), such views should show up in the platforms of congressional challengers. The ability to assess such views, the degree to which they are distinct, and the degree to which they find representation within Congress, can tell us much about the representativeness, in both the descriptive and the "action-oriented" senses, of our government. I make no claims to have answered this question here, but I would argue that I have established a groundwork and a theoretical rationale for doing so.

Fourth, and finally, I direct the reader's attention back to the justifications for the study of congressional challengers—and of political "losers" more generally—that I provide in the introductory chapter. Several of the reasons I provide there for concern with congressional challengers—the fact that they do occasionally win, that they keep incumbents busy, that they can send messages to incumbents, that they can assist other candidates—are difficult to prove empirically. All of these functions are outcome-oriented; that is, they go beyond the campaign itself. Each of these potential reasons proposes a link, however tenuous it may be, between the issues raised in the campaign and the legislative activity of an officeholder, whether that office holder be the challenger himself or herself (following an election victory), the incumbent being challenged, or another, more successful, candidate of the challenger's party.

It seems easier, however, to simply say that these candidates are here, and that for this reason alone they are worthy of understanding. As I noted in chapter 1, political theorists have sought to provide justifications for political participation *for its own sake,* irrespective of its instrumental consequences. These candidates provide an example of such participation. I certainly saw much of this in my research. During one interview, our conversation was frequently interrupted as the candidate's neighbors stopped by to drop off checks intended to help defray campaign costs; another interview took place following a sparsely attended yet boisterous meeting of the Butler County, Ohio, Democratic Party; and still another took place at the annual convention of the Democratic Socialists. Each of these interviews featured candidates who had been defeated handily, yet the enthusiastic reception these candidates received (after their election defeat) from neighbors, friends, and colleagues was proof that these candidates and their allies were enthusiastic political participants, not single-minded seekers of election. Such participation may be said to provide a channeling of dissent for disenchanted ideological minorities, a voice for the unrepresented, a legitimization of minority views, or merely an opportunity to exercise free speech. We cannot prove empirically that these candidacies served any purpose, but the observations I have made here seem to provide evidence that they fulfill this function.

In a similar manner, academics and nonacademics of all political viewpoints frequently hold competition to be a good in and of itself in American life. It is possible to argue that competition is valuable without overly concerning ourselves with the ideas placed into the competition. In *Federalist #53,* James Madison argues forcefully that the heterogeneity of economic and cultural circumstances within the United States ought to be fully represented within the American Congress (Madison 1961 [1787],

333). Investigating the campaigns of nonincumbent candidates is, as I argue above, a crucial means of verifying whether or not this is so. According to the argument I have presented here, expressions of such heterogeneity only occur, again, where the competition is particularly unbalanced.

Another early theorist of American democracy, Thomas Jefferson, might be seen as arguing that even in such cases the ideas presented are still worthy of study, that they make us all stronger even where we do not share them. Writing on the necessity of tolerance of and freedom for minority religious viewpoints in the early American Republic, Jefferson argues that "It does me no injury for my neighbour to say that there are twenty gods, or no god. It neither picks my pocket or breaks my leg. . . . Truth can stand by itself. Why subject it to coercion? To produce uniformity. But is uniformity of opinion desirable? No more than of face and stature" (Jefferson 1999 [1785], 165–66).

Jefferson's argument can easily be read as an argument for the introduction of diverse viewpoints into political debate. These ideas can inform us, can shape our own thinking, even where they are not successful at the ballot box. At the very least, they can make us question our own opinions, even if we are only to reaffirm these same opinions after thinking about them. No more powerful argument for the importance of candidate divergence need be made. In this book I have argued that competitive elections and governmental behavior are not the correct place to look for divergent, contrasting views. This does not mean that such views do not, or should not, exist in American elections. It is easy to argue that our public policy is ill-served by the advantage incumbents hold in American elections. It is harder to see virtue in the same phenomena. I would not argue that my theory provides a rationale for identifying virtue in such circumstances, but I would argue that it provides a rationale for applying more careful scrutiny to both candidates in such elections and, in the end, for seeking to understand the rational motivations behind the campaigns of candidates even where these campaigns are unlikely to end in victory.

Notes

Notes to Introduction

1. The answer to the inevitable trivia question here is William Howard Taft, Herbert Hoover, Gerald Ford, Jimmy Carter, and George H. W. Bush.

2. Even Senate races tend to draw more attention from party leaders—see Westlye 1991 and Krasno 1994, 72–102 for a comparison of House and Senate races on this point.

Notes to Chapter 1

1. In fact, Zaller (1998) argues that the incumbency advantage has been dramatically overstated, and that what appears to be an incumbency advantage is merely the fact that electoral selection produces incumbents who generally tend to be better politicians than their opponents.

2. Banks and Kiewiet (1989) argue that these political "amateurs" appear precisely because they have the best chance to win in such races—that were the incumbent expected to be vulnerable, they would not be viable candidates for their party's nomination and thus can only surmount this first hurdle toward winning election in races expected to be uncompetitive.

3. See Wittman (1973) for a more formal treatment of this argument.

4. Putnam (2000, 41) is an exception to this rule. For other political participation works, this omission is not due to an oversight by authors, but, most likely, due to the extremely small number of citizens who run for office.

Notes to Chapter 2

1. While simultaneous positioning, as in a one-shot game, is certainly not the same as a game with endless iterations, or unrestricted ability to reposition, the results here are identical. Where candidates take positions simultaneously, one candidate does not know what position the other candidate will take; if there is no limit to the number of moves that can be made, a candidate cannot know how his opponent will respond to any position taken. The result in both cases is convergence at the median. For simplicity, I refer to such a scenario in this chapter as simultaneous positioning.

2. This type of division-of-benefits framework is also used in Aldrich's (1995) conditional party government model.

3. These are circumstances that drive models in which information asymmetries lead to divergence, as is the case in Ferejohn and Noll 1978.

Notes to Chapter 3

1. For a discussion of problems in using ADA scores and a review of major works that have used ADA scores to measure the positions of members of Congress, see Groseclose, Levitt, and Snyder 1999.

2. For other work using media surveys of congressional candidates in this fashion, see Erikson and Wright 1989; Wright 1986; Wright and Berkman 1986.

3. For evidence on the relationship between these issues and 1996 congressional voting, see Ferejohn 1998.

4. On the gays in the military question, it appears that incumbents may have viewed the "don't ask, don't tell" policy as a compromise position that was to the right of what the Clinton administration had initially proposed. A majority of Democratic incumbents, including most of those in the more liberal wing of the party, opposed the policy, while a majority of Republican incumbents supported it. It appears—and I have verified this in conversation with nonincumbents of each party—that nonincumbents viewed this question as a comparison of the "don't ask, don't tell" policy with the status quo ante, the ban on homosexuals in the military that had been in place prior to the Clinton administration's proposal to lift the ban entirely.

The differences in the EPA question are somewhat less subtle; the overwhelming difference between incumbents and nonincumbents in each party suggests that, insofar as incumbents could refer to their voting on the particular bill in question while nonincumbents could not, many nonincumbents misunderstood the question. The question is phrased in a confusing manner, with a double negative that may have caused many respondents to give the exact opposite response of what they intended. Again, I have tested this on a selection of the candidates themselves.

5. This was conservative Texas Democrat Ralph Hall's reelection bid. Hall won easily.

6. Several candidates who declined to answer the questions on the *Time/Congressional Quarterly* survey attached written statements making a similar argument when they returned their uncompleted surveys.

7. The correlation between the competitiveness categories and 1992 party presidential vote share is .559 for the fifty-seven candidates considered here. The mean 1992 party presidential vote share in the districts of long-shot candidates was 29.95 percent; for somewhat competitive candidates, 36.76 percent; and for very competitive candidates, 43.07 percent.

8. See Westlye (1991) for a similar distinction in analyzing Senate challengers' campaigns.

Note to Chapter 4

1. This district was substantially redrawn after the 2000 elections; the majority of it is now in the Nineteenth District.

Notes to Chapter 5

1. Data from Herrnson's 1998 survey (in Herrnson 2000, 195) are much more ambiguous; there is no significant difference in the degree to which competitive and uncompetitive challengers focused on issues, and incumbents are less likely to focus on image or personality.

2. The issue categories I use in figure 5.1 do not precisely parallel those of the *Time/Congressional Quarterly* survey, but given the question wording, the Brady Bill question could be categorized as a measure of attitudes on crime and on guns, while the Clinton Budget question mentions healthcare issues. The FMLA question also could capture attitudes on healthcare.

3. The absence of references to Clinton's gays in the military proposal is also interesting in light of Ferejohn's (1998, 57) finding that gays in the military was among the strongest issue-based predictors of candidates' 1994 vote share.

4. Four of them were right.

5. Following the 2000 redistricting, this district became the Fifth District. The partisan composition of the district was not substantially changed.

6. In the 1996 elections, minor parties were permitted to cross-endorse major party candidates in Minnesota. A subsequent Supreme Court ruling, *Timmons v. Twin City Area New Party*, overturned this policy after the election (see Ryden 1999).

Notes to Chapter 6

1. Herrnson and Patterson (2002), for instance, find that in 2000, 82 percent of DCCC hard-money contributions and 91 percent of NRCC hard-money contributions went to candidates in competitive races; a total of ninety challengers received contributions from the DCCC or NRCC.

2. As is the case with Mary Rieder in chapter 5, this candidate was cross-endorsed by the Reform Party.

3. See Burden 2001a for a similar argument regarding congressional primaries.

4. Costello did face a tougher opponent in 1998; the Republican nominee was the son of Costello's Democratic predecessor, Melvin Price. Although the NRCC purchased advertisements attacking Costello for his ethics problems, Costello still won with 60 percent of the vote (Duncan and Nutting 1999, 455).

Notes to Chapter 7

1. Five of these were in Louisiana, where a winner of the majority of the vote in the state's "jungle primary" does not face opposition in the general election. Excluding Louisiana, the figure for uncontested incumbents is 23.0 percent.

2. Personal communication from Barry C. Burden, December 19, 2003.

Interviews

(All interviews are unpublished. They are arranged by year, state, and House district.)

1996 Interviews

Illinois

Noel Naughton. Republican challenger to Representative Bobby Rush (IL-1). Evergreen Park, Illinois. January 23, 1997.
Jim Nalepa. Republican challenger to Representative William Lipinski (IL-3). LaGrange, Illinois. November 19, 1996.
Deanne Benos, press secretary to Representative Rod Blagojevich, Democratic challenger to Representative Michael Flanagan (IL-5). Washington, DC. April 28, 1997.
Steve de la Rosa. Democratic challenger to Representative Henry Hyde (IL-6). Chicago, Illinois. November 16, 1996.
Randy Borow. Republican open seat candidate (IL-7). North Riverside, Illinois, December 16, 1996.
Ira Cohen, district press secretary to Representative Danny Davis, Democrat, open seat candidate (IL-7). Chicago, Illinois. May 15, 1997.
Elizabeth Hull. Democratic challenger to Representative Phillip Crane (IL-8). Palatine, Illinois. November 21, 1996.
Joseph Walsh. Republican challenger to Representative Sidney Yates (IL-9). Chicago, Illinois. November 20, 1996.
Phillip Torf. Democratic challenger to Representative John Porter (IL-10). Deerfield, Illinois. December 4, 1996.
Clem Balanoff. Democratic challenger to Representative Jerry Weller (IL-11). Chicago, Illinois. December 6, 1996.
Shapley Hunter. Republican challenger to Representative Jerry Costello (IL-12). Tamms, Illinois. February 5, 1997.
Susan Hynes. Democratic challenger to Representative Harris Fawell. (IL-13). Naperville, Illinois. December 19, 1996.
Douglas Mains. Democratic challenger to Representative Dennis Hastert (IL-14). West Chicago, Illinois. December 10, 1996.
Laurel Lunt Prussing. Democratic challenger to Representative Thomas Ewing (IL-15). By telephone. January 28, 1997.
Catherine Lee. Democratic challenger to Representative Donald Manzullo (IL-16). Barrington, Illinois. December 12, 1996.
Mark Baker. Republican challenger to Representative Lane Evans (IL-17). Quincy, Illinois. February 10, 1997.

Mike Curran. Democratic challenger to Representative Ray LaHood (IL-18). Springfield, Illinois. February 10, 1997.

Jay Hoffman. Democratic open seat candidate (IL-20). Belleville, Illinois. February 5, 1997.

Craig Roberts, chief of staff to Representative John Shimkus, Republican open seat candidate (IL-20). Washington, DC. April 30, 1997.

Minnesota

Mary Rieder. Democratic challenger to Representative Gil Gutknecht (MN-1). Eyota, Minnesota. February 28, 1997.

Gary Revier. Republican challenger to Representative David Minge (MN-2). Redwood Falls, Minnesota. February 28, 1997.

Dennis Newinski. Republican challenger to Representative Bruce Vento (MN-4). Maplewood, Minnesota. March 4, 1997.

Jack Uldrich. Republican challenger to Representative Martin Sabo (MN-5). St. Paul, Minnesota. March 3, 1997.

Tad Jude. Republican challenger to Representative Bill Luther (MN-6). Fridley, Minnesota. March 1, 1997.

Darrell McKigney. Republican challenger to Representative Colin Peterson (MN-7). White Bear Lake, Minnesota. June 19, 1997.

Andy Larson. Republican challenger to Representative James Oberstar (MN-8). Duluth, Minnesota. June 19, 1997.

Ohio

Mark Longabaugh. Democratic challenger to Representative Steve Chabot (OH-1). By telephone. July 17, 1997.

Tom Chandler. Democratic challenger to Representative Rob Portman (OH-2). Cincinnati, Ohio. April 23, 1997.

David Westbrock. Republican challenger to Representative Tony Hall (OH-3). Dayton, Ohio. July 1, 1997.

Paul McClain. Democratic challenger to Representative Mike Oxley (OH-4). Mansfield, Ohio. April 22, 1997.

Annie Saunders. Democratic challenger to Representative Paul Gillmor (OH-5). Norwalk, Ohio. April 22, 1997.

Jess Goode, press secretary to Representative Ted Strickland, Democratic challenger to Representative Frank Cremeans (OH-6). Washington, DC. April 29, 1997.

Richard Blain. Democratic challenger to Representative David Hobson (OH-7). Springfield, Ohio. July 2, 1997.

Jeffrey Kitchen. Democratic challenger to Representative John Boehner (OH-8). Hamilton, Ohio. July 1, 1997.

Randy Whitman. Republican challenger to Representative Marcy Kaptur (OH-9). Toledo, Ohio. April 22, 1997.

Cynthia Ruccia. Democratic challenger to Representative John Kasich (OH-12). Bexley, Ohio. April 23, 1997.

Ken Blair. Republican challenger to Representative Sherrod Brown (OH-13). Newbury, Ohio. April 21, 1997.
Joyce George. Republican challenger to Representative Tom Sawyer (OH-14). Akron, Ohio. April 25, 1997.
Cliff Arnebeck. Democratic challenger to Representative Deborah Pryce (OH-15). Columbus, Ohio. April 23, 1997.
Thomas Burkhart. Democratic challenger to Representative Ralph Regula (OH-16). Ashland, Ohio. April 25, 1997.
Robert Burch. Democratic challenger to Representative Robert Ney (OH-18). By telephone. August 6, 1997.
Thomas Coyne. Democratic challenger to Representative Steve LaTourette (OH-19). Brook Park, Ohio. December 23, 1996.

Wisconsin

Lydia Spottswood. Democratic challenger to Representative Mark Neumann (WI-1). Kenosha, Wisconsin. December 17, 1996.
Paul Uebehler, campaign manager to Paul Soglin, Democratic challenger to Representative Scott Klug (WI-2). Madison, Wisconsin. May 20, 1997.
James Harsdorf. Republican open seat candidate (WI-3). Beldenville, Wisconsin. June 18, 1997.
Mike Fahey, press secretary to Representative Ron Kind, Democratic open seat candidate (WI-3). Washington, DC. April 29, 1997.
Tom Reynolds. Republican, challenger to Representative Jerry Kleczka (WI-4). West Allis, Wisconsin. January 23, 1997.
Paul Melotik. Republican challenger to Representative Thomas Barrett (WI-5). Milwaukee, Wisconsin. February 25, 1997.
Scott West. Republican challenger to Representative David Obey (WI-7). Stevens Point, Wisconsin. May 20, 1997.
Karissa Johnson, chief of staff to Representative Jay Johnson, Democratic open seat candidate (WI-8). Washington, DC. April 28, 1997.
David Prosser. Republican open seat candidate (WI-8). Madison, Wisconsin. July 22, 1997.
Floyd Brenholt. Democratic challenger to Representative James Sensenbrenner (WI-9). West Bend, Wisconsin. February 25, 1997.

Party Campaign Committees

Julie Dwyer. Deputy Field Director, Democratic Congressional Campaign Committee. Washington, DC. May 3, 1996.
Terry Nelson. Midwestern Field Representative, National Republican Congressional Committee. Washington, DC. May 3, 1996.

2000 Interviews

Delaware

Michael Miller. Democratic challenger to Representative Michael Castle (DE-AL). Lewes, Delaware. February 5, 2001.

Maryland

Don Dearmon. Democratic challenger to Representative Roscoe Bartlett (MD-6). Washington, DC. March 9, 2001.
Terry Lierman. Democratic challenger to Representative Connie Morella (MD-8). Bethesda, Maryland. April 30, 2001.

New Jersey

Charlene Cathcart. Republican challenger to Representative Rob Andrews (NJ-1). Audubon, New Jersey. May 30, 2001.
Reed Gusciora. Democratic challenger to Representative Chris Smith (NJ-4). Trenton, New Jersey. April 16, 2001.
Dan Quinonez, campaign manager for Representative Mike Ferguson, Republican open seat candidate (NJ-7). Hackensack, New Jersey. April 23, 2001.
Dick Zimmer. Republican challenger to Representative Rush Holt (NJ-12). Lawrenceville, New Jersey. April 6, 2001.

Pennsylvania

Christian Marchand, campaign manager for Representative Melissa Hart, Republican open seat candidate (PA-4). Washington, DC, March 9, 2001.
Tom Kopel. Republican challenger to Representative Tim Holden (PA-6). Reading, Pennsylvania. January 17, 2001.
Ron Strouse. Democratic challenger to Representative Jim Greenwood (PA-8). Doylestown, Pennsylvania. January 26, 2001.
Stephen Urban. Republican challenger to Representative Paul Kanjorski (PA-11). Wilkes-Barre, Pennsylvania. February 26, 2001.
Ed O'Brien. Democratic challenger to Representative Pat Toomey (PA-15). Bethlehem, Pennsylvania. March 26, 2001.
Bob Yorczyk. Democratic challenger to Representative Joseph Pitts (PA-16). Exton, Pennsylvania. January 7, 2001.
Leslye Hess Herrmann. Democratic challenger to Representative George Gekas (PA-17). Harrisburg, Pennsylvania. February 23, 2001.

Works Cited

Adams, James, and Samuel Merrill III. 2003. "Voter Turnout and Candidate Strategies in American Elections." *Journal of Politics* 65: 161–89.
Aldrich, John H. 1995. *Why Parties?* Chicago: University of Chicago Press.
Alford, John R., and David W. Brady. 1989. "Personal and Partisan Advantages in U. S. Congressional Elections." In *Congress Reconsidered.* 4th ed., edited by Lawrence C. Dodd and Bruce I. Oppenheimer, 153–69. Washington, DC: Congressional Quarterly Press.
American Political Science Association. 1950. *Towards a More Responsible Two-Party System.* New York: Rinehart.
Ansolabehere, Stephen, and James M. Snyder. 2001. "The Incumbency Advantage in U.S. Elections: An Analysis of State and Federal Offices, 1942–2000." Unpublished ms, Massachusetts Institute of Technology.
Arendt, Hannah. 1958. *The Human Condition.* Chicago: University of Chicago Press.
Asher, Herbert B. 2001. *Polling and the Public.* Washington, DC: Congressional Quarterly Press.
Bachrach, Peter, and Morton S. Baratz. 1962. "The Two Faces of Power." *American Political Science Review* 56: 947–52.
Banks, Jeffrey S., and D. Roderick Kiewiet. 1989. "Explaining Patterns of Candidate Competition in Congressional Elections." *American Journal of Political Science* 33: 997–1015.
Baron, David P. 1995. "A Sequential Choice Theory of Legislative Organization." In *Positive Theories of Congressional Institutions,* edited by Kenneth A. Shepsle and Barry R. Weingast, 71–100. Ann Arbor: University of Michigan Press.
Barone, Michael, and Grant Ujifusa. 1997. *The Almanac of American Politics 1998.* Washington, DC: National Journal Group.
Barone, Michael, Richard E. Cohen, and Grant Ujifusa. 2001. *The Almanac of American Politics 2002.* Washington, DC: National Journal Group.
Barry, Brian M. 1970. *Sociologists, Economists, and Democracy.* Chicago: University of Chicago Press.
Bartels, Larry M. 1988. *Presidential Primaries and the Dynamics of Public Choice.* Princeton, NJ: Princeton University Press.
Berinsky, Adam J., and Susan S. Lederman. 2003. "The 2000 New Jersey 12th Congressional District Race." In *The Other Campaign: Soft Money and Issue Advocacy in the 2000 Congressional Elections,* edited by David B. Magleby, 183–96. Lanham, MD: Rowman and Littlefield.
Boatright, Robert G., and Andrew J. Taylor. 2001. "Same Candidates, Different Year: Repeat Match-Ups in House Elections." Paper presented at the Annual Meeting of the American Political Science Association, San Francisco, CA.
Bond, Jon R., Cary R. Covington, and Richard Fleisher. 1985. "Explaining Challenger Quality in Congressional Elections." *Journal of Politics* 41: 510–29.

Born, Richard J. 1986. "Strategic Politicians and Unresponsive Voters." *American Political Science Review* 80: 599–612.
Bradburn, Norman M., and Seymour Sudman. 1989. *Polls and Surveys*. San Francisco: Jossey-Bass.
Brady, David W., John F. Cogan, and Morris P. Fiorina. 2000. "Epilogue: 1998 and Beyond." In *Continuity and Change in House Elections*, edited by David W. Brady, John F. Cogan, and Morris P. Fiorina, 235–48. Stanford, CA: Stanford University Press.
Brown, Clifford W., Lynda W. Powell, and Clyde Wilcox. 1995. *Serious Money: Fundraising and Contributing in Presidential Nomination Campaigns*. New York: Cambridge University Press.
Bruner, Jerome S. 1944. *Mandate from the People*. New York: Duell, Sloan, and Pierce.
Burden, Barry C. 2001a. "The Polarizing Effect of Congressional Primaries." In *Congressional Primaries and the Politics of Representation*, edited by Peter Galderisi, Marni Ezra, and Michael Lyons, 95–115. Lanham, MD: Rowman and Littlefield.
———. 2001b. "Candidate Positioning in American Elections." Paper presented at the Annual Meeting of the American Political Science Association, San Francisco, CA.
Campbell, James E. 1993. *The Presidential Pulse of Congressional Elections*. Lexington: University of Kentucky Press.
———. 2003. "The Stagnation of Congressional Elections." In *Life After Reform: When the Bipartisan Campaign Reform Act Meets Politics*, edited by Michael J. Malbin, 141–58. Lanham, MD: Rowman and Littlefield.
Canon, David T. 1990. *Actors, Athletes, and Astronauts: Political Amateurs in the United States Congress*. Chicago: University of Chicago Press.
———. 1993. "Sacrificial Lambs or Strategic Politicians? Political Amateurs in the United States Congress." *American Journal of Political Science* 37: 1119–41.
Cantril, Albert H. 1991. *The Opinion Connection: Polling, Politics, and the Press*. Washington, DC: Congressional Quarterly Press.
Chappell, Henry W., and William R. Keech. 1986. "Policy Motivation and Party Differences in a Dynamic Spatial Model of Party Competition." *American Political Science Review* 80: 881–99.
Chicago Tribune. 1996. "The Tribune's Endorsements." October 14.
Coates, Dennis C. 1995. "Measuring the 'Personal Vote' of Members of Congress." *Public Choice* 85: 227–48.
Coleman, John J. 2000. "Congressional Campaign Spending and the Quality of Democracy." *Journal of Politics* 62: 757–89.
Collet, Christian, and Martin P. Wattenberg. 1999. "Strategically Unambitious: Minor Party and Independent Candidates in the 1996 Congressional Elections." In *The State of the Parties*. 3d ed., edited by John C. Green and Daniel M. Shea, 229–48. Lanham, MD: Rowman and Littlefield.
Converse, Jean M., and Howard Schuman. 1974. *Conversations at Random: Survey Research as Interviewers See It*. New York: John Wiley and Sons.
Cox, Gary W. 1997. *Making Votes Count: Strategic Coordination in the World's Electoral Systems*. New York: Cambridge University Press.

———, and Jonathan N. Katz. 1996. "Why Did the Incumbency Advantage in U. S. House Elections Grow?" *American Journal of Political Science* 40: 478–97.
Crespi, Irving. 1989. *Public Opinion, Polls, and Democracy*. Boulder, CO: Westview Press.
Curran, John. 2000. "For Retiree, Political Life Begins at 82; Race Against LoBiondo Keeps Widower Busy." *Bergen County Record*, November 1.
Dahl, Robert A. 1961. *Who Governs? Democracy and Power in an American City*. New Haven, CT: Yale University Press.
DeClercq, Eugene. 1978. "The Use of Polling in Congressional Campaigns." *Public Opinion Quarterly* 42: 247–58.
DeFiebre, Conrad. 1996. "Gutknecht Vows Self-improvement after Tight Win; Defeated DFLer Mary Rieder Did Not Rule Out Making Another Run at the First District U.S. House Seat: 'I Told My Supporters Not to Throw Away Their Lawn Signs.'" *Minnesota Star Tribune*, November 7.
Diamond, Martin.1959. Review of *An Economic Theory of Democracy*, by Anthony Downs. *Journal of Political Economy* 67: 208–12.
Diemer, Tom. 1994. "Ohio in Washington: The Congressional Delegation." In *Ohio Politics*, edited by Alexander P. Lamis, 196–232. Kent, OH: Kent State University Press.
Downs, Anthony. 1957. *An Economic Theory of Democracy*. New York: HarperCollins.
Duncan, Philip D., and Christine C. Lawrence. 1997. *Politics in America 1998*. Washington, DC: Congressional Quarterly Press.
———, and Brian Nutting. 1999. *Politics in America 2000*. Washington, DC: Congressional Quarterly Press.
Eaton, Sabrina. 1996. "Opponent Challenges Kasich on Financial Ties to Chief Aide." *Cleveland Plain Dealer*, September 13.
Eisinger, Robert M. 2003. *The Evolution of Presidential Polling*. New York: Cambridge University Press.
Elazar, Daniel J. 1972. *American Federalism: A View from the States*. 2d ed. New York: Thomas Y. Crowell.
Enelow, James M., and Melvin J. Hinich. 1984. *The Spatial Theory of Voting*. New York: Cambridge University Press.
Erikson, Robert S. 1971. "The Advantage of Incumbency in Congressional Elections." *Polity* 3: 395–405.
———, and Gerald C. Wright. 1989. "Voters, Candidates, and Issues in Congressional Elections." In *Congress Reconsidered*. 4th ed., edited by Lawrence C. Dodd and Bruce I. Oppenheimer. Washington, DC: Congressional Quarterly Press.
Feld, Scott L., and Bernard Grofman. 1991. "Incumbency Advantage, Voter Loyalty, and the Benefit of the Doubt." *Journal of Theoretical Politics* 3: 115–37.
Fenno, Richard F. 1978. *Home Style: House Members in Their Districts*. Boston: Little, Brown, and Co.
———. 1990. *Watching Politicians: Essays on Participant Observation*. Berkeley, CA: Institute of Governmental Studies.
———. 1997. *Learning to Govern: An Institutional View of the 104th Congress*. Washington, DC: Brookings Institution.

Fenton, John H. 1957. *Politics in the Border States.* New Orleans, LA: Galleon Press.
———. 1966. *Midwest Politics.* New York: Holt, Rinehart, and Winston.
Ferejohn, John A. 1993. "The Spatial Model and Elections." In *Information, Participation, and Choice: An Economic Theory of Democracy in Perspective,* edited by Bernard Grofman, 107–24. Ann Arbor: University of Michigan Press.
———. 1998. "A Tale of Two Congresses: Social Policy in the Clinton Years." In *The Social Divide: Political Parties and the Future of Activist Government,* edited by Margaret Weir, 49–82. Washington, DC: Brookings Institution.
———, and Robert G. Noll. 1978. "Uncertainty and the Formal Theory of Political Campaigns." *American Political Science Review* 72: 492–505.
Fiorina, Morris P. 1981. *Retrospective Voting in American National Elections.* New Haven, CT: Yale University Press.
———. 1989. *Congress: Keystone of the Washington Establishment.* New Haven, CT: Yale University Press.
Fishel, Jeff. 1973. *Party and Opposition: Congressional Challengers in American Politics.* New York: David McKay Company.
Fishkin, James S. 1997. *The Voice of the People: Public Opinion and Democracy.* New Haven, CT: Yale University Press.
Fowler, Linda L. 1993. *Candidates, Congress, and American Democracy.* Ann Arbor: University of Michigan Press.
———, and Robert D. McClure. 1989. *Political Ambition: Who Decides to Run for Congress.* New Haven, CT: Yale University Press.
Gallup, George H., and Saul F. Rae. 1940. *The Pulse of Democracy.* New York: Simon and Schuster.
Garand, James C., and Donald A. Gross. 1983. "Changes in the Vote Margins for Congressional Candidates: A Specification of Historical Trends." *American Political Science Review* 78: 17–30.
Gaventa, John. 1980. *Power and Powerlessness.* Urbana: University of Illinois Press.
Geer, John G. 1996. *From Tea Leaves to Opinion Polls.* New York: Columbia University Press.
Gerber, Alan S. 1998. "Estimating the Effect of Campaign Spending on Senate Election Outcomes Using Instrumental Variables." *American Political Science Review* 92: 401–11.
Gillon, Steven M. 1992. *The Democrats' Dilemma: Walter F. Mondale and the Liberal Legacy.* New York: Columbia University Press.
Goldberg, Robert Alan. 1995. *Barry Goldwater.* New Haven, CT: Yale University Press.
Green, Donald P., and Ian Shapiro. 1994. *Pathologies of Rational Choice Theory.* New Haven, CT: Yale University Press.
Greenberg, Joseph, and Kenneth A. Shepsle. 1987. "The Effect of Electoral Awards in a Multiparty Competition with Entry." *American Political Science Review* 81: 525–37.
Grofman, Bernard. 1993. "Toward an Institution-Rich Theory of Political Competition with a Supply-Side Component." In *Information, Participation, and Choice: An Economic Theory of Democracy in Perspective,* edited by Bernard Grofman, 179–196. Ann Arbor: University of Michigan Press.
Groseclose, Timothy J. 2001. "A Model of Candidate Location When One Candi-

date Has a Valence Advantage." *American Journal of Political Science* 45: 862–86.

———, Steven D. Levitt, and James M. Snyder. 1999. "Comparing Interest Group Scores Across Time and Chambers: Adjusted ADA Scores for the U.S. Congress." *American Political Science Review* 93: 15–32.

Hall, Richard L. 1995. "Empiricism and Progress in Positive Theories of Legislative Institutions." In *Positive Theories of Congressional Institutions*, edited by Kenneth A. Shepsle and Barry R. Weingast, 273–302. Ann Arbor: University of Michigan Press.

Hamburger, Tom. 1996. "Race Pits Adept Pol, Moderate Newcomer; Gutknecht: Energetic Orator." *Minnesota Star Tribune*, October 25.

Hamilton, William R. 1995. "Political Polling: From the Beginning to the Center." In *Campaigns and Elections American Style*, edited by James A. Thurber and Candice J. Nelson, 161–80. Boulder, CO: Westview Press.

Herbst, Susan. 1993. *Numbered Voices*. Chicago: University of Chicago Press.

———. 1998. *Reading Public Opinion: How Political Actors View the Democratic Process*. Chicago: University of Chicago Press.

Herrnson, Paul S. 1988. *Party Campaigning in the 1980s*. Cambridge, MA: Harvard University Press.

———. 1995. *Congressional Elections*. 2d ed. Washington, DC: Congressional Quarterly Press.

———. 2000. *Congressional Elections*. 3d ed. Washington, DC: Congressional Quarterly Press.

———. 2001. "The Congressional Elections." In *The Elections of 2000*, edited by Gerald M. Pomper, 155–76. New York: Chatham House Publishers.

———, and Kelly D. Patterson. 2002. "Financing the 2000 Congressional Elections." In *Financing the 2000 Elections*, edited by David B. Magleby, 106–32. Washington, DC: Brookings Institution.

Hershey, Marjorie Random. 1974. *The Making of Campaign Strategy*. Lexington, MA: D. C. Heath and Co.

———. 1984. *Running for Office: The Political Education of Campaigners*. Chatham, NJ: Chatham House.

Hibbs, Douglas A. 1987. *The American Political Economy: Macroeconomics and Electoral Politics*. Cambridge, MA: Harvard University Press.

Hinich, Melvin J., and Michael C. Munger. 1994. *Ideology and the Theory of Political Choice*. Ann Arbor: University of Michigan Press.

Hirschman, Albert O. 1970. *Exit, Voice, and Loyalty*. Cambridge, MA: Harvard University Press.

Hollander, Sidney, et al. 1971. "Toward Responsibility in Reporting Opinion Surveys." *Public Opinion Quarterly* 35: 335–49.

Hotelling, Harold. 1929. "Stability in Competition." *Economic Journal* 39: 41–57.

Huckshorn, Robert J., and Robert C. Spencer. 1971. *The Politics of Defeat*. Boston: University of Massachusetts Press.

Hunterdon Review. 2000. "Zimmer for Congress." October 27.

Jacobs, Lawrence R., and Robert Y. Shapiro. 2000. *Politicians Don't Pander: Political Manipulation and the Loss of Democratic Responsiveness*. Chicago: University of Chicago Press.

Jacobson, Gary C. 1990. *The Electoral Origins of Divided Government.* Boulder, CO: Westview Press.
———. 1997a. *The Politics of Congressional Elections.* New York: Addison-Wesley.
———. 1997b. "The 105th Congress: Unprecedented and Unsurprising." In *The Elections of 1996,* edited by Michael Nelson, 143–66. Washington, DC: Congressional Quarterly.
———. 1998. "The Declining Salience of U. S. House Candidates, 1958–1994." Paper presented at the Annual Meeting of the American Political Science Association, Boston, MA.
———. 1999. "The Effect of the AFL-CIO's 'Voter Education' Campaigns on the 1996 House Elections." *Journal of Politics* 61: 185–94.
———. 2001. "Congress: Election and Stalemate." In *The Elections of 2000,* edited by Michael Nelson, 185–209. Washington, DC: Congressional Quarterly Press.
Jefferson, Thomas. 1999 [1785]. *Notes on the State of Virginia.* New York: Penguin Books.
Johnson, James D. 1991. "Rational Choice as a Reconstructive Theory." In *The Economic Approach to Politics : A Critical Reassessment of the Theory of Rational Action,* edited by Kristen Renwick Monroe. New York: HarperCollins.
Jones, Charles O. 1962. "A Suggested Scheme for Classifying Congressional Campaigns." *Public Opinion Quarterly* 26: 126–31.
Kazee, Thomas A. 1980. "The Decision to Run for the U.S. Congress: Challenger Attitudes in the 1970s." *Legislative Studies Quarterly* 5: 79–100.
———, ed. 1994. *Who Runs for Congress? Ambition, Context, and Candidate Experience.* Washington, DC: Congressional Quarterly Press.
Key, V. O. 1958. *Politics, Parties, and Pressure Groups.* New York: Thomas Y. Crowell.
King, Gary, and Andrew Gelman. 1991. "Systematic Consequences of Incumbency Advantage in U. S. House Elections." *American Journal of Political Science* 35: 110–38.
Kingdon, John W. 1966. *Candidates for Office: Beliefs and Strategies.* New York: Random House.
Klingemann, Hans-Dieter, Richard I. Hofferbert, and Ian Budge. 1994. *Parties, Policies, and Democracy.* Boulder, CO: Westview Press.
Klinkner, Philip A. 1994. *The Losing Parties: Out-Party National Committees, 1956–1993.* New Haven, CT: Yale University Press.
Kolodny, Robin . 1998. *Pursuing Majorities: Congressional Campaign Committees in American Politics.* Norman: University of Oklahoma Press.
Kramer, Gerald H. 1971. "Short-term Fluctuations in American Voting Behavior, 1896–1964." *American Political Science Review* 65: 131–43.
Krasno, Jonathan S. 1994. *Challengers, Competition, and Reelection: Comparing Senate and House Elections.* New Haven, CT: Yale University Press.
Krehbiel, Keith. 1998. *Pivotal Politics: A Theory of U.S. Lawmaking.* Chicago: University of Chicago Press.
Layzell, Anne C., and L. Marvin Overby. 1994. "Biding Their Time in the Illinois 9th." In *Who Runs for Congress,* edited by Thomas A. Kazee, 150–64. Washington, DC: Congressional Quarterly Press.

Leuthold, David A. 1968. *Electioneering in a Democracy.* New York: John Wiley and Sons.
Levitt, Steven D. 1994. "Using Repeat Challengers to Estimate the Effect of Campaign Spending on Election Outcomes in the U.S. House." *Journal of Political Economy* 102: 777–98.
Lindblom, Charles E. 1958. "In Praise of Political Science." *World Politics* 9: 240–53.
———. 1977. *Politics and Markets: The World's Political-Economic Systems.* New York: Basic Books.
MacDonald, Stuart Elaine, and George Rabinowitz. 1993a. "Ideology and Candidate Evaluation." *Public Choice* 76: 59–78.
———. 1993b. "Direction and Uncertainty in a Model of Issue Voting." *Journal of Theoretical Politics* 5: 61–87.
———. 1998. "Solving the Paradox of Nonconvergence: Valence, Position, and Direction in Democratic Politics." *Electoral Studies* 17: 281–300.
Mack, W. R. 1998. "Repeat Challengers: Are They the Best Challengers Around?" *American Politics Quarterly* 26: 308–43.
Madison, James. [1787] 1961. *Federalist #53.* In *The Federalist Papers,* edited by Clinton L. Rossiter, 330–36. New York: Mentor Books.
Maisel, L. Sandy. 1986. *From Obscurity to Oblivion: Running in the Congressional Primary.* Knoxville: University of Tennessee Press.
———, and Walter J. Stone. 1997. "Determinants of Candidate Emergence in U.S. House Elections: An Exploratory Study." *Legislative Studies Quarterly* 22: 79–96.
Mansbridge, Jane J. 1986. *Why We Lost the ERA.* Chicago: University of Chicago Press.
———. 2003. "Rethinking Representation." *American Political Science Review* 97: 515–28.
Mayhew, David R. 1974. *Congress: The Electoral Connection.* New Haven, CT: Yale University Press.
———. 1986. *Placing Parties in American Politics.* Princeton, NJ: Princeton University Press.
McAdams, John C., and John R. Johannes. 1987. "Determinants of Spending by House Challengers, 1974–1984." *American Journal of Political Science* 31: 457–83.
McKeever, Porter. 1994. "Adlai Stevenson and the Campaigns of 1952 and 1956." In *Lessons from Defeated Presidential Candidates,* edited by Kenneth W. Thompson, 115–34. Lanham, MD: University Press of America.
McKelvey, Richard D., and Peter C. Ordeshook. 1976. "Symmetric Spatial Games without Majority Rule Equilibria." *American Political Science Review* 70: 1172–84.
McWilliams, Wilson Carey. 2001. "The Meaning of the Election." In *The Election of 2000,* edited by Gerald Pomper, 177–201. New York: Chatham House.
Merrill, Samuel, and Bernard Grofman. 1997. "Directional and Proximity Models of Voter Utility and Choice: A New Synthesis and an Illustrative Test of Competing Models." *Journal of Theoretical Politics* 9: 25–48.
Miller, Arthur H., Warren E. Miller, Alden S. Raine, and Thad A. Brown. 1976. "A

Majority Party in Disarray: Policy Polarization in the 1972 Election." *American Political Science Review* 70: 753–78.

Milyo, Jeffrey D. 1998. "The Electoral Effects of Campaign Spending in House Elections: A Natural Experiment Approach." Unpublished manuscript. Department of Economics, Tufts University.

Moakley, Maureen W. 1986. "Political Parties." In *The Political State of New Jersey*, edited by Gerald M. Pomper. New Brunswick, NJ: Rutgers University Press.

Neal, Steve. 1996. "In Search of Sidney Yates." *Chicago Sun-Times*, October 15.

Newsweek. 1972. "Campaign '72: The Homestretch." October 30, pp. 36–37.

Ornstein, Norman J., Thomas E. Mann, and Michael J. Malbin. 2002. *Vital Statistics on Congress 1999–2000*. Washington, DC: American Enterprise Institute.

Paddock, Joel. 1998. "Explaining State Variation in Interparty Ideological Differences." *Political Research Quarterly* 51: 765–80.

Page, Benjamin I. 1978. *Choices and Echoes in Presidential Elections*. Chicago: University of Chicago Press.

Perlstein, Rick. 2001. *Before the Storm: Barry Goldwater and the Unmaking of the American Consensus*. New York: Hill and Wang.

Pitkin, Hanna Fenichel. 1967. *The Concept of Representation*. Berkeley: University of California Press.

Przeworski, Adam, and John D. Sprague. 1971. "Concepts in Search of Explicit Formulation: A Study in Measurement." *Midwest Journal of Political Science* 15: 199–212.

———. 1986. *Paper Stones: A History of Electoral Socialism*. Chicago: University of Chicago Press.

Putnam, Robert D. 2000. *Bowling Alone: The Collapse and Revival of American Community*. New York: Simon and Schuster.

Rabinowitz, George, and Stuart Elaine MacDonald. 1989. "A Directional Theory of Issue Voting." *American Political Science Review* 83: 93–121.

Rae, Nicol C. 1998. *Conservative Reformers: The Republican Freshmen and the Lessons of the 104th Congress*. Armonk, NY: M. E. Sharpe.

Riker, William H. 1982a. "The Two-Party System and Duverger's Law: An Essay on the History of Political Science." *American Political Science Review* 76: 753–66.

———. 1982b. *Liberalism Against Populism*. Prospect Heights, IL: Waveland Press.

———. 1997. "The Ferment of the 1950s and the Development of Rational Choice Theory." In *Contemporary Empirical Theory*, edited by Kristen Renwick Monroe, 191–201. Berkeley: University of California Press.

———, and Peter C. Ordeshook. 1973. *An Introduction to Positive Political Theory*. Englewood Cliffs, NJ: Prentice Hall.

Robertson, David B. 1976. *A Theory of Party Competition*. New York: John Wiley.

Robinson, James A. 1960. "Survey Interviewing Among Members of Congress." *Public Opinion Quarterly* 24: 127–38.

Roemer, John E. 2001. *Political Competition: Theory and Applications*. Cambridge, MA: Harvard University Press.

Rosenstone, Steven J. 1983. *Forecasting Presidential Elections*. New Haven, CT: Yale University Press.

Ryden, David K. 1999. "'The Good, the Bad, and the Ugly': The Judicial Shaping of

Party Activities." In *The State of the Parties: The Changing Role of Contemporary American Parties*. 3d ed., edited by John C. Green and Daniel M. Shea, 50–65. Lanham, MD: Rowman and Littlefield.
Salisbury, Robert H. 1970. "An Exchange Theory of Interest Groups." In *Interest Group Politics in America,* edited by Robert Salisbury, 32–68. New York: Harper and Row.
Sapiro, Virginia, Steven J. Rosenstone, and the National Election Studies. 2001. *1948–2000 Cumulative Data File* (dataset). Ann Arbor: University of Michigan, Center for Political Studies (producer and distributor).
Sartori, Giovanni. 1976. *Parties and Party Systems.* New York: Cambridge University Press.
Schlesinger, Joseph A. 1975. "The Primary Goals of Political Parties: A Clarification of Positive Theory." *American Political Science Review* 69: 840–49.
———. 1994. *Political Parties and the Winning of Office.* Ann Arbor: University of Michigan Press.
Schoenberg, Bernard. 1996a. "'Long Game Ahead of Us' Says Poll Leader Shimkus." *State Journal-Register,* June 13.
———. 1996b. "20th District Candidates Have Common Ground: A Close Look at Shimkus, Hoffman Finds a Number of Similarities." *State Journal-Register,* October 21.
———. 1996c. "Hoffman-Shimkus House Race Likely to Be Close." *State Journal-Register,* October 24.
Schuessler, Alexander A. 2000. *A Logic of Expressive Choice.* New York: Cambridge University Press.
Schultze, Steve. 1996. "Race Shows Power of TV Attack Ads." *Milwaukee Journal Sentinel,* November 7.
Schwartz, Mildred A. 1990. *The Party Network: The Robust Organization of Illinois Republicans.* Madison: University of Wisconsin Press.
Scolaro, Joseph. 1996. "Neumann Eager to Get Back to Congress." *Wisconsin State Journal,* November 10.
Shadegg, Stephen C. 1965. *What Happened to Goldwater: The Inside Story of the 1964 Republican Campaign.* New York: Holt, Rinehart, and Winston.
Shepsle, Kenneth A. 1972. "The Strategy of Ambiguity: Uncertainty and Electoral Competition." *American Political Science Review* 66: 555–68.
Shklar, Judith N. 1991. *American Citizenship: The Quest for Inclusion.* Cambridge, MA: Harvard University Press.
Siegel, Ralph. 2000. "Zimmer Concedes 12th District Race to Holt." *Bergen County Record,* November 30.
Sievers, Scott. 1996. "Hoffman Pushes Debates; Shimkus Says He's Ready." *St. Louis Post-Dispatch,* June 5.
Simon, Adam F. 2002. *The Winning Message: Candidate Behavior, Campaign Discourse, and Democracy.* New York: Cambridge University Press.
Snyder, James M. 1994. "Safe Seats, Marginal Seats, and Party Platforms: The Logic of Platform Differentiation." *Economics and Politics* 6: 201–11.
Sorauf, Frank J. 1963. *Party and Representation: Legislative Politics in Pennsylvania.* New York: Atherton Books.
———. 1992. *Inside Campaign Finance.* New Haven, CT: Yale University Press.

Squire, Peverill, and Eric R. A. N. Smith. 1984. "Repeat Challengers in Congressional Elections." *American Politics Quarterly* 12: 51–70.

State Journal-Register. 1996. "Shimkus Merits Election to 20th Congressional Seat." October 21.

Stokes, Donald E. 1963. "Spatial Theories of Party Competition." *American Political Science Review* 57: 368–77.

Stone, Irving F. 1943. *They Also Ran: The Story of the Men Who Were Defeated for the Presidency.* New York: Doubleday.

Stone, Walter J., L. Sandy Maisel, and Cherie Maestas. 1998. "Candidate Emergence in U.S. House Elections." Paper presented at the annual meeting of the American Political Science Association, Boston, MA.

Stone, Walter, and L. Sandy Maisel. 2003. "The Not-So-Simple Calculus of Winning: Potential U.S. House Candidates' Nomination and General Election Prospects." *Journal of Politics* 65: 951–77.

Talbott, Basil. 1996. "Area GOP Congressmen Like Majority's Clout." *Chicago Sun-Times,* October 13.

Thompson, Kenneth W., ed. 1994. *Lessons from Defeated Presidential Candidates.* Lanham, MD: University Press of America.

Tufte, Edward R. 1978. *Political Control of the Economy.* Princeton, NJ: Princeton University Press.

Tullock, Gordon. 1981. "Why So Much Stability?" *Public Choice* 37: 189–202.

Westlye, Mark C. 1991. *Senate Elections and Campaign Intensity.* Baltimore, MD: Johns Hopkins University Press.

Wittman, Donald A. 1973. "Parties as Utility Maximizers." *American Political Science Review* 67: 490–98.

———. 1977. "Candidates with Policy Preferences: A Dynamic Model." *Journal of Economic Theory* 14: 180–89.

———. 1983. "Candidate Motivation: A Synthesis of Alternative Theories." *American Political Science Review* 77: 142–57.

Wolfinger, Raymond E., and Steven J. Rosenstone. 1980. *Who Votes?* New Haven, CT: Yale University Press.

Wright, Gerald C. 1986. "Elections and the Potential for Policy Change in the U.S. House of Representatives." In *Congress and Policy Change,* edited by Gerald C. Wright, Leroy N. Rieselbach, and Lawrence C. Dodd, 94–119. New York: Agathon.

———, and Michael B. Berkman. 1986. "Candidates and Policy in United States Senate Elections." *American Political Science Review* 80: 567–88.

———, Robert S. Erikson, and John P. McIver. 1985. "Measuring State Partisanship and Ideology with Survey Data." *Journal of Politics* 47: 469–89.

Wright, John R. 2003. *Interest Groups and Congress: Lobbying, Contributions, and Influence.* New York: Longman.

Zaller, John R. 1998. "Politicians as Prize Fighters: Electoral Selection and Incumbency Advantage." In *Politicians and Party Politics,* edited by John G. Geer, 125–85. Baltimore, MD: Johns Hopkins University Press.

Zukin, Cliff. 1986. "Political Culture and Public Opinion." In *The Political State of New Jersey,* edited by Gerald M. Pomper. New Brunswick, NJ: Rutgers University Press.

Index

abortion, xii, 53, 72, 112–13, 116, 121, 123, 134, 135–36, 138
Adams, James, 45
AFL-CIO, 66–67, 136–37, 176, 187
agriculture (as campaign issue), 116, 137
autoimmune deficiency syndrome (AIDS), 137
Akron, 69
Alabama, 183
Aldrich, John H., 227n2 (ch. 2)
Alexander County, IL, 170–71
Alford, John R., 3
Almanac of American Politics (Barone, Cohen, and Ujifusa), 190
amateur politicians, xxii, 8, 182, 227n2 (ch. 1)
American National Election Studies (ANES), 105, 151
American Political Science Association (APSA), 9–10, 145
Americans for Democratic Action (ADA), 50, 54, 228n1 (ch. 3)
Andrews, Robert, xii, xiii
Ansolabehere, Stephen, 3
Arendt, Hannah 16
arts, government funding of, 134–35
Asher, Herbert B., 84, 86
Aspin, Les, 176

B-2 Bomber, 53, 72
Babbitt, Bruce, 137
Bachrach, Peter, 12, 24
Baltimore, 191, 201
Banks, Jeffrey S., 227n2 (ch. 1)
Baratz, Morton S., 12, 24
Barca, Peter, 176, 177
Baron, David P., 215
Barone, Michael, 69, 189–91
Barrett, Tom, 177

Barry, Brian M., 26
Bartels, Larry M, 164
Belleville, IL, 169
Beloit, WI, 176
benchmark poll, 81, 84, 89–92
Berinsky, Adam J., xii
Berkman, Michael B., 55, 228n2
Bexley, OH, 173
Bipartisan Campaign Reform Act (BCRA), 222. *See also* campaign finance reform
Blair, Kenneth, 77, 79–80, 83, 88
Blue Dog Democrats, 136
Boatright, Robert G., 220
Bond, Jon R., 105
Born, Richard J., 105
Bosnia, 53, 54, 73
Bradburn, Norman M., 86
Brady Bill, 53, 73, 135, 229n2 (ch. 5)
Brady, David W., 3, 185
Brenholt, Floyd, 130–31, 140, 141, 185, 211
Brown, Clifford W., 15
Brown, Sherrod, 79, 162
Brown, Thad A., xv
Bruner, Jerome S., 85
Budge, Ian, 12
budget (as campaign issue), 53, 72, 98, 116, 136, 229n (ch. 7)
Burden, Barry C., 188, 229
Bush, George H. W., 173, 176, 227n1 (intro.)
Bush, George W., xii, 189, 197, 204
Butler County, OH, 224

Cairo, IL, 69, 169
California, 183
Camden, NJ, xii, 189
campaign finance reform 116, 132, 222. *See also* Bipartisan Campaign

246 Index

Reform Act
Campbell, James E., 107, 222
candidate quality, 7, 76, 151–52, 194, 222
candidate recruitment, 147, 152, 155–56, 176, 204
Canon, David T. xv, xxi–xxii, 8, 36–37, 161
Cantril, Albert H., 69, 85–86
Cape May, NJ, xii
Carter, Jimmy, 227n1 (intro.)
Casey, Patrick, 202
Castle, Mike, 191
Cathcart, Charlene, xxii–xxiii
challengers: competitiveness of, 105–6, 205; fundraising of, 66, 187; issue positions of, 53, 54, 58–62, 188, 200, 213–15; previous research on, 4, 8, 105–8, 218, 229n1 (ch. 5); views on incumbents, 109–15, 126–40, 198
Champaign, IL, 186
Chappell, Henry W., 36
Chicago Tribune, 133
Chicago, 69–70, 78, 133, 166, 169, 181, 186
Cincinnati, 69
civil rights, xii
Clean Air Act, 127
Cleveland, 69, 79
Clinton Bill, 113, 158; administration of, xi, 228n4, 229nn2–3 (ch. 5); budget proposals of, 53, 72, 137; impeachment of, 187, 199; 1992 presidential campaign of, 79, 170, 173–74, 176; 1996 presidential campaign of, 93–94, 116, 136, 142, 161, 166, 170, 173–74, 176, 178
Clinton, Hillary, 137
Club for Growth, 11
Coates, Dennis C., 3
Cogan, John F., 185
Cohen, Richard E., 69, 189–90
Coleman, John J., 3
Collet, Christian, 15
Collinsville, IL, 80
Columbus, OH, 69, 173–74

conditional party government, 217, 227n2 (ch. 2)
congratulation/rationalization effect, 6, 63
Congressional Quarterly, 53, 72, 73, 148
Congressional Quarterly, candidate survey, xvii, 50–52, 61, 117, 144, 147, 186–88, 218, 228nn4, 6, 229n2 (ch. 5); competitiveness ratings, 51
Converse, Jean M., 63
Convington, Cary R., 105
Conyers, John, 174
Cook Report, 51
corporate welfare (as campaign issue), 130, 133
Corzine, Jon, 189
Costello, Jerry, 170–72, 186, 211, 229n4 (ch. 6)
Cox, Gary W., 3, 215
Crane, Philip, 78–79, 211
Crespi, Irving, 86
crime (as campaign issue), 116, 229n2 (ch. 5)
Curran, John, xii

Dahl, Robert A., 12
Dean, Howard, 11
death penalty, 199
Decatur, IL, 69
DeClercq, Eugene, 86
defense policy, 117
DeFiebre, Conrad, 138
Delaware, 184, 191–92, 194, 200, 205, 207; candidate quotations from, 198; political culture of, 190–91
Democratic Congressional Campaign Committee (DCCC), 144–45, 150, 152, 157–60, 162, 166, 173–78, 180, 187, 194, 197, 201–2, 204, 229n1 (ch. 6)
Democratic Party, 11, 26, 66, 143, 148–49, 151, 162, 185; congressional candidates of, xi, xii, 53–59, 65, 67, 79, 112–19, 123, 128–139, 153, 156–61, 163, 166, 169, 173–79, 192, 198–99, 203–4, 208; in Illinois, 69–70; in Maryland, 191,

202; in Minnesota, 69–70, 163, 181; in New Jersey, 202; in Ohio, 69–70, 162–63, 173–75, 224; in Pennsylvania, 190, 202; in Wisconsin, 69–70, 160, 175–79
Democratic Socialists of America, 224
Department of Education, 131
Diamond, Martin, 18–19, 47
Diemer, Tom, 69
Dingells, John, 162
directional voting model, 44
Dole, Robert, 93, 117, 142, 176, 188
Downs, Anthony, 10, 12, 15–16, 18–20, 26, 30, 32–33, 35, 43–46, 145
Dukakis, Michael, 176
Duncan, Philip, D., 69, 78, 81, 129, 132, 169, 185, 229n4 (ch. 6)
Durbin, Richard, 80–81
DW-NOMINATE, 50. *See also* W-NOMINATE

East St. Louis, IL, 69, 169–70
Eaton, Sabrina, 173
Economic Theory of Democracy, An (Downs), 9–10, 16
Edgar, Jim, 172
education, 115–16, 119, 130, 136, 139, 189
Eisinger, Robert M., 87–88
Elazar, Daniel J., 147–50, 180
Elyria, OH, 79
Enelow, James M., 33
energy (as campaign issue), 193
environment (as campaign issue), 113, 116, 125, 130, 136, 189
Environmental Protection Agency (EPA), 53, 72, 228n2
Erikson, Robert S., 3, 68, 147, 228n2
Evanston, IL, 133
Ewing, Tom, 162
ex ante preferred positions, 41, 103, 216, 219, 223
expressive campaign, xvi, xix, 14, 15, 19, 33, 37–40, 46–48, 64, 71, 104, 105, 123, 125, 129, 131–32, 140–41, 143, 150–51, 192, 194, 200, 204, 206, 210, 214, 217, 219, 221

expressive preferences. *See* noninstrumental policy preferences
Eyota, MN, 138

Family and Medical Leave Act (FMLA), 53, 54, 72, 229n2 (ch. 5)
Federal Election Commission (FEC), 65, 66
Federalist #53, 224–25
Feingold, Russell, 185
Feld, Scott L., 34–35, 215
Feldman Group, 81
Fenno, Richard F., xxii, 12, 63, 81, 107, 213
Fenton, John H., 69, 147, 166, 180–81, 191
Ferejohn, John A., 44–45, 227n3 (ch. 2), 228n3 (ch. 5), 229n3 (ch. 5)
Fiorina, Morris P., xiv, 3, 185
Fishel, Jeff, xv, 6–7
Fishkin, James S., 16
Flanagan, Michael, 135
Fleisher, Richard, 105
Ford, Gerald, 173, 227n1 (intro.)
foreign policy, 117
formal theory. *See* median voter model; positive political theory; spatial theory
Fowler, Linda L., 5, 7, 161
Frank, Barney, xxi

Gallup, George H., 85–86
Garand, James C., 3
Gaventa, John, 12, 13, 24
gay rights (as campaign issue), 133
gays in the military, 52–53, 73, 117, 228n4, 229n3 (ch. 5)
Geer, John G., 21, 75
Gelman, Andrew, 3
Georgia, 26
Gephardt, Richard, 160, 178
Gerber, Alan S., 7
Gillon, Steven M., 212
Gingrich, Newt, 98, 112–13, 126, 133
Goldberg, Robert Alan, 211
Goldwater, Barry, xx, 25, 211–12
GOPAC, 93, 158

248   Index

Gore, Albert, 137, 170, 176, 197, 202, 204
Gore, Tipper, 178
government reform (as campaign issue), 133
Green, Donald P., 11–12
Greenberg, Joseph, 215
Greenleaf, Stewart, 202
Grofman, Bernard, 34–35, 215
Groseclose, Timothy J., 34–36, 215, 228n1 (ch. 3)
Gross, Donald A., 3
gun control, xii, 113, 116, 122, 136, 229n2 (ch. 5). *See also* Brady Bill
Gusciora, Reed, xii–xxiii
Gutknecht, Gil, 136–39, 186

Hall, Ralph, 228n5
Hall, Richard L., 215
Hamburger, Tom, 137
Hamilton, William R., 84–85
Hart, Melissa, 202
Hastert, J. Dennis, 162, 203
healthcare (as campaign issue), xi–xii, 116, 130, 136, 229n2 (ch. 5)
health maintenance organizations (HMOs), 196
Herbst, Susan, 75, 86–88
Heritage Foundation, 93
Herrnson, Paul S., 7–8, 52, 84–85, 106, 111, 145–46, 187–88, 194, 229n1 (ch. 6)
Hershey, Marjorie Random, 6, 146
Hess, Karl, 211–12
Hibbs, Douglas A., 10
Hinich, Melvin J., 10, 33
Hirschman, Albert O., 36
Hofferbert, Richard I., 12
Hoffman, Jay, 77, 80–83, 87–88, 97
Hollander, Sidney, 87
Holt, Rush, xi–xiii
Hoover, Herbert, 227n1 (intro.)
Hotelling, Harold, 10
House of Representatives: Appropriations Committee, 132; Budget Committee, xi, 129, 139, 173; committees in, 185–186; elections to, 1, 21, 227n2 (intro.); elections of 1990, 187; elections of 1992, 67; elections of 1994, xxii, 66, 94, 158, 163, 164, 169, 172–76, 229n3 (ch. 5); elections of 1996, xvii, 24, 52–53, 63, 66, 67, 112, 174, 181, 183–87, 192–94, 228n3, 229n6; elections of 1998, 184–87; elections of 2000, xiii, 24, 184, 186–88, 192–94, 206, 228n1 (ch. 4); Science Committee, 129; 104th Congress, 50, 136, 137, 158, 162; 106th Congress, 187, 206. *See also* Republican Party
Huckshorn, Robert J., xv, 6–8, 106, 146, 218
Hull, Elizabeth, 77, 79, 83, 88, 211
Human Condition, The (Arendt), 16
Hunter, Shapley, 170–73, 176, 179, 211
Hunterdon Review, xi
Hyde, Henry, xxi

Illinois, 62, 77, 143, 150, 162, 167, 169, 183, 200; candidate quotations from, 89, 91, 109, 112–14, 118–22, 124–28, 153, 155, 157–60, 164, 166, 168–73; congressional districts in, 68, 78–79, 80–83, 116, 132–35, 139, 169–73, 179, 180, 185, 186; political culture of, 69–70, 148, 150, 154, 161
impeachment (as campaign issue), 187, 193, 199
incumbency advantage, xiv, 2–4, 28, 32, 34, 183, 213, 225
incumbents: challengers' references to, 108–15, 124–28, 139, 198; fundraising of, 3, 66, 187; issue positions of, 53–60, 106, 200, 213–15; reelection rate of, xiv, 23, 63, 65, 185–86
information, xviii, 25, 46, 51, 75, 87, 89, 92, 93, 100–103, 107, 195–96, 215–16, 218–19
informational polling, 94–96
instrumental policy preferences, 27, 28, 213
interest groups, 46, 50, 76, 77, 87, 92, 93, 95, 98, 138

issue positions, xviii, 5, 8, 13, 20–25, 30, 47, 48–60, 102–8, 111, 115–24, 126, 129–41, 143–44, 179, 147, 193, 198, 199, 212, 216, 219–20

Jackson, Jesse, 174
Jacobs, Lawrence R., 2
Jacobson, Gary C., xiv, 4, 5, 7, 67, 105, 112, 151, 186–88, 206, 222
Janesville, WI, 176
Janosik, Edward, xii–xiii
Jefferson, Thomas, 225
jobs (as campaign issue), 116
Johannes, John R., 105
Johnson, James D., 17, 32–33
Jones, Charles O., 63

Kaptur, Marcy, 162
Kasich, John, 173–75, 186
Katz, Jonathan N., 3
Kazee, Thomas A., xv, 5, 7, 133, 220
Keech, William R., 36
Keene, Karlyn, 86
Kennedy, Edward, 223
Kennedy, Mark, 186
Kenosha, WI, 176
Kentucky, 170
Key, V. O., 145, 147
Kiewiet, D. Roderick, 227n2 (ch. 1)
King, Gary, 3
Kingdon, John W., xv, 6–8, 63, 106, 146, 218
Kleczka, Gerald, 177
Klingemann, Hans-Dieter, 12
Klinkner, Philip A., 212
Kolodny, Robin, x, 146
Kramer, Gerald H., xiv
Krasno, Jonathan S., 227n2 (intro.)
Krehbiel, Keith, 217
Kucinich, Dennis, 174
Kustra, Robert, 172

labor issues, 116, 189
LaFollette, Doug, 177
LaFollette, Robert, 177
Lautenberg, Frank, 202
Lawrence, Christine C., 81, 133, 169

Layzell, Anne C., 133
Lederman, Susan S., xii
Leland, David, 174
Leuthold, David A., xv, 6, 146, 218
Levitt, Steven D., 220, 228n1 (ch. 3)
liberalism quotient (LQ), 50–51, 55–59, 65, 149
liberalism quotient differential (LQD), 50–51, 55, 57–59, 148–50
Lincoln, Abraham, 126
Lindblom, Charles E., 10, 12
LoBiondo, Frank, xii–xiii
Lorain, OH, 79
Louisiana, 5, 148, 188, 229n1 (ch. 7)

MacDonald, Stuart Elaine, 44
Mack W. R., 220
Madison, James, 224–25
Madison, WI, 68
Maestas, Cherie, 5, 218
Maine, 183
Maisel, Louis Sandy, xv, xx, 5, 7–8, 146, 218–19
Malbin, Michael J., 2, 3
Mann, Thomas E., 2, 3
Mansbridge, Jane J., 46, 223
Maryland, 184, 192, 194–96, 205–7; candidate quotations from, 197, 199, 202–4, 208; political culture of, 191, 200–201
Massachusetts, 26
material benefits, 145
Mayhew, David R., 4, 12, 19, 21–22, 29, 68–69, 145, 147–50, 166, 180–81, 190–91, 212–13
McAdams, John C., 105
McClure, Robert D., 5, 7, 161
McGovern, George, xv, xx, 25, 87, 211–12
McIver, John P., 68
McKeever, Porter, xxiii
McKelvey, Richard D., xiv, 34
McWilliams, Wilson Carey, 199
median voter, xxii, 22, 35, 37, 39, 49, 104, 106, 111, 139–40, 210, 212, 214–16
median voter model, xiv, xvi, xvii, xix,

9–13, 17–21, 24, 27, 29–33, 44–47, 48, 59–60, 222
Medicaid (as campaign issue), 98
Medicare (as campaign issue), 53, 54, 72, 94, 98, 117, 187
Megan's Law, xi
Merrill, Samuel, 34, 45
military spending, 130
Miller, Arthur H., xv, 87
Miller, Warren E., xv
Milwaukee, 70, 129
Milwaukee Journal-Sentinel, 178
Milyo, Jeffrey D., 220
Minge, David, 136, 186
minimum wage, 113, 131
mining (as campaign issue), 193
Minneapolis, 70, 98, 137, 186
Minnesota, 62, 64, 143, 150, 162, 183, 200, 229n6; candidate quotations from, 90, 94, 96–99, 109, 113, 128, 154, 161, 163, 166–67, 203; congressional districts in, 68, 135–40, 186; political culture of, 69–70, 136–37, 148, 167, 181
Minnesota Star-Tribune, 138
minor party candidates, 14
Mississippi River, 169
Missouri, 170, 171
Moakley, Maureen W., 189
Mondale, Walter, 211–12
Munger, Michael C., 10, 33

National Republican Congressional Committee (NRCC), 144–45, 150, 152, 157–60, 162, 175, 180, 187, 194, 197, 202–3, 229nn1, 4 (ch. 6)
Neal, Steve, 134
Neumann, Mark, 176, 178, 185
New Castle County, DE, 191
New Jersey, xii–xiii, 184, 192, 194, 198, 202, 205, 207, 209; candidate quotations from, 201–3; congressional districts in, 12; political culture of, 189–90
New Madrid County, MO, 171–72
New York, 189
Newark, NJ, 189

Newsweek, 212
Niles, IL, 133
Nixon, Richard M., xv
Noll, Robert G., 45, 227n3 (ch. 2)
noninstrumental policy preferences, 18, 19, 24, 27, 28, 37, 46, 105, 216
North American Free Trade Agreement (NAFTA), 53, 54, 61, 73, 117
Nutting, Brian, 69, 78, 130, 185, 229n4 (ch. 6)

Obey, David, 177
Ohio, 62, 68, 143, 150, 164, 167, 169, 183, 200, 224; candidate quotations from, 96–97, 111–14, 117–18, 120–25, 127, 153, 155, 157, 159, 160, 162, 163, 168, 173–75; congressional districts in, 79–80, 173–75, 179, 186; political culture of, 69–70, 148, 164, 181, 189
open seat elections, xxi, 52, 105, 107, 187, 192, 198
Ordeshook, Peter C., xiv, 26, 33–34
Ornstein, Norman J., 2, 3
Overby, L. Marvin, 133

Paddock, Joel, 147
Page, Benjamin I., xx, 12
Pallone, Frank, 202
Pappas, Mike, xi
party-based campaign, 33, 40–43, 60, 71, 214
Patterson, Kelly D., 229n1 (ch. 6)
Pennsylvania, 184, 191–92, 194, 202, 205, 207; candidate quotations from, 196, 198, 199, 201, 203–4, 208–9; political culture of, 190
Penny, Tim, 136–37
pensions (as campaign issue), 117
Perlstein, Rick, 211
Perot, H. Ross, 52, 79
persuasive polling, 94–96, 98
Peterson, Colin, 136
Pew Charitable Trusts, 196
Philadelphia, 189–90
Pitkin, Hanna Fenichel, 15–16
Pittsburgh, 190, 209

pluralism, 12, 13, 15
political culture, 148, 149, 171, 180, 189
political experience, 14, 92, 93, 109, 152, 153, 206
political participation, 14, 224, 227n4
political parties: candidates' views on, 123, 142–44, 151–79, 201–5; functions of, xix, 64, 71, 95, 143–51, 156–63, 179–82, 193, 194, 200–205, 209, 217, 220; in rational choice models, 12, 37, 40–43, 48, 214, 221; strength of, xix, 31, 69, 143–49, 156, 163, 167, 169, 179–81, 189, 191–92
Politics in America (Duncan and Lawrence), 78, 133, 169
Politics of Defeat, The (Huckshorn and Spencer), 6–7, 106
polling, xviii, 39, 51, 75–101, 152, 158–60, 166, 193–97, 200, 219
Poshard, Glenn, 170
positive political theory, 217, 221. *See also* median voter model; rational choice theory; spatial theory
Powell, Lynda W., 15
presidential elections, xiii, 64, 68, 77; of 1964, 211; of 1972, xv, 66, 212; of 1984, 66, 212; of 1988, 52, 55, 57, 58, 176; of 1992, 52, 56–59, 170, 173, 176, 196, 228n7; of 1996, 92, 93, 99, 116, 155, 160, 166, 170, 173, 176, 178, 187; of 2000, xi, 170, 176, 187, 189, 191, 197, 204
Price, Melvin, 229n4 (ch. 6)
primary elections, 7, 152, 163–69, 201, 229n3 (ch. 6), n1 (ch. 7); in Illinois, 81, 170; in Minnesota, 166–67; in New Jersey, xi; in Ohio, 168–69; in Pennsylvania, 202; in Wisconsin, 165, 176–78
Princeton, NJ, 189
probability of winning: candidate beliefs about, 48, 49, 51, 71, 74, 75, 99, 102–4, 108, 128–31, 175, 181, 182, 196, 210, 214, 217, 219, 222; in rational choice models, xviii, 18, 23, 24, 26–33, 36–43, 46–47
Project Vote Smart, 188
Przeworski, Adam, 21, 26
public housing (as campaign issue), 116
public opinion, xviii, 76, 87, 103, 104, 107, 131, 132, 140, 195, 197
purposive benefits, 145
push polling, 95–96
Putnam, Robert D., 227n4

Rabinowitz, George, 44
Racine, WI, 176
Rae, Nicol C., xxii, 85–86
Raine, Alden S., xv
rational choice theory, 10, 13, 17. *See also* median voter model; positive political theory; spatial theory
Reagan, Ronald, 170, 173
redistricting, 52; cycles of, xix, 2, 188, 206; in Maryland, 191, 208–10; in New Jersey, 190, 209; in Ohio, 68; in Pennsylvania, 190, 207–9; of 1992, 173; of 2002, 184, 190, 191, 194, 207–10, 228n1 (ch. 4), 229n5
Reform Party, 136, 154, 201, 205, 229n2 (ch. 6)
Republican National Committee (RNC), 171, 211–12
Republican Party, 11, 143, 148–49, 151, 211; congressional candidates of, xi, xii, 53–59, 65, 112–19, 123, 129–39, 154–61, 164, 166–73, 185, 192, 204–8, 229n4 (ch. 6); in Illinois, 69–70, 143, 160–62, 169–73, 179–81; in Maryland, 191; in Minnesota, 69–70, 166–67, 181; in New Jersey, 189; in Ohio, 69–70; in Pennsylvania, 190, 207–8; and victorious 1994 candidates, 49, 58–60, 114–15, 136, 158, 160, 176; in Wisconsin, 69–70
responsible party government, 9–10, 217, 221, 222
retrospective voting, xiv
Rieder, Mary, 136–40, 186, 220, 229n2 (ch. 6)
Riker, William H., 26, 33, 145, 221

Ripon, WI, 70
Roberts, Craig, 81–83
Robertson, David B., 12
Robinson, James A., 63
Rochester, MN, 136
Roemer, John E., 36
Rosenstone, Steven J., xiv, 45, 151
Rostenkowski, Dan, 68
Ruccia, Cynthia, 173–76, 179, 186, 220
Russia, 53, 54, 61–62, 73
Ryden, David K., 229n6

Salisbury, Robert H., 46–47
Salvi, Al, 172
San Francisco, 6
Sapiro, Virginia, 151
Sarbanes, Paul, 202
Sartori, Giovanni, 12, 212–13
Schlesinger, Joseph A., 36
Schoenberg, Bernard, 80–82
school choice, 133
Schuessler, Alexander A., 15, 39–40
Schultze, Steve, 178–79
Schuman, Howard, 63
Schwartz, Mildred A., 143, 146, 150, 161, 169, 171
Scolaro, Joseph, 178–79
selective mobilization, 45, 107
senate elections, xi, xiii, 7, 53, 68, 99, 155, 172, 189–90, 194, 202, 227n2 (intro.), 228n8
Sensenbrenner, James, 130, 131–32, 140, 185–86, 211
sequential positioning, xvii, 19, 23, 24, 28, 32–37, 42, 49, 59, 105, 140, 175, 213–15, 222, 227n1 (ch. 2)
Shadegg, Stephen C., 211
Shalala, Donna, 137
Shamansky, Robert, 173–75
Shapiro, Ian, 11–12
Shapiro, Robert Y., 21
Sheboygan, WI, 130
Shepsle, Kenneth A., 10, 215
Shimkus, John, 77, 80–83, 85, 88, 97, 185, 220
Shklar, Judith K., 16
Siegel, Ralph, xi

Sierra Club, 93
Sievers, Scott, 82
Simon, Adam F., 16
simultaneous positioning, 18, 19, 33, 35, 213, 227n1 (ch. 2)
Skokie, IL, 133
Smith, Chris, xii–xiii
Smith, Eric R. A. N., 220
Snyder, James M., 3, 35, 228n1 (ch. 3)
Social Security, 117
Sorauf, Frank J., 151, 190
spatial models, 9, 10, 13, 18, 34, 36, 213, 216, 221. *See also* median voter model; positive political theory; rational choice theory
Spencer, Robert C., xv, 6–8, 106, 146, 218
Spottswood, Lydia, 175–79, 185, 220
Sprague, John D., 21, 26
Springfield, IL, 80–81
Squire, Peverill, 220
St. Clair County, IL, 169
St. Louis, 81, 171
St. Louis Post-Dispatch, 82
St. Paul, MN, 70
State Journal-Register (Springfield, IL), 80, 82
state legislators, xii, 83, 155, 161, 167, 173, 175, 177, 189, 191, 194, 201, 205, 209
Stevenson, Adlai, xxiii
Stokes, Donald E., 11
Stone, Irving F., xx
Stone, Walter, 5, 218–19
Strickland, Ted, 173–74
Sudman, Norman M., 86
Supreme Court, 229n6

Taft, William Howard, 227n1 (intro.)
Talbott, Basil, 79
Tamms, IL, 170
tax policy, 116, 136, 198–99
Taylor, Andrew J., 220
term limits, 53, 54, 72, 117, 133, 186, 187
Thompson, Kenneth W., xx
Time, xvii, 50–53, 61, 72, 73 117, 144,

147, 148, 188, 218, 228n6, 229n2 (ch. 5)
Timmons v. Twin City Area New Party, 229n6
tobacco farming, 192
Toledo, OH, 69
Torricelli, Robert, 189, 202
tracking poll, 81, 85, 89–92
transportation (as campaign issue), 116
Trenton, NJ, xii, 189
Tufte, Edward R., xiv, 10
Tullock, Gordon, xiv

Ujifusa, Grant, 69, 189–91
uncontested seats, 5, 52, 67, 181, 185, 188
Urbana, IL, 186

Van Horne, Terry, 202
vote maximization, 24–27, 30–33, 35–36, 43, 143, 209, 212, 214, 219
voter preferences, xviii, 18–26, 30, 43, 48, 74, 76, 88, 98, 102, 112, 139, 193, 204, 212–14, 218

Walsh, Joseph, 133–36, 140, 185
Washington, DC, 83, 86, 89, 91, 113, 154, 158, 166, 175, 178, 184, 191, 195, 201, 204, 218
Wattenberg, Martin P., 15
welfare reform, 53, 54, 73, 116, 128

Wellstone, Paul, 136, 137, 223
West Point, 91
Westlye, Mark C., 227n2 (intro.), 228n8
Who Runs for Congress (Kazee), 133
Wilcox, Clyde, 15
Wilmington, DE, 191
Winona State University, 136
Wirthlin Group, 81
Wisconsin, 62, 143, 150, 162, 169, 183, 200; candidate quotations from, 91–93, 97–99, 109, 112–14, 119, 121, 122, 127, 154, 157–61, 163, 165–67, 175–79; congressional districts in, 68, 116, 129–32, 140, 175–79, 185; political culture of, 69–70, 148, 164, 181
Wittman, Donald A., 36, 227n3 (ch. 1)
W-NOMINATE, 188. *See also* DW-NOMINATE
Wolfinger, Raymond E., 45
Wright, Gerald, 3, 55, 68, 147, 228
Wright, John R., 87, 228n2
Wyoming, 183

Yates, Sidney, 132–35, 185
Youngstown, OH, 69

Zaller, John R., 227n1 (ch. 1)
Zimmer, Dick, xi–xiii
Zukin, Cliff, 189